WOMEN IN CHRISTIAN TRADITIONS

WOMEN IN RELIGIONS
Series Editor: Catherine Wessinger

Women in Christian Traditions
Rebecca Moore

Women in Christian Traditions

Rebecca Moore

NEW YORK UNIVERSITY PRESS

New York and London

NEW YORK UNIVERSITY PRESS
New York and London
www.nyupress.org

References to Internet websites (URLs) were accurate at the time of writing.
Neither the author nor New York University Press is responsible for URLs that
may have expired or changed since the manuscript was prepared.

Library of Congress Cataloging-in-Publication Data
Moore, Rebecca, 1951–
Women in Christian traditions / Rebecca Moore.
pages cm. — (Women in religions)
Includes bibliographical references and index.
ISBN 978-1-4798-2961-3 (cl : alk. paper) — ISBN 978-1-4798-2175-4 (pb : alk. paper)
1. Women in Christianity—History. I. Title.
BV639.W7M594   2015
270.082--dc23   2014040539

New York University Press books are printed on acid-free paper,
and their binding materials are chosen for strength and durability.
We strive to use environmentally responsible suppliers and materials
to the greatest extent possible in publishing our books.

Manufactured in the United States of America

10 9 8 7 6 5 4 3 2 1

Also available as an ebook

In memory of my grandmothers

my mother

my sisters

and my younger daughter

In honor of my elder daughter

my granddaughter

and all those to come

CONTENTS

ACKNOWLEDGMENTS

There are many people to thank who helped in the development, writing, and production of this book. I could not have written it without receiving a sabbatical grant from the College of Arts and Letters at San Diego State University. I appreciate the support of the Religious Studies Department chair Risa Levitt Kohn in arranging for my absence.

Catherine Wessinger, the editor of the Women in Religions series, has made useful comments throughout the process. I thank her and Professor Elizabeth Goodine at Loyola University New Orleans for test-driving the raw manuscript in courses on women in Christianity.

Certainly the staff at New York University Press, especially the acquisitions editor Jennifer Hammer, have been exceptionally helpful in making decisions on the look and feel of the finished product. I want to express appreciation to Constance Grady, Dorothea Halliday, and all of those at the press who brought the book to completion.

Undying gratitude goes to Mary Ann Foley, assistant professor of theology at the University of Scranton, and to E. Nicholas Genovese, professor emeritus of classics at San Diego State University. Their insights into all things religious, classical, and textual have immeasurably improved the final product. I want to thank the Reverend Darin Johnson, campus minister at Agape House at San Diego State University, who steered me in a number of fruitful directions. The anonymous readers of the initial manuscript also provided helpful insights and suggestions, for which I am grateful.

Finally, great appreciation goes to my father, John V Moore, and my husband, Fielding M. McGehee III, who patiently listened to me throughout the research and writing process. With great forbearance they gently raised questions and kindly made suggestions. Their love and understanding have made this book possible.

Introduction

Why Study Women in Christian Traditions?

Any book that offers itself as a history of a subject that scores—if not hundreds—of books have already considered must negotiate two seemingly contradictory challenges. First, it must differentiate itself from previous works. Second, it must recognize, respect, and incorporate what they have taught us. These tasks are even more important when the subject itself is somewhat controversial or misunderstood, as is the case with women's contributions to the development of a major world religion such as Christianity. Thus, this volume approaches the topic of women in Christian traditions by respecting the past but also facing the future.

This book interprets a vast body of scholarly studies in an accessible and relatively brief way. It gives a broad overview of the complete sweep of history rather than focusing on a particular moment, issue, or individual. It relies almost exclusively on feminist scholarship of the last several decades, yet also departs from some of the assumptions of that scholarship. It raises questions that challenge our thinking about how women shaped beliefs and practices during two thousand years of church history. For example, did the emphasis on virginity in the early church empower Christian women? Did the emphasis on marriage during the Reformations of the sixteenth century improve their status?

These questions and others have important implications for women in Christianity in particular and women in religion in general, since they go to the heart of the human condition. Who are we and how are we to live? Societies and cultures provide their own answers with which various religious groups may agree or disagree. When we consider the history of Christianity, we find moments when believers clashed with prevailing cultural views and behaviors, and other times when they supported societal values and prejudices. In various epochs we find women taking both conservative steps backward and revolutionary leaps forward. While some of the women discussed in this book might have seen themselves as self-conscious radicals, most of them merely believed they were being true to their faith in God and to their understanding of Jesus Christ. At the same time, their answers to the questions posed above diverged dramatically.

A traditional study of Christianity might begin with an examination of its biblical roots, or with the cultural context of first-century Judea under Roman occupation. But since this book takes a feminist approach to the subject, it needs to preface a rereading of the conventional history by starting with a discussion of leading theories and scholars. This introduction to contemporary feminist theology will inform our understanding of what follows.

Introducing Feminist Theologies

Feminism is sometimes called the other f-word. It makes both women and men uncomfortable as they think about the gender roles they have accepted. Misunderstanding as well as misogyny masks what most feminists mean when they use the word "feminism." In the late twentieth century fewer young women identified themselves as feminists than had their mothers, believing that such women were man-hating, braburning radicals. A movement called postfeminism arose in part as a backlash against women's efforts to achieve social equality.

According to the bumper sticker definition, "Feminism is the radical notion that women are people." This quote has been attributed to several women, including the British journalist Rebecca West, the African American novelist Gloria Naylor, and two American professors of women's studies, Cheris Kramarae and Paula Treichler. The fact that so many women might have said it suggests the larger proposition that many women do say it. Even if they do not identify themselves as feminists, most women believe in social equality, unbiased job opportunities, and a level playing field for advancement in all realms of society. By this definition, men can be feminists too.

A more formal definition of feminism is "the political and social efforts of women and men directed toward ending sexist *domination*— with all that the latter may imply in terms of racial, economic and other patterns of stratification."[1] By this definition, feminism is a political movement of women and men who are working to eliminate structures of authority based on gender discrimination. The pattern in which men hold the power and women are disenfranchised or excluded from power is called patriarchy. Patriarchy may even dominate other men, especially those of ethnic, racial, or sexual minorities. Although patriarchy can also simply be defined as a male-headed household, its use here indicates a social hierarchy that governs all human relations.

Related to patriarchy is androcentrism, that is, the belief that the male or masculine view is normative. Androcentrism is so constitutive a part of many human cultures, including those of Western Europe and North America, that we are often not even aware of it. Yet it dictates our ideas about what is normal and natural, and until the twentieth century it has generally controlled scholarship by deciding what is important and worth studying, and what is trivial and not worth considering.

Feminist theology, a branch within the larger discipline of feminist studies, reflects upon the structure of patriarchy and androcentrism within a particular religious tradition, in this particular book, Christianity. It recovers the hidden and suppressed past; it constructs a vision that provides for human flourishing by including women from start to finish; it advocates for change; and it creates structures that enable change to occur. In other words, it is not only a theoretical endeavor, it involves practice or action as well.

Historically, feminist theologians adopted three main approaches toward the assessment of Christianity.[2] The reformist school, primarily Evangelical in orientation, believes that gender equality can be achieved in the churches without a complete overhaul of existing structures. Reformist theologians such as Letha Scanzoni (b. 1935) and Nancy Hardesty (1941–2011), cofounders of the Evangelical Women's Caucus (now the Evangelical and Ecumenical Women's Caucus), argue that the message of the Bible, and especially of Jesus, has been distorted, but that it can be reclaimed through a biblical hermeneutics—that is, principles of interpretation of scripture—that sees Jesus as a countercultural feminist.[3]

The reconstructionist school believes that Christian institutions need radical change, not just reform, in order to ameliorate deep structural flaws. These feminist theologians see the recovery of a suppressed Christian tradition that includes women—along with the development of a hermeneutics that rereads the Bible through the lenses of women's experience—as essential for liberating Christianity from patriarchy and androcentrism. Letty M. Russell (1929–2007), an ordained Presbyterian minister and faculty member at Yale University, was a pioneer reconstructionist. Like the reformists, she emphasized scripture and the liberating attitudes of Jesus, but went further to develop a theology of partnership that called for changes in church life and ministry.[4] Another reconstructionist, Delores Williams, professor emerita at Union Theological Seminary in New York, criticizes some of the African American denominational churches for their failure to address a number of issues crucial to the flourishing of all African Americans. She advances a Christology, or conception of Christ, that emphasizes his ministerial vision, rather than a Christology that sees him as a scapegoat or surrogate for others, which she finds destructive of African American female personhood.[5]

Reformist and reconstructionist feminists regard themselves as faithful Christians who wish to remain in a transformed church. In contrast, the final group, revolutionary feminists, who are also called rejectionists, believe that the patriarchal nature of Christianity, grounded in a male deity and a male savior, and controlled throughout history by males who want to maintain their power, can never advance the position of women, either in heaven or on earth. They may call themselves post-Christian feminists, and some turn to Goddess religions as more emancipating for women than Christianity ever could be.

An important revolutionary feminist was Mary Daly (1928–2010), who began her academic career as a Catholic theologian and philosopher and ended it as a post-Christian radical. In her first book, *The Church and the Second Sex* (1968), she examined the French feminist writer Simone de Beauvoir's attack on Christianity.[6] While she acknowledged the truth of de Beauvoir's criticisms, Daly nonetheless retained hope that the Roman Catholic Church could be redeemed. But by the time she wrote *Beyond God the Father*, five years later, she had abandoned Christianity. "Under the conditions of patriarchy the role of liberating the human race from the original sin of sexism would seem to be precisely the role that a male symbol *cannot* perform."[7] Jesus could never be a beneficial model for women, she wrote, since the very qualities that he exemplified—self-sacrifice, humility, meekness, passivity—were the exact characteristics that kept women oppressed. While eventually falling outside Christian theology, Daly's revolutionary feminism is nonetheless foundational for understanding all succeeding feminist considerations of Christian thought and history.

The outpouring of feminist scholarship on women in Christianity and the development of a feminist theology in the last third of the twentieth century can be divided into three distinct periods.[8] The classical period ran from 1968 through 1977 and is characterized primarily by its critique of patriarchy and misogyny. A good example of this type of literature is *Religion and Sexism*, which asked the question, "To what extent did Judaism and Christianity contribute directly to and promote this heritage of misogynism?" Edited by Rosemary Radford Ruether (b. 1936), visiting professor of feminist theology at Claremont Graduate University, the volume provided detailed answers in ten essays and a parable.[9] The second period, extending from 1978 through 1985, included defining works of historical recovery. The suppressed history of women in Christianity became visible in such works as *In Memory of Her*, by Elisabeth Schüssler Fiorenza (b. 1938), professor of divinity at Harvard Divinity School. "The attempt to 'write women back into early Christian history' should not only restore early Christian history to women," she observed, "but also lead to a richer and more accurate perception of early Christian beginnings."[10]

The third period in the development of feminist theology encompassed 1986 through the late 1990s, and focused on theological reconstruction, that is, "recasting of Christian themes and symbolizations along the lines of explicitly feminist ethical and feminist theological emphases."[11] Feminist theologians reconsidered Christian teachings about the Trinity, Christ, salvation, anthropology (that is, the theology of humanity, as opposed to the academic discipline), and other dogmas that seemed to circumscribe women's full participation in Christianity. For example, the Roman Catholic theologian and woman religious Elizabeth A. Johnson (b. 1941)[12] and the Protestant theologian Sallie McFague (b. 1933) both created visions of the divine that utilized inclusive language for God. They agreed that speech about God is metaphorical and analogous to human life. Johnson adopted the language "Holy Wisdom" to describe the Holy Spirit, Jesus, and the Creator Mother, while McFague proposed the language of mother, lover, and friend to describe the relationships one might have with the divine.[13] By getting at the underlying nature of God, both writers constructed a new theology in order to avoid the effects of an exclusively male deity upon the expression of full human equality.

A backlash to reconstructions like these arose, with some writers wondering whether feminist theology could even be called Christian. Kathryn Greene-McCreight, an Episcopal priest in New Haven, Connecticut, differentiated between biblical feminists, who read the Bible as the inspired witness to God's grace, and feminist theologians, who view the Bible primarily as a tool for advancing patriarchy.[14] Although Greene-McCreight admitted that the critique of patriarchy is legitimate, she found that the method some feminists use takes Christians outside the biblical tradition. Moreover, she argued that feminist theology "reinscribes totalizing assumptions about 'women' and reinforces stereotypes about women's submissiveness rather than overcoming and subverting them."[15]

In the twenty-first century, a new wave of feminist theologians is building upon the foundations laid by their foresisters, yet addressing some of the concerns expressed by Greene-McCreight. They are providing "bold reinterpretations of Christianity that seek to renew the life of the church and its witness to the world," according to Joy Ann McDougall, professor of systematics at Candler School of Theology.[16] She notes three features these newer theologians share. First, they are including women's lived experiences as sources of embodied knowledge. Just as men's experiences once served as the primary means by which Christians understood church teachings, women's experiences are indispensable for developing theology today. Second, they are "directing their energies toward the church's central doctrines and practices." Rather than abandon the struggle to make sense of Christian tradition for modern churchwomen, they are engaged in the same process of theological reflection that has engrossed male theologians for two millennia. Finally, they are utilizing the insights of feminist theory to confront contemporary issues that threaten to overwhelm all of humanity, not just Christians or women. McDougall believes that these new theologians are engaged in "saving work" by offering fresh readings of Christianity.[17]

What became evident in the first feminist theological writings was the failure to account for or to include the experiences of nonwhite women in the new theology. If "living realities are the takeoff point for theological elaboration," as the Brazilian feminist Ivone Gebara asserted,[18] it was clear that the experiences of white North American women did not encompass those of African American, Asian, or African women, nor of South American women as well as North American Latinas. Women of color have had to face discrimination not only on the basis of gender but also on the basis of race and class. For these reasons, a variety of alternative feminist theologies began to emerge in the late 1970s and early 1980s.

"Judging by what is written in the historic black denominations the black woman is invisible," Theressa Hoover (b. 1925), the former associate general secretary of the Women's Division of the United Methodist Church, wrote in 1974.[19] Given the fact that African American women were the backbone of the black church, making up three-quarters of its membership, their invisibility was troubling. In reaction to the silence of male African American theologians and the neglect by white feminist theologians, a womanist theology arose. "Womanist theology begins with the experiences of Black women as its point of departure," according to Jacquelyn Grant (b. 1948), an ordained minister and professor at the Interdenominational Theological Center. "This experience includes not only Black women's activities in the larger society but also in the churches and reveals that Black women have often rejected the oppressive structure in the church as well."[20]

While African American churchwomen tend to work within the Protestant church, Latina churchwomen tend to work within Roman Catholic Christianity. *Mujerista* theology, articulated by Ada María Isasi-Díaz (1943–2012), a theologian at Drew University, is "a theology *from* the perspective of Latinas that is an intrinsic element of Hispanic/ Latino theology in the USA."[21] In contrast, the theology of women living in Central and South America comes out of the political and religious struggle for liberation in Latin America. A major exponent of this theology is María Pilar Aquino (b. 1956), a woman religious and professor of theology at the University of San Diego. Her book *Our Cry for Life* (*Nuestro clamor por la vida*) presented a systematic analysis of the state of the question of women and theology before providing a constructive methodology for feminist theology in Latin America.[22] Isasi-Díaz and Aquino agreed that the starting point for feminist theology is the centrality of daily life, which is linked to the problems of "division of labor by sexes; the split between the public and private spheres; and the creation of the sex-gender system, which affirms male superiority."[23] Isasi-Díaz called this *lo cotidiano* (the everyday), that is, the daily experience of Hispanic women.[24]

Latin America was missionized in the sixteenth and seventeenth centuries primarily by male Catholic friars and priests from Spain,

Portugal, and France: Dominicans, Franciscans, Jesuits, and others. Africa and Asia, in contrast, were missionized primarily in the nineteenth and twentieth centuries by English and American Protestants, both men and women, although there are exceptions to these generalizations. Missionary work gave some women a limited amount of control, especially in the proselytizing and control of other women. While we cannot say that women missionaries were necessarily feminist in outlook, their presence nonetheless revealed the subjugation that their sisters abroad were experiencing. "Their daily exposures to some of the oppression Asian women faced, such as arranged marriage, bonded labour, and female infanticide, made them more aware of their own subordination and the harmful effects of sexual exploitation," according to Kwok Pui-lan, a professor at Episcopal Divinity School in Cambridge, Massachusetts.[25]

Asia is an enormous continent, with diverse nations and peoples. As a result, the feminist theologies that have arisen there are quite varied, reflecting the particular churches, denominations, and cultural contexts from which they have grown. In the 1970s, women began to develop feminist theology in South Korea—a highly Christianized Asian nation, with half of the population professing Christianity today—in response to an androcentric church that controlled access to biblical interpretation.[26] Virginia Fabella, a Maryknoll sister and Catholic theologian, said that feminists in the Philippines, another Asian nation with a large Christian population, have done the same. "For too long, what we are to believe about Jesus Christ and what he is to mean for us have been imposed on us by our colonizers, by the Western world, by a patriarchal church, and by male scholars and spiritual advisers."[27] Asian feminists identified the effects of oppression through economic and religious colonization as serious problems rarely addressed by indigenous male or non-Asian theologians.

The situation was similar in African nations, where Christianity served as both a liberating and an oppressing force for women. Mercy Amba Oduyoye (b. 1934) argued that it is a myth that the church brought liberation to African women: what it brought instead were European, middle-class values. "Faced with the vastly complicated, hydra-headed challenges of living in today's world," she wrote, "Africa finds little sustenance in the continuing importation of uncritical forms of Christianity with answers that were neatly packaged in another part of the world."[28] The director of the Institute of African Women in Religion and Culture at Trinity Theological Seminary in Ghana, Oduyoye today contends that Christianity has fueled the cultural sexism that already existed in Africa and notes that some of the strongest African religious women have left historic Christianity to establish independent churches. She argues for the affirmation of African traditions within Christianity and for the full participation of women in the life of churches: in leadership, in ritual, and in religious language.

All of these feminist theologies and more—such as ecofeminism, queer theology, and feminist spirituality, which comes from women's lived experiences rather than from normative masculinized practices—fall within the larger rubric of liberation theology. Arising in the 1960s primarily within the Roman Catholic Church, liberation theology, broadly conceived, asserts that God has a "special option" for the poor and the marginalized. "God opts for the poor to overthrow unjust relationships," writes Ruether. "This makes the poor the preferential locus for understanding who and where the Church actually is."[29] Salvation occurs in the concrete reality of human history, not in a far-distant afterlife. Previous theologies that neglected the poor or postponed salvation, failed to rightly speak the Word of God. According to the liberationists, theology must be tested in the crucible of practice: If theology does not lift up humanity in the here and now, if it does not make justice an imperative, it is inadequate if not inauthentic.

Feminist theologians operate within the paradigm of liberation theology but emphasize the retrieval of the full humanity of women. They provide new readings of ancient texts; they expose theologies that justify the subservience of women; they highlight women as significant foresisters whose life and work had fallen into obscurity. All of this activity occurs within the idea that praxis confirms or denies the validity of theology. Another way to say this is with the adage "The proof is in the pudding"—that is, we can ascertain the quality or truth of an idea only by putting it into practice.

BF: Before Feminism

What did people know about women in Christianity prior to the rise of feminist scholarship? Christians always appreciated the great women of the Hebrew Bible,[30] where stories abound about strong matriarchs like Sarah, Rebecca, Leah, and Rachel; women warriors like Miriam, Deborah, and Jael; and schemers and plotters like Tamar, Ruth, Delilah, and Jezebel. The Old Testament narratives provide glimpses of women who think and act and who affect the outcome of salvation history. As Edith Deen asserted in *All of the Women of the Bible*, "Here in this Bible portrait gallery—the greatest in all literature—are women of our common humanity."[31] Deen, the editor of the women's section of a daily newspaper, whose interest in biblical women began with a short series of portraits she published in the paper, created an encyclopedic work in 1955. Feminist biblical scholarship, especially *Women in Scripture*, has superseded Deen's faith-based chronicle, but for its time, the book was a breakthrough.[32]

The New Testament, a much shorter collection of books, also contains narratives about women, beginning with the four Gospels. Throughout the books of Matthew, Mark, Luke, and John, which present theological reflections on the life, teachings, and death of Jesus of Nazareth, we catch sight of women interacting with him or serving as illustrations in the parables with which he instructs the crowds. Feminist biblical scholars have pointed out that women in the Gospels make up a large part of the story of Jesus and the early church. The Acts of the Apostles—an adventure story after the fashion of a Greek novel—continues the narrative begun in the Gospels and describes a number of early female converts to Christianity.

This book could not have been written if it had not been for the rise of the feminist movements—sometimes called women's liberation—of the 1960s and 1970s. It took a new generation of women scholars to earn their doctorates in the 1960s and to begin to write and publish in the fields of Christian theology, ethics, and biblical studies beginning in the 1970s. The contribution of these founding foresisters to our current understanding of women in Christianity is inestimable. A brief glance at the catalogs from several university libraries in the metropolitan area in which I live gives an excellent example of the stark contrast between "before" and "after" feminist scholarship.

My home university has seventy-eight titles on the subject "women in Christianity." Nine of them predate Mary Daly's book *The Church and the Second Sex*, originally published in 1968. Of those, only a single work—*Women in the World of Religion*, published in 1967 by Elsie Thomas Culver—comes from the twentieth century.[33] The remaining volumes are e-books reprinting essays from the seventeenth century. When we look at the consortium of area university libraries—which includes three public universities and one private Catholic university—we find a total of 148 titles, with only 37 books predating *The Church and the Second Sex*. A book from 1966 titled *Woman Is the Glory of Man* justified the "distinction in missions" between men and women, who are equal in dignity but have complementary domains of responsibility.[34] *Christ and Womankind*, written thirty-one years earlier, made the argument that under Christ, women are exactly on the same level as that of man: "As moral personalities man and woman are not subordinated but co-ordinated."[35] By "coordinated," the German theologian Peter Ketter meant that each gender has its own duties, and that the task of women is to serve in love. "It is in accordance with feminine nature and with the explicitly revealed will of God that woman should be the servant of humanity, but not the slave of the man," he wrote. "She shall develop her individual personality in personal freedom while serving as companion and helpmate."[36]

A Feminist Approach

This book's particular feminist account of Christianity considers previous ways the story of Christianity has been told and identifies patterns of domination within the religion. The most obvious example of this has been the use of the Bible and religious authority to justify patriarchal institutions and the oppression of women. Just as important as providing information about Christianity's sexist past, however, is illuminating the ways women have developed a global and diverse religious movement. We might subtitle this volume "Triumph and Tragedy" or "Promise and Pathos" to indicate the dual vision that it contains. Nevertheless, the overarching purpose is to highlight women and their efforts to shape the beliefs and practices of Christianity over a period of two thousand years. It recovers forgotten and obscured moments in history so that a richer and fuller interpretation may be realized: an interpretation that includes women as well as men.

A better subtitle would be "Saints, Seers, and Scholars" to indicate the various responsibilities women have undertaken throughout Christian history. "Saints" refers to the missionaries and martyrs who have braved danger and death in order to witness to their faith. The category "Seers" includes prophets and mystics, those women throughout the centuries whose reputed openness to the divine has given them unique messages to communicate to the rest of us. Finally, "Scholars" refers to women whose intellectual pursuits seem noteworthy. They wrote, or dictated, their view of theology, current events, or church controversies. We find saints, seers, and scholars in every age.

The temptation immediately faced in such a project is replacing a theory of great men in Christianity with a theory of great women in Christianity. This is especially problematic given the fact that, until recently, most of the reports of great women in the past were written by men. These narratives generally served to promote a patriarchal agenda by limiting women to particular gender behaviors. A notable exception was Edith Deen's *Great Women of the Christian Faith* (1959), which she wrote to accompany *All of the Women of the Bible* (1955).[37] Deen discussed women who were important in their own right, as well as those who were wives and mothers of famous men. By examining themes, movements, and events in their historical contexts, and by locating outstanding women within the broader developments that shape Christianity, an author may avoid the "great woman" pitfall. Weaving the story of two New Testament disciples—Martha and Mary—throughout the narrative also dodges this trap. They exemplify two different—and modest—ways women have been Christians through the centuries.

This book also combines history with historiography, which means providing a recitation of past events and, at the same time, examining how history is written. In addition, it uses contemporary sociological and anthropological methods that look at groups of people and their behaviors. Traditional historical and theological methods focused on individuals and ideas by reading texts of the past. These texts tell us a great deal, both explicitly by what they include, and implicitly by what they leave out. Sociology, anthropology, archaeology, and other disciplines look at additional types of evidence: physical items, human interactions, and cultural artifacts, such as music, paintings, and sculpture. This volume utilizes all of these tools, and more, because unearthing the story of women in Christianity requires diverse tactics. This process is similar to what is known as triangulation at sea: In order to determine the exact whereabouts of the ship, the captain must locate it at the intersection of three geographical points. In navigating our way through history, we need to adopt the same method, using multiple sources of data to arrive at a rough reconstruction of what happened and why.

As noted, texts do not tell the whole story of women in Christianity. Catholic and Orthodox Christians have the advantage of enjoying an extensive tradition of female saints. At baptism, if not before, Catholic girls are given a saint's name. Until rather recently, both Catholic and Orthodox Christians grew up hearing about important women in church history: monastic leaders, martyrs, mystics, and missionaries. "What I wanted most in the world was to be a saint," writes the San Diego State University women's studies professor emerita Oliva Espín:

> The saints who stimulated my imagination most were women. The intricacies of these women's lives have stayed with me: their courage as well as their weakness, their childishness as well as their maturity, their loves and fears, and above all, their focus on doing what they believed God wanted from them regardless of the opinions of others, including the male authorities of Church and family.[38]

Feast days mark the comings and goings of these famous women: Saint Monica, the mother of the famous Christian theologian Saint Augustine, whom she instructed in the fundamentals of Christianity (May 4); Saint Catherine of Alexandria, who was brutally tortured and martyred for her Christian beliefs (November 25); Saint Clare, who served the poor with Francis of Assisi (August 12); and hundreds of other interesting and important saints. This historical perspective enriches Catholic and Orthodox appreciation of the work women have done in the past.

In addition, Catholics, especially Catholic girls, benefit from the real-life models of nuns. While media portrayals are not always accurate or fair, they often present nuns and sisters as clear religious leaders: strong, spunky, and at times scary. Women religious also wear a uniform that sets them apart, at least until recently, and some orders of nuns continue to dress in a distinctive habit. Even Protestant girls can aspire to the strength they see in the sisterhood: from the world-weary, chain-smoking mother superior played by Anne Bancroft in *Agnes of God*, to the fallible, romantic, and beautiful Deborah Kerr in *Black Narcissus*, to the unworldly but socially active nuns in the Whoopi Goldberg hit movie *Sister Act*.

Protestant Christians, in contrast, have the advantage of ordaining women to the ministry. Many Protestants, though not all, can hear women preach, see women administer the sacraments, lead the liturgy, and serve as pastors to their congregations. Some Protestant denominations, like their Catholic and Orthodox counterparts, deny women the rite of ordination, but those that do allow it enrich appreciation of women's ministerial service in the church today.

Organization of the Book

Chapter 1 examines the biblical figure of Eve and the impact that subsequent interpretations of her status and her sin have had on theology. Chapter 2 presents the historical context of the Jesus movement, and the countercultural attitude that Jesus adopted in his day by ministering to women and by including women disciples. It compares and contrasts Mary the mother of Jesus and Mary Magdalene. Chapter 3 describes the ministries women had in the early church. These forms of service were gradually restricted and replaced by a theology of asceticism and martyrdom that narrowed the options women had for being faithful Christians.

In the Middle Ages, however, which chapter 4 covers, women saw expanded opportunities for leadership both as professed religious and as lay sisters. They labored as missionaries, teachers, copyists, nurses, and in other fields of endeavor, despite conflicts with church authorities regarding their work outside the cloister. Chapter 5 details the radical shifts that occurred during the Reformations of the sixteenth century, with the elevation of marriage as a valued vocation for females. Many of those who were not married were demonized and persecuted as witches, and executed by the thousands, if not millions. At the same time, some women took advantage of the new spirit of reform to evangelize in public and function as ministers in Protestant churches and as missionaries in Catholic churches.

This enlargement of women's visibility in the public sphere is seen in chapter 6, which focuses on the nineteenth century. Women founded Christian denominations, influenced Christian men in reform movements, and traveled the world as missionaries. Chapter 7 discusses the effect of this enlargement upon global Christianity. It considers how women have challenged traditional theological constructs and how Christianity has changed as a result, especially in regard to the ordination of women.

Readers seeking a treatment of specific Christian dogmas concerning Christology, soteriology, theology, anthropology, eschatology (the theology of Endtimes or Last Things), sacramentology, and ecclesiology (doctrines about the nature of the church) will find these discussed throughout the volume.[39] Each chapter addresses one of these areas, and sometimes more than one. At the same time, it is important to remember that this book concentrates on women in Christian traditions; thus doctrinal issues are treated primarily as they pertain to women in the church.

An examination of the way that women have determined the construction and practice of Christian traditions reveals that this major world religion owes an enormous debt to its female followers. From the earliest disciples to the latest theologians, from the missionaries to the martyrs, women have kept the faith alive. This book helps to show how they have done that.

FIGURE 1.1. Painting of Adam and Eve inside Abreha and Atsbeha Church, Ethiopia. Photo by Bernard Gagnon. Reproduced under Creative Commons License.

1

In the Beginning . . . Eve

If we read the first three chapters of Genesis in the Bible without reading the later accumulation of interpretation into it, we find a story told by nomadic peoples undoubtedly intended to explain the origins of their world and the place of men and women in it. When we read it through two thousand years of Christian and Jewish interpretive history, however, we find that the simple etiology has acquired multiple layers of meaning that the original storytellers probably did not anticipate.

The story of the Garden of Eden is important to Christian theology for two reasons. First, it establishes the need for a soteriology by which Christians explain Jesus's mission and purpose on earth. Soteriology answers the question "How does Jesus save?" (*sōtēr* being the Greek for savior). The Eden story has been interpreted to describe a cosmic fall from original perfection into sin and death that needed supernatural help to correct. Jesus was the one who came to solve the problem. Second, Christian theologians throughout the centuries have used the story to explain, and to justify, women's subordinate status. An anthropology that privileged men over women relied upon Genesis as its rationale.

Given the prominence that men enjoy in the Hebrew Bible and the Christian New Testament, it seems almost inconceivable that the actions of a single woman, Eve, changed the destiny of humankind forever. Yet her actions necessitated the coming of Jesus to restore order out of the chaos she created, according to some theologians. "The Bible teaches that woman brought sin and death into the world," according to Elizabeth Cady Stanton (1815–1902), writing in *The Woman's Bible* (1895), one of the earliest feminist critiques of misogynistic biblical interpretation:

[T]hat she precipitated the fall of the race, that she was arraigned
before the judgment seat of Heaven, tried, condemned and sentenced.
Marriage for her was to be a condition of bondage, maternity a period of suffering and anguish, and in silence and subjection, she was
to play the role of a dependent on man's bounty for all her material
wants.[1]

Although Stanton is not accurate in her description of "what the Bible
teaches," she does faithfully reproduce the *interpretation* of the story
that many, if not most, theologians have taught for centuries. Without
Eve's ill-fated chat with the serpent in the Garden of Eden in Genesis
3 of the Hebrew Bible, humanity would not have been expelled from
Paradise and cursed by hard work, painful pregnancy, and death.

Before focusing on the first woman, we need to take a look at the
story of the first human couple. It is surprising for some to learn that
Genesis contains two stories of creation. The first account presents the
six days of creation, and the seventh day, the Sabbath, as a day of rest
(1:1–2:4). In this narrative God creates the elements of the world—light,
waters, land, vegetation, animals, humans—in a very systematic and organized fashion. Humans do not appear until the end of the process,
when God says,

> "Let us make humankind in our image, according to our likeness; and let
> them have dominion over the fish of the sea, and over the birds of the air,
> and over the cattle, and over all the wild animals of the earth, and over
> every creeping thing that creeps upon the earth."
>
> So God created humankind in his image, in the image of God he cre-
> ated them; male and female he created them.
>
> God blessed them, and God said to them, "Be fruitful and multiply,
> and fill the earth and subdue it; and have dominion over the fish of the
> sea and over the birds of the air and over every living thing that moves
> upon the earth." (Gen. 1:26–27)[2]

This statement of primordial equality shows that God creates men and women at the same moment, and both are in the image and likeness of the divine (Gen. 1:27). "No lesson of women's subjection can be fairly drawn from the first chapter of the Old Testament," remarks Stanton.[3]

The second creation tells a different story. In that version, a nongendered human is created out of dust and set within a garden full of good things to eat (Gen. 2:4–25). The Lord God instructs the human—some interpreters translate the word *ādām* as "earthling" because the creature is made out of earth, *adamah*—that the fruit of every tree is available except from the "tree of the knowledge of good and evil . . . for in the day that you eat of it you shall die." The Lord God sees that the *ādām* is alone and decides to "make him a helper as his partner." The noun translated helper "is a relational term, [designating] a beneficial relationship," according to the biblical scholar Phyllis Trible (b. 1932). Given the context, in which God is a superior helper and animals are inferior helpers, the Hebrew word here shows that "woman is the helper equal to man."[4] After creating animals and birds and presenting them to the human as possible companions, the Lord God finally forms a woman from a rib taken from the sleeping human. "This at last is bone of my bones and flesh of my flesh," says the man (*ish*, in Hebrew); "this one shall be called Woman (*ishah*) for out of Man this one was taken" (Gen. 2:23). Thus we have the creation of gender, and, one could argue, an etiology for sexual intercourse, since the Bible then says, "*Therefore* a man leaves his father and his mother and clings to his wife, and they become one flesh" (italics mine). The biblical author is careful to note that the couple "were both naked, and were not ashamed," to presage what will follow.

The question that later interpreters asked was whether this story indicates the primary and superior nature of men, being the first human created, or whether this indicates that women are the crowning achievement of creation, being the last. Saint Thomas Aquinas (1225–1274), writing in the thirteenth century, argues that it was more suitable for the woman to be made from the man, since it conferred a certain dignity upon the first man. Moreover, the man might love the woman all the more, and, finally, they are united not only for procreation but also for domestic life. In addition, Aquinas writes that it was entirely appropriate for the woman to come from the side, or rib, since if she came from the head she might exert supremacy over the man, while if she came from the feet, she might be a slave.[5] Trible agrees, asserting that "the rib means solidarity and equality."[6] She argues that the parallel literary structure of Genesis 2, which begins with God's creation of a man and ends with God's creation of a woman, demonstrates the same organic equality evident in Genesis 1.

In Genesis 3, "a wonderful tale about a trickster snake, a woman who believes it, and a rather passive, even comical man, biblical writers comment on the inevitability of reality as they perceived it, wistfully presenting an image of an easier, smoother life."[7] In the third chapter of Genesis, the first woman—not yet named Eve—has a conversation with a serpent about the fruit on the tree of knowledge of good and evil. She takes a bite and offers it to her husband. "Then the eyes of both were opened, and they knew that they were naked" (3:7). Stanton points out that the serpent did not attempt to beguile the woman with jewels, rich dresses, or worldly luxuries; rather, the woman was tempted by the acquisition of knowledge. "Compared with Adam she appears to great advantage through the entire drama."[8] Indeed, the woman is an independent agent, interpreting God's command, acting decisively, and, when confronted by God, accepting responsibility. "By contrast," writes Trible, "the man is a silent, passive, and bland recipient."[9]

The story functions etiologically, explaining why the snake will slither on its belly, why the woman will experience painful pregnancies but will nonetheless desire her husband, and why the man will have to work hard to cultivate the land. It also explains the origin of death, since the Lord God expels the first couple from Eden: he seems to express the fear that, like gods, they will live forever. Later interpreters, such as the author of the New Testament book of Revelation, see the snake as a symbol, or disguise, for Satan (Rev. 12:9, 20:2). At the end of the Genesis story, the *ādām* gives the woman the name Eve, *Hawwāh* (from the Hebrew word for "to live") because, as the biblical author explains, "she was the mother of all living."

The temptation narrative suggests that an original equality between women and men was lost, and that the present order of gender relations is not the way they were meant to be. Martin Luther (1483–1546), the sixteenth-century Protestant reformer, states this explicitly when he writes, "If Eve had persisted in the truth, she would not only not have been subjected to the rule of her husband, but she herself would also have been a partner in the rule which is now entirely the concern of males."[10] God had planned for equality between the sexes, but it was lost due to the disobedience of the first humans. Some contemporary Christians would disagree with Luther, however, such as the Council on Biblical Manhood and Womanhood, which affirmed in 1987 that "Adam's headship in marriage was established by God before the Fall, and was not a result of sin."[11]

The first three chapters of Genesis establish the paradigms by which Christians will understand gender relations in the future. Genesis 1 illustrates what is called sex equality or gender equality, in which men and women exist together in a nonhierarchical affiliation. It can be, and has been, argued that Genesis 2 appears to show sex complementarity. Women and men are equal but have differing though complementary roles: the woman is a partner, but also a helper in the man's projects rather than her own. Genesis 3 demonstrates sex polarity, which seems to justify a subordinate role for women under the domination of men because of their intrinsically inferior nature. Although male theologians throughout the centuries could have argued for women's equality, and at times have advocated a complementary role, they gravitated toward the position of sex polarity largely because of social and cultural norms. Moreover, they made Eve a scapegoat.

In *Eve: A Biography*, the literary critic Pamela Norris finds that by the second century CE,[12] Jewish rabbis and Christian theologians tended to blame women in general, and Eve in particular, for a variety of ills in the world. "The myth of Adam, Eve and the serpent was a key text for the founders of the Christian church, anxious to establish a link between the redemptive powers of Christ and the origins of human bad behavior."[13] Two centuries before the birth of Jesus, the deuterocanonical book of Sirach seems to attribute the origin of sin and death to Eve: "From a woman sin had its beginning, and because of her we all die" (Sir. 25:24).[14] The apocryphal *Life of Adam and Eve* (*Vita Adae et Evae*), a Latin version of the Greek text *Apocalypse of Moses* (*Apocalypsis Mosis*), is more explicit in attributing blame to Eve.[15] After they have been ousted from the garden, Adam and Eve wander about, searching for food—which was plentiful in Eden—and discuss what penitence they should undergo. Eve asks Adam, "My lord, how much did you intend to repent, since I have brought toil and tribulation on you?" Eve appears to accept total responsibility for their situation. During her own penitence of fasting and purifying herself in a cold river, she is tricked by Satan, who has disguised himself and tricks her again.[16] The text explains that Satan had appeared as the serpent in the biblical story.

The New Testament record concerning Eve is rather mixed. Jesus refers to the first couple only in a discussion of divorce that suggests that procreation may not be the sole reason for sex (Matt. 19:4–6). Paul the apostle blames Adam, rather than Eve, for introducing death and sin into the world (1 Cor. 15:21–22; Rom. 5:12, 19). He also maintains that woman is the reflection of man, since she was made from man (1 Cor. 11:7–8). "Nevertheless," Paul adds, "in the Lord woman is not independent of man or man independent of woman. For just as woman came from man, so man comes through woman; but all things come from God" (1 Cor. 11:11–12). In contrast, the letter 1 Timothy, which has been attributed to Paul, relies on Genesis 3 to justify excluding women from church administration.[17] The writer says that "Adam was not deceived, but the woman was deceived and became a transgressor" (1 Tim. 2:14). It was Eve and not Adam who was responsible for human sin. While Paul sees salvation for women and men in Christ, the author of 1 Timothy says that women "will be saved through childbearing, provided they continue in faith and love and holiness, with modesty" (1 Tim. 2:15).

The church writers of the patristic era—which dates from the second century to the fifth or even eighth century, depending on the source—continue to blame Eve and the daughters of Eve for the problems besetting humanity. The North African theologian Tertullian (d. ca. 220)[18] stresses in the second century that each woman is an Eve:

> *You* are the devil's gateway: *you* are the unsealer of that [forbidden] tree; *you* are the first deserter of the divine law; *you* are she who persuaded him whom the devil was not valiant enough to attack. *You* destroyed so easily God's image, man. On account of *your* desert—that is, death—even the Son of God had to die.[19]

Despite Tertullian's vigorous condemnation of Eve for "unsealing" the tree, eating from the tree of knowledge could be interpreted as an act of free will, courage, and necessity. This is how members of the Church of Jesus Christ, Latter-day Saints read the story. Eve was faced with two commandments: be fruitful and multiply, and do not eat from the tree of knowledge. She chose to disobey the second mandate in order to obey the first, since it was only with knowledge that the first couple perceived their nakedness. Nevertheless, the dominant Christian view from the time of Paul to the present is that eating from the tree of knowledge was the first, and therefore the worst possible, act of disobedience. The original perfection intended by God was damaged, and because of their expulsion from the Garden of Eden, humans no longer bore the image and likeness of the divine in their persons.

While the apostle Paul believed that Adam's rebellion introduced sin and death into the world—he simply ignored Eve in his analysis—subsequent theologians elaborated a doctrine of original sin. As articulated by Saint Augustine of Hippo (354–430), this sin is transmitted from Adam through the man's sperm during sexual intercourse. This understanding of human nature asserts that humans are ontologically evil: they are born with their free will impaired and with an inclination toward immoral behavior.

From this pessimistic anthropology developed the soteriology that declared that only Jesus could restore human perfection by erasing the sin of disobedience through his perfect obedience to God, even to the point of dying. As the first transgressor, Eve opened the path to salvation, for the fall from primeval perfection necessitated the restoration of the lost image and likeness of God. Jesus's sacrificial death wiped the slate clean, and enabled humans to reconcile themselves with God.

Eve informs ensuing theology in two far-reaching ways. First, she inevitably accompanies discussions of gender in later theological discussions about the nature of women and the justification of men's power. Christian anthropology, for better and worse, hinges upon interpretations of the first humans. Second, the rebellion against God's injunction provides not only the etiology for understanding the human condition, but also the explanation for the incarnation; that is, the reason why God needed to assume human flesh in the person of Jesus. Christian soteriology looks to Genesis for its ideas about creation and how the world came to be, and for its ideas about the need for redemption, due to the actions of Adam and Eve.

Thus, Eve leads to Jesus. And though she seems not to have been important to the earthly man of Nazareth, she becomes very important to his successors.

2

The Women Disciples in the Kingdom of God

Christianity began as a movement within first-century Palestinian Juda-ism to bring about the kingdom of God. Led by an itinerant charismatic preacher, Jesus of Nazareth, the movement adopted an egalitarian orga-nization that included Torah-observant women and men, as well as those living on the fringes of respectable society. Women served at the core of the movement. The oldest gospel, Mark, states that a number of women "used to follow [Jesus] and provided for him when he was in Galilee; and there were many other women who had come up with him to Jerusalem" (15:41). Jesus's female disciples not only financed the movement, they undoubtedly cooked and washed for the male disciples as they traveled throughout Judea, Galilee, and beyond.

What can we learn about these people, given that the texts we have were written in the first and second centuries by those living within a patriarchal culture? Clearly the New Testament authors had clear-cut audiences and definite purposes in mind, and their writing was care-fully crafted to communicate specific messages. To restore women to the earliest history of Christianity does not require discovering new sources, but "rereading the available sources in a different key," according to Elis-abeth Schüssler Fiorenza.[1]

The four Gospels depict women in a great variety of modes: as actors and agents of their own destinies, recipients of healing, models of faith, and characters in Jesus's parables about the kingdom of God. They pres-ent Martha and Mary, two sisters who respond to Jesus through different forms of discipleship. They also show Mary of Nazareth, the mother of Jesus, and Mary of Magdala, the first witness to the empty tomb. Femi-nist scholars have noted the strikingly distinctive models of Christian womanhood that these two Marys offer.

FIGURE 2.1. Mural depicting the Virgin of Guadalupe, Tijuana, B.C., Mexico. Photo by author.

The Kingdom of God

The sources of information about Jesus's life and teachings are few, and those that exist are subjective. "Gospel" means good news, or good message, good report; thus, the Gospels are not impartial biographies or eyewitness accounts, but rather theological presentations of different interpretations of who Jesus was (the theological idea of Christology) and what Jesus did (the theological idea of soteriology). Extrabiblical sources—that is, nonbiblical historical texts—are few, and say more about John the Baptizer (who lived concurrently with Jesus and who also had a large group of followers) than about Jesus himself.

Christian theologians have attempted to identify what they believe to be actual historical elements embedded in the four Gospels. They differentiate between the Jesus of history and the Christ of faith. The Jesus of history is Jesus of Nazareth, the human being who walked the earth teaching and preaching the coming kingdom of God. The Christ of faith is the exalted figure who is the Word of God Incarnate and the second person of the Trinity, the Son of God. The Gospels intermingle both visions of Jesus: the lowly human and the exalted divinity.

The historical Jesus was the one who dealt directly with women and men from every level of society. Who was he? Paula Fredriksen, professor of scripture emerita at Boston University, begins her book *From Jesus to Christ* with this brief summary:

> Sometime around the year 30 C.E., Jesus, a Nazarene peasant and charismatic religious leader, was executed in Jerusalem as a political agitator by the Roman prefect Pontius Pilate. . . . Despite his death, however, his followers did not disband. They grouped together, preserving some of Jesus' teachings and some stories about him, which became part of the substance of their preaching as they continued his mission to prepare Israel for the coming Kingdom of God.[2]

Most Christians agree that Jesus did indeed preach the kingdom of God (*he basileia tou theou*, e.g., Luke 18:12), but they do not necessarily agree on the nature of that realm. New Testament scholars have provided different translations of the original Greek in order to indicate a nonhierarchical state of being rather than a form of governance. Thus, we have reign of God, realm of God, kindom (without the letter *g*, to indicate kinship) of God, and commonweal of God. (I will use the most literal translation, kingdom of God.) The Jewish expectation was that God's reign would occur on earth, not in an afterlife. Both the canonical gospels and the noncanonical gospels (those that do not make it into the New Testament canon) provide ample evidence in Jesus's life and teachings that he was part of a movement that sought to restructure human relations in an egalitarian and antihierarchical way. "To some extent, speaking of the 'Jesus movement' inevitably reinscribes the heroic isolation of Jesus within the tradition," says Mary Rose D'Angelo, professor of theology at the University of Notre Dame:

> I prefer to speak of the reign-of-God movement on the grounds of the older critical insight that insisted that Jesus preached not himself, but God's reign, and to see God's reign as a movement of Jewish spiritual resistance to the violent and idolatrous reign of Caesar.[3]

When we focus on the kingdom of God in the Gospels, rather than on Jesus, we find that women are intimately involved in a movement greater than a single person. There are the Twelve, the dozen men handpicked by Jesus to be his closest companions; there are also other disciples, both women and men, named and unnamed; and, after Jesus's death, there are apostles, that is, evangelists sent out by the movement to spread the word about the Jesus the Messiah, the Anointed One; or, in Greek, the Christ.

Women and Jesus

Jesus's encounter with a Samaritan woman at a well shows that a woman is the first person to recognize Jesus as a prophet and a messiah in John's gospel (John 4:1–42), suggesting female proselytizing to the Gentiles. In this story, Jesus asks a lone woman at a well for some water. Although she is surprised, since animosity exists between Jews and Samaritans, she engages in a theological discussion with Jesus, asking him for the "living water" that he promises, and wondering where the proper location for the worship of God is, an issue of conflict for Jews and Samaritans.[4] While the male disciples express amazement at finding Jesus talking to an unchaperoned woman, the woman herself returns to her community and tells everyone to "Come and see a man who told me everything I have ever done! He cannot be the Messiah, can he?" (John 4:29). The gospel narrative then states, "Many Samaritans from that city believed in him because of the woman's testimony," and concludes that "many more believed because of his word" (John 4:39, 41). Thus, a Samaritan woman serves as an important evangelist in this story.

Jesus's confrontation in Mark's gospel with another Gentile woman—a Phoenician from Syria—signals a dramatic turning point in his ministry. The unnamed woman crashes a dinner party Jesus is attending, begging him to heal her daughter, who is afflicted with a demon (Mark 7:24–30). Jesus refuses, saying, "Let the children be fed first, for it is not fair to take the children's food and throw it to the dogs." But the woman perseveres and retorts, "Yes, Lord, even the dogs under the table eat the children's crumbs." Jesus is stung by this: "Then he said to her, 'For saying that, you may go—the demon has left your daughter.' So she went home, found the child lying on the bed, and the demon gone."

Why does Jesus initially refuse to perform this particular healing? He had already healed a foreign man (Mark 5:1–13); and he had raised the daughter of the leader of the synagogue (Mark 5:21–43). The woman is respectful, bowing down before him, but her conduct is also eccentric, especially when she responds in kind to Jesus's metaphor about dogs.

Moreover, it is not faith that has healed the woman's daughter, but it is her "word," her retort, that changes Jesus's mind. "The Syrophoenician woman has led the Markan Jesus to enlarge the boundaries to include even Gentiles."[5]

Yet faith does typify the women with whom Jesus engages, especially the faith of two sisters in the Gospel of John (John 11:1–44): Martha and Mary of Bethany, a village on the Mount of Olives to the east of Jerusalem. When their brother Lazarus dies, Martha goes out to meet Jesus, who apparently arrives too late to save him. "But even now I know that God will give you whatever you ask of him," she says to Jesus (John 11:22). Jesus asks her whether she believes in him. She proclaims, "Yes, Lord, I believe that you are the Messiah, the Son of God, the one coming into the world" (John 11:27). While other individuals in John's gospel have wondered whether Jesus were the Messiah, Martha is the first to declare this belief explicitly. Jesus tells the weeping women to roll away the stone covering the entrance to the tomb of Lazarus, where his enshrouded body had been buried for four days. Martha remonstrates, saying there is already a stench, but Jesus commands Lazarus to come out, and he does. This resuscitation causes a number of those present to believe in Jesus.

While Martha demonstrates faith in this first pericope, or scriptural unit, about the sisters, Mary demonstrates deep understanding of the nature of Jesus's mission in a second. Six days before Passover, Jesus returns to Bethany to have dinner with Lazarus, Martha, and Mary (John 12:1–8). Martha serves the food and Mary anoints Jesus's feet with expensive perfume. When Judas objects to the expense, Jesus reproves him by saying, "Leave her alone. She bought it so that she might keep it for the day of my burial" (John 12:7). There is no indication in John's gospel that the Twelve, unlike Mary, recognize Jesus's impending death. "Martha's confession and Mary's act of anointing suggest that they are disciples," writes Adele Reinhartz, professor of religious studies at the University of Ottawa. "That they hosted a dinner for Jesus, at which others of his inner circle were present, implies that the sisters, or women like them, were also part of, or close to, this inner circle."[6]

All four Gospels include a story about an anointing woman, but they recast it to suit their theological purposes. John has Mary of Bethany, an upstanding disciple, anoint his feet, while Luke has a sinful woman do it. Matthew follows the oldest account, that given in Mark, by having a woman pour costly oil on Jesus's head. In Mark and Matthew, the disciples berate the woman for wasting the money on an extravagance, but Jesus chides them.

> "Let her alone; why do you trouble her? . . . She has done what she could; she has anointed my body beforehand for its burial. Truly I tell you, wherever the good news is proclaimed in the whole world, what she has done will be told in remembrance of her" (Mark 14:6–9).

Why will this anonymous woman be remembered? She has performed a prophetic action, states Schüssler Fiorenza, and thus emerges as the true disciple. "While Peter had confessed, without truly understanding it, 'you are the anointed one,' the woman anointing Jesus recognizes clearly that Jesus's messiahship means suffering and death."[7]

Luke's gospel portrays Mary and Martha rather differently (10:38–42) than John's gospel. When Jesus pays the women a visit, Mary silently sits listening to what he is saying, while Martha bustles about doing chores. "So she came to him and asked, 'Lord, do you not care that my sister has left me to do all the work by myself?'" Martha begs Jesus to tell Mary to help her, but Jesus defends Mary and tells Martha she needs to focus on what's important. "She is the loser, with whom the reader is not supposed to identify, but with whom many readers do."[8] Feminist theologians have argued that the author of Luke was attempting to discourage women from participating in the preaching ministry in the early church. Somewhat incongruously, though, Martha seems to be a *diakonos*, that is, a church leader. Furthermore, both Luke and John present Martha as the host who receives Jesus, thus suggesting that she is the head of the household.[9]

Despite Luke's negative portrayal of the sisters—Martha the distracted one and Mary the passive one—they reappear throughout subsequent history as ideal types or models of two ways of being a Christian. Mary leads the contemplative life, serving God through prayer and meditation; Martha leads the active life, serving God through works of charity. Later interpreters will argue that nuns and monks embody Mary in contemplation and that ordinary laypeople live in the world of action like Martha; still others, that Christians must incarnate both women.

In addition to interacting with Jesus, women serve as exemplary figures in Jesus's parables, his metaphorical stories that draw on the real-life experiences of Jewish Mediterranean peasants. In Matthew, Jesus says, "The kingdom of heaven is like yeast that a woman took and mixed in with three measures of flour until all of it was leavened" (Matt. 13:33; also in Luke 13:20–21). The story suggests that work traditionally done by women has value. The three measures of flour could feed about a hundred people, and was about the largest amount of dough a person could knead. Thus, the kingdom of God, or kingdom of Heaven, in Matthew's gospel, "although hidden like a small bit of leaven in a mound of dough, will become—through this woman's effort—the bread of life."[10]

In Luke, Jesus asks, "What woman having ten silver coins, if she loses one of them, does not light a lamp, sweep the house, and search carefully until she finds it?" When she does find it, she rejoices with her friends. "Just so, I tell you, there is joy in the presence of the angels of God over one sinner who repents" (Luke 15:8–10). The story of the woman and the lost coin is one of a dozen couplets that pair a story about a woman with a story about a man in Luke's gospel.[11] Luke also presents a parable of a widow who persistently appeals for justice from a judge who refuses her case; eventually the judge relents and grants her the request. "Because this widow keeps bothering me, I will grant her justice so that she may not wear me out by continually coming" (Luke 18:2–8). Jesus contrasts this judge—"not a wise man of beneficent power"—with God, who grants "justice to his chosen ones who cry to him day and night" if they are as determined as the widow.[12] Jesus points to another widow—a poor woman who offers two copper coins worth a penny that were "all she had to live on"—as a model of generosity far greater than the offerings of rich people who put in large sums (Mark 12:41–44).

These examples give a brief glimpse into the significant presence of women participating in the kingdom of God movement. Two women stand well above the rest, though: Mary the mother of Jesus and Mary Magdalene.[13] It would be difficult to find two more different types of followers.

Mary the Mother of Jesus

The theology of the Virgin Mary, or Mariology, was built upon exceedingly short sketches of Mary given in the Gospels. The entire New Testament refers to Mary, the mother of Jesus, by name just eighteen times.[14] There are a few additional generic references to the mother of Jesus, such as those that appear in the Gospel of John (2:1–10, 19:25–27). On the other hand, the Gospels include five additional women named Mary as being followers of Jesus: "Mary mother of James the less and Joses, the 'other Mary,' Mary of Bethany, Mary Cleopas, and of course Mary Magdalene."[15] This proliferation of Marys (our Anglicization of Mariamme or Mariam) reflects the popularity of the name Miriam at that time.[16] One reason for its widespread acceptance was that Moses's sister, Miriam, was the great heroine of the escape from Egypt (Exod. 15:20–21).

Only two gospels, Matthew and Luke, describe the miraculous conception of Jesus, while Mark starts with Jesus as an adult and John begins with Jesus as the preexistent Word of God.[17] In Matthew, Joseph, Mary's betrothed, learns that she is pregnant and decides to quietly divorce her once they get married (Matt. 1:18–25). But an angel tells him in a dream that the child is conceived from the Holy Spirit. "She will bear a son, and you are to name him Jesus, for he will save his people from their sins" (Matt. 1:20–21). The angel quotes the Hebrew prophet Isaiah as evidence: "Therefore the Lord himself will give you a sign. Look, the young woman is with child and shall bear a son, and shall name him Immanuel" (Isa. 7:14). While the literal translation of the Hebrew word *almah* means maiden or young woman, the Septuagint—the authoritative Greek version of the Hebrew Bible written between 300 and 200 BCE—translates the same word as *parthenos*, which means virgin.

In Luke's gospel, Mary is a young woman who is engaged to Joseph, but she is not yet pregnant (Luke 1:26–56). In this story, the angel Gabriel comes to Mary and announces that she will conceive a son, that she will call him Jesus, and that he will be great—if she assents. But Mary asks, "How can this be, since I am a virgin [*parthenos*]?" The angel explains, "The Holy Spirit will come upon you, and the power of the Most High will overshadow you; therefore the child to be born will be holy; he will be called Son of God." While Matthew's gospel presents the conception as a *fait accompli*, Luke's gospel gives Mary a choice: yes or no. "Here am I, the servant [slave] of the Lord," says Mary, "Let it be done to me according to your word" (Luke 1:38). She then praises God in a song now called the Magnificat (Luke 1:46–55), one of the strongest statements of God's concern for the poor to appear in the Bible:

> He has brought down the powerful from their thrones, and lifted up the lowly;
>
> He has filled the hungry with good things, and sent the rich away empty.

Mary's *fiat*—her "let it be done"—has been the source of debate among feminist theologians. Is this the assertive decision of a self-possessed woman? Or is it the meek acquiescence of an adolescent girl? "There is no more matriarchal image than the Christian mother of God who bore a child without male assistance," declares the literary critic Marina Warner, author of one of the earliest reconsiderations of Mary.[18] Warner infers from ancient mythology that the virginity of goddesses did not denote a biological quality but rather symbolized their autonomy. "[Their] virginity signified [they] had retained freedom of choice: to take lovers or to reject them."[19] Thus virginity conferred strength and did not necessarily have a moral connotation.

On the other hand, critics stress that Mary adopts a passive stance. Unlike the mother goddesses or divine virgins of ancient mythology, Mary seems disconnected from sexuality. Her asexuality helped to shape Marian devotion through the centuries because it fulfilled Oedipal desires within men and Electra impulses among women, according to one psychoanalytical hypothesis.[20] The Norwegian theologian Kari Børresen argues that making Mary a feminist icon is absurd, "if the essential ecclesiological and Mariological connection between femininity and subordination is ignored or not known."[21] The feminist biblical scholar Jane Schaberg states, "As the male projection of idealized femininity, a patriarchal construction, she is the good woman, stripped of all dangerous elements; she receives worship, not equality."[22] In *Sexism and God-Talk*, Rosemary Radford Ruether observes that traditional Mariology reflects the ideology of the "patriarchal feminine," which sees woman as responsible for sin and death in its exaltation of Mary as the one individual undeformed by sin.[23] Yet Ruether also finds an alternative Mariology in Luke's gospel, where "Mary does not consult Joseph, but makes her own decision. Luke sees this free choice as an expression of her faith."[24]

Mary's centrality for Christianity initially existed in her relationship with Jesus. Bishops meeting in Nicaea in 325 reaffirmed the early Christian belief that the Son of God was fully human. At the same time, they also recognized the full divinity of the Son of God. In 381, bishops gathered at the Council of Constantinople and further clarified this by professing that the Son of God "was incarnate by the Holy Spirit and the Virgin Mary and became human [*enanthrōpēsanta*]."[25] They also enunciated Christian belief in a Trinitarian deity comprising the Father, the Son, and the Holy Spirit. Once the complete divinity and humanity of the Son of God was established, the question arose as to which nature Mary brought forth: the divine or the human? Debate raged over whether she was the *Christotokos* (the Christ Bearer) or the *Theotokos* (the God Bearer). Christian bishops meeting at Ephesus in 431 came down on the side of *Theotokos*, which has since come to be interpreted as "Mother of God."

The doctrine of the *Theotokos* led inexorably to the idea of the perpetual virginity of Mary, although the Gospels clearly refer to Jesus's brothers and sisters;[26] the apostle Paul mentions "James the Lord's brother" (Gal. 1:19); and a church history written by Eusebius of Caesarea in the fourth century relates the martyrdom of James, the brother of the Lord, in Jerusalem. A second-century book, the Proto-Gospel of James, explains that these brothers and sisters were the children of Joseph by a previous marriage. This text also states that Mary's virginity remained intact after the birth of Jesus. Writing in the third century, Tertullian challenged this view by providing a graphic and detailed picture of Jesus's birth and its effect on Mary's womb. Tertullian's contemporaries nevertheless began to accept the idea of Mary's perpetual virginity.

Popular devotion and ascetical practices also served to elevate Mary's status. In the early church, monastic sisterhoods, which required virginity for young women and chastity for widows, looked to Mary as the supreme example of holiness. In the European Middle Ages, she became the iconic mother who suffers for her children. Michelangelo's famous *Pietà* (1498–99/1500), in which Mary holds the dead body of Jesus, captures the maternal grief that Mary symbolized.

Catholic Church leaders call the century between 1850 and 1950 the "Marian Age" because it was marked by two infallible papal dogmas, that is, official statements of church teachings, and by the rise of Marian apparitions.[27] In 1854 Pope Pius IX issued the papal bull *Ineffabilis Deus* (*Indescribable God*), which proclaimed the Immaculate Conception of Mary—that is, that Mary was conceived without original sin. The pope issued this bull, and others, to mobilize the faithful in response to the assaults of modernity upon the Roman Catholic Church, such as the French Revolution (1789–1799) and the subsequent revolutions of 1848 in Europe and Latin America. The second Marian dogma was

pronounced at the end of World War II, another time of social dislocation, when Pope Pius XII issued the bull *Munificentissimus Deus* (*Most
Generous God*) in 1950. Called the dogma of the Assumption, it states
that at her death Mary was taken up, body and soul, into heaven, where
she now sits beside Jesus.

Although the Immaculate Conception and the Assumption seem to
divinize Mary of Nazareth and to exalt her status tremendously, she nevertheless remains close to the hearts of the faithful whom she left behind
on earth. More than 20,000 Marian apparitions have been recorded
since the fourth century,[28] including 210 appearances between 1928 and
1971.[29] Dozens of apparitions that occurred in nineteenth-century Europe gained church approval, including those of Paris (1830), LaSalette
(1846), and most famously Lourdes (1858) in France. Twentieth-century
apparitions have had more difficulty receiving formal church support,
with Fátima, Portugal (1917), being a notable exception.

The most significant apparition of all time is arguably the vision of
the Virgin of Guadalupe reported by Saint Juan Diego (1474–1548) in
1531 in what is now Mexico City. The Virgin had instructed the Indian to
present roses blooming in December to the bishop of Mexico as a sign
that a church should be built on the hill of Tepeyac, former shrine to the
Aztec goddess Tonantzin. Juan Diego carried the roses in a *tilma*, his
native cloak, "but when he spilled out the roses before the great Bishop
in his episcopal palace in Mexico City, the real sign appeared: a full-
length painting of the Virgin Mary miraculously imprinted on his *tilma*
itself."[30] The image of Guadalupe was not appreciably different from
other images of the Immaculate Conception painted in sixteenth- and
seventeenth-century Spain, with one important distinction: she was an
Indian wearing a star-covered cloak in an Aztec style. Initially only indigenous peoples accepted her: she spoke in their language, she looked
like them, and she too suffered the violence, rape, and death that marked
the colonization of Latin America.[31] But when she was credited with
saving Mexico City from a devastating plague in 1737, Spaniards, creoles,
and mixed-race inhabitants also recognized her as their national patron.

Catholic Christians in Latin America appreciate Jesus but seem to value Mary much more, according to the liberation theologians Ivone Gebara and Maria Clara Bingemer.[32] The American Roman Catholic priest Virgilio Elizondo declares that "It is an undeniable fact that devotion to Mary is the most popular, persistent, and original characteristic of Latin American Christianity."[33] Twentieth- and twenty-first-century popes have encouraged Marian devotion among the faithful. Most Protestant Christians, with a different view of scripture and tradition, stand outside this practice, while Orthodox Christians fall somewhere in the middle. "Whether we regard the Virgin Mary as the most sublime and beautiful image in man's struggle towards the good and the pure, or the most pitiable production of ignorance and superstition, she represents a central theme in the history of Western attitudes to women."[34]

Mary of Magdala

Mary Magdalene burst into popular consciousness with the 2003 publication of Dan Brown's novel *The Da Vinci Code*. This work of fiction repackages the arguments made in the 1982 nonfiction work *Holy Blood, Holy Grail*, namely, that Jesus and Mary Magdalene were married and that their descendants were protected throughout the centuries by various knights and religious orders.[35] In 2012 Karen King, a biblical scholar at Harvard Divinity School, made known the discovery of a small papyrus fragment written in Coptic in which Jesus, referring to Mary, says "my wife" (*tahime*).[36] King is careful to point out that this does not necessarily mean that Jesus was married—though it would be rare for a Jewish male not to marry in Jesus's day—but rather that one Christian community as early as the second century believed that he was.

The rise of assertions that Jesus and Mary were married—like the exaltation of the Virgin Mary—has little to do with Mary Magdalene and everything to do with Jesus. Increasing the purity and virginity of Mary of Nazareth served to make Jesus more divine in the early church. Increasing the stature of Mary of Magdala, making her a disciple, a wife, and a leader after Jesus's death, serve to make Jesus more human in to-day's culture. Thus, in the late twentieth century, Mary Magdalene began growing in popularity among feminist and other progressive Christians who view her as a model of discipleship and as an opponent to the church of Peter, that is, the Roman Catholic Church.

Just as Jesus was identified by his hometown, Nazareth, and called the Nazarene, Mary was identified by her hometown, Magdala, and is there-fore called the Magdalene or Magdalen. Today Magdala is the city of Migdal in Israel, about five kilometers north of Tiberias on the western shore of Lake Kinnaret (the Sea of Galilee). In the first century, Migdal was located at an urban crossroads, where Jews and non-Jews mixed. It had a reputation for wealth, luxury, and loose morals.[37] To say one was from Magdala has the same connotation as saying one is from San Fran-cisco or New Orleans: it was hardly Pittsburgh or Peoria.

With the exception of Luke, the Gospels first present Mary Magda-lene at the very end of the narratives, as witness to Jesus's death, burial, and the empty tomb. Luke, however, identifies her early in the gospel as one of the women "who had been cured of evil spirits and infirmities: Mary, called Magdalene, from whom seven demons had gone out, and Joanna, the wife of Herod's steward Chuza, and Susanna, and many oth-ers, who provided for them out of their resources" (Luke 8:2–3). Unlike the other gospels, Luke does not include her by name among the wit-nesses to the crucifixion or the entombment, though he does say, "All his acquaintances, including the women who had followed him from Galilee, stood at a distance, watching these things" (Luke 23:49). John's gospel provides an extended discussion of Mary's encounter with Jesus at the tomb (20:1–18). At first she does not recognize the risen Christ, but when he calls her name, she says in Aramaic, "*Rabbouni!*" (Teacher). John writes, "Mary Magdalene went and announced to the disciples, 'I have seen the Lord'; and she told them that he had said these things to her" (20:18).

The question of witnesses to the resurrection became an important political issue in the early church. Those among the first to see the risen

Christ had more weight than those who came later. Paul the apostle lists the people to whom Jesus appeared: "First to Cephas [Peter], then to the twelve. Then he appeared to more than five hundred brothers and sisters at one time. . . . Then he appeared to James, then to all the apostles. Last of all . . . he appeared also to me" (1 Cor. 15:5–8). Yet the fact that all four Gospels list Mary Magdalene as a witness to the crucifixion and resurrection—which even Luke reluctantly admits—suggests a tradition that Paul either did not know of (since he became an apostle ten years after Jesus's death) or chose to ignore.

Nonbiblical Apocrypha—the books that did not qualify for inclusion in the New Testament—provide many more details about Mary Magdalene. These texts emerged from distinctive Christian communities scattered across North Africa, the Eastern Mediterranean, and the European continent. Although the victors in the early Christological and Trinitarian debates attempted to write the losers out of history by excommunicating dissenters and by destroying their writings, a number of works survived.

In 1945, forty-six papyrus books were discovered in Nag Hammadi, along the upper Nile River in Egypt. Five of these texts give Mary Magdalene "a startlingly prominent role."[38] These include the Gospel of Thomas, the Dialogue of the Savior, the First Apocalypse of James, the Gospel of Philip, and the Sophia of Jesus Christ. Other texts long known to Christian tradition also contain references to Mary Magdalene, including the Pistis Sophia, the Gospel of Peter, and the Gospel of Mary. Although it is possible that some of these texts refer to Mary of Nazareth,[39] most scholars believe that the texts noted above are discussing Mary Magdalene.

The writings in the Nag Hammadi library and some of the early apocryphal texts are usually called Gnostic, a term that is becoming increasingly problematic. Gnosticism has been an umbrella expression that demarcates texts that frequently include a cosmological myth that explains the human fall from wisdom as spiritual beings into the world of ignorance and matter. The Greek term *gnōsis*, or knowledge, characterizes the desire that Gnostics had for recovering their original perfection through attainment of wisdom, or *sophia*. Karen King traces the scholarly construction of Gnosticism as an entity within, or opposed to, Christianity, and predicts that the term Gnosticism will eventually be abandoned, because it is imprecise and distorts contemporary efforts to reconstruct ancient religion.[40]

Whatever we call these texts, it is clear that Mary Magdalene appears in tension with some of the disciples, particularly Peter. In the Pistis Sophia, a text from the third century, Peter complains to Jesus about Mary: "My Lord, we are not able to suffer this woman who takes the opportunity from us, and does not allow anyone of us to speak, but she speaks many times" (36:57–58).[41] Mary in turn complains to Jesus about Peter's intimidation:

> My Lord, my mind is understanding at all times that I should come forward at any time and give the interpretation of the words which she [Pistis Sophia] spoke, but I am afraid of Peter, for he threatens me and hates our race. (72:160–61)[42]

The question of who has the right to speak and teach in Jesus's name also arises in these texts. In the Gospel of Mary (5:5, 9:4–8), a second-century text, Peter admits that "the Savior loved you more than the rest of women," but he and Andrew express disbelief when they hear the teachings Mary imparts. "Did he, then, speak with a woman in private without our knowing about it?" Peter wonders. "Are we to turn around and listen to her? Did he choose her over us?"[43] Mary responds by asking tearfully whether they think she made it all up. Levi comes to her assistance and berates Peter, saying the disciple has always been an angry person. "If the Savior made her worthy, who are you then for your part to reject her?"[44] The so-called Gnostic texts present Mary Magdalene as part of the discipleship team; in fact, given her close relationship with the Master, she is a leader of the team.

Early iconography reveals a progressive exaltation of Mary Magdalene. She is frequently shown in the loose garments worn by consecrated virgins, especially when she appears along with the Virgin Mary. One representation depicts the two Marys approaching an altar, a symbol for the empty tomb. Amulets from the sixth century sold to pilgrims to the Holy Land also show these women in the act of censing an altar.[45] Stone coffins depict Mary Magdalene as the original witness to the resurrection, and early church theologians agreed that she was the first to impart the good news to the other disciples. This testimony earned her the honorific of "apostle to the apostles."

The reverence for Mary Magdalene as the apostle to the apostles changed in 591, however, when Pope Gregory the Great (p. 590–604)[46] preached a series of homilies on chapter 7 of Luke. In that story, Jesus forgives a sinful woman who washes his feet with her hair. In one of his sermons, Gregory stated unequivocally, "We believe that this woman [Mary Magdalene] whom Luke calls a female sinner, whom John [the Evangelist] calls Mary, is the same Mary from whom Mark [Mark 16:9] says seven demons were cast out."[47] Gregory was attempting to conclusively terminate the confusion about all of the Marys named in the Gospels, but the effect was to turn Mary Magdalene into a repentant prostitute. As a result, European art frequently presents images of Mary as a pathetic, seminude figure. Painters liked to emphasize her hair and her breasts as she knelt before Jesus in positions of prostration or repentance.

Mary Magdalene nevertheless lived on as the patron of churches, religious orders, and charitable outreach to women, most notably prostitutes. Magdalen homes opened throughout Great Britain in the eighteenth and nineteenth centuries, operated by some who saw sex work as caused by poverty, and by others who saw poverty as caused by sex work. The popular press called rescue workers and sex workers alike magdalens. But nineteenth-century British and American feminists also found in the Magdalene a model of a biblical woman they might emulate, an apostle engaged in missionary work.

When the Council of Trent (1545–1563) of the Catholic Church produced a Roman Missal, or Order of Service, in 1570, it identified Mary

Magdalene as a penitent.[48] When the Second Vatican Council (1962–1965) of the Church commissioned a new missal, which came out in 1970, the word "penitent" no longer appeared. The scripture readings assigned for her saint's day, July 22, are dramatically different: pre–Vatican II told the story of the sinful woman in Luke 7; post–Vatican II gives the account of Mary's encounter with the risen Christ in John 20.

Mary Magdalene's recovery by contemporary feminist theologians is an example of how women scholars can visit ancient texts and find new meaning in them. Shorn of two thousand years of art and culture, Mary Magdalene now comes to us as an authentic evangelist, speaking out even when disbelieved. As a rival to Peter, she resonates with those criticizing today's Church of Peter. She was valiant, she was respected, she seemed to have an important position among the disciples, and she was female. All of these qualities make her an attractive saint for the twenty-first century.

Conclusions

The kingdom of God movement that Jesus led included female and male disciples. Feminist theologians have presented evidence, only briefly touched upon here, demonstrating that the movement was egalitarian, nonhierarchical, and gender-inclusive. Two remarkable women support this argument. Mary of Nazareth responded to God's call with trust and faithfulness, making her a model believer. Subsequent interpretations of Mary, though, seemed to create an impossible model for women to follow: virgin *and* mother? But the Blessed Virgin Mary hears the cries of the poor, and so remains the dominant figure of divine compassion for millions of Roman Catholics around the world. Mary Magdalene, in contrast, was only too human, suffering for centuries the false accusation that she was a reformed prostitute. Modern reconstructions portray her as a lively, engaged, and challenging disciple, and perhaps the wife of Jesus. Contemporary feminists find the apostle to the apostles an exemplary figure for Christians today.

FIGURE 3.1. *Saints Perpetua and Felicity*, by Robert Lentz, O.F.M.
© Robert Lentz. Courtesy of Trinity Stores, www.trinitystores.com.

3

Women and the Conversion of an Empire

Women were crucial to the spread of Christianity in its earliest centuries. Inscriptions, iconography, and material culture testify to the continuing and influential presence of Christian, Jewish, and pagan women throughout the Greco-Roman world. Texts written by Christian women, as by any female writers in antiquity, are extremely scarce, however. Notable exceptions include the diary of Vibia Perpetua, who was martyred in Carthage around 203;[1] the journal of Egeria, who made a pilgrimage to the Holy Land between 381 and 384;[2] and the *cento* (in Latin, patchwork) of Faltonia Betitia Proba, written in the mid-fourth century, which used verses of Vergil to retell the biblical story of Genesis and the birth, life, and death of Jesus.[3] Legends and oral traditions featuring heroines were shared in communities of women before being committed to writing and may offer some glimpses into the lives and beliefs of other women.

Scholars must therefore piece together a history from various sources to make some deductions about how women shaped early Christianity. In addition to scrutinizing the artifacts of material culture, we must read between the lines of texts written by men. One analysis of Paul's first letter to the church at Corinth, for example, reconstructs the actions of Corinthian women prophets by deconstructing Pauline rhetoric.[4] If the apostle Paul advises women in Corinth to cover their hair when prophesying (1 Cor. 11:4–7), then it is likely that they were prophesying without covering their hair. If he writes that "women should be silent in the churches" (1 Cor. 14:34), then it seems likely that women were actually speaking in the churches. Granted, there are a number of good reasons for thinking that Paul might not have written this prohibition,[5] or that he was quoting from a letter he had received from the men in Corinth,[6] or that he was addressing a specific problem unique to Corinth, given his praise of women leaders in his letter to the Romans;[7] nevertheless, subsequent interpreters have used this verse to exclude women from ministry. "It is precisely in the context of such contentious passages that the whole question of scriptural authority is raised with considerable urgency."[8]

The first four centuries of Christianity saw both the expansion and the contraction of women's leadership of the early church. Under Paul, women directed house churches, and after his death they were ordained to particular church offices. The Roman torture of Christians—which did not discriminate between women and men—paradoxically enlarged Christianity by laying the foundation for a cult of martyrs, which women generated and supported. With the end of the repression, Christians sought another way to imitate Christ's sufferings: asceticism. One of the enduring debates about the status of women in the early church concerns the freedom and autonomy that women achieved through renunciation: Did women gain more or lose more by giving up home and family in order to be Christians? The question became moot by the end of the fourth century, however, when a centralized, hierarchical church radically reduced women's ecclesial independence. Women had converted an empire, but in the end, their very success led to their marginalization.

Women in the Pauline Churches

As one feminist commentator has observed, "[Saint] Paul, to put it mildly, doesn't have a great deal of street credibility with feminists."[9] In addition to telling women that they should cover their heads and keep silent in churches, he says that the husband has authority over his wife, that celibacy is preferable to marriage, and that a Christian wife should not divorce her unbelieving husband—unless he divorces her first. Yet the picture of Paul as an unrepentant sexist is inaccurate, for he also says that conjugal rights are mutual: A husband or a wife cannot suddenly decide to become celibate (1 Cor. 7:4–5). He also quotes words from a baptismal formula that "are the clearest statement of women's equality to be found in the Christian scriptures."[10]

> There is no longer Jew or Greek, there is no longer slave or free, there is no longer male and female; for all of you are one in Christ Jesus. (Gal. 3:28)

Furthermore, he distinctly names women among ministers, coworkers, missionaries, and apostles whom he admires. Thus, Paul is a very complicated figure who is difficult to interpret and impossible to categorize.

Much of what Paul says must be considered in light of his expectation that Jesus was returning very soon, that is, within his own lifetime. This eschatological view explains, in part, some of Paul's reluctance to change the status quo. Paul was a Diaspora Jew from what is now Turkey, "a Hebrew born of Hebrews; as to the law, a Pharisee; as to zeal, a persecutor of the church" (Phil. 3:5–6). A nascent movement of Jews and Gentiles who believed that Jesus was the expected messiah—who called themselves followers of The Way—had existed for about a decade before Paul received his revelation from Jesus (Gal. 1:15–16) and joined their numbers. He then embarked upon a missionary odyssey to proclaim the good news to Gentiles, which took him from the Arabian Peninsula to the cities of Asia Minor and Greece, and finally to Rome. The New Testament book called Acts of the Apostles sketches some of these travels, as do Paul's own letters. What is immediately apparent from both Acts and Paul is the vital presence of women in the church.

Acts describes a number of apostles—that is, individuals who were sent out to teach, preach, administer rites, and perform other duties—but focuses on two figures who dominate the imagination of the later church: the disciple Peter and the apostle Paul.[11] The book begins with the Ascension of Jesus, after which the disciples, "together with certain women, including Mary the mother of Jesus, as well as his brothers," retire to a room to pray (1:14). At Pentecost, when the Holy Spirit descends on a large number of women and men assembled in Jerusalem, the author indicates that the spirit of prophecy has come to all people alike. He quotes the prophet Joel: "In the last days it will be, God declares, that I will pour out my Spirit upon all flesh, and your sons and your daughters shall prophesy" (2:17). Acts notes that Philip the evangelist had four un-married daughters who "had the gift of prophecy" (21:9).

Although Acts features a number of women—reporting that "not a few of the leading women" who were devout Greeks joined the new movement (17:4, 12)—three stand out. Lydia, a merchant and dye-seller, invites Paul to stay at her home after she hears him preach one Sabbath to a group of women who had gathered by the river in Philippi (16:13). It seems that once she and her household are baptized, she hosts community gatherings at her home. "For the author of Acts, Lydia no doubt serves as a fine example of the women of high standing who were drawn to early Christianity and who benefited the community in various ways acting as patrons."[12] Tabitha (or Dorcas, in Greek) is "a disciple" in Joppa who is "devoted to good works and acts of charity" (9:36). When she dies of illness, other disciples send for Peter, who tells her to get up, which she does with his assistance. Neither Lydia nor Tabitha appear to have husbands, and they move about with great freedom, so it is likely that they are widows.

Priscilla and her missionary partner—probably her husband—Aquila is the third important woman described in Acts (and in 1 Cor. 16:19; Rom. 16:3; and 2 Tim. 4:19). There are several interesting things about Priscilla, or more properly Prisca, as Paul refers to her. First, in four out of six New Testament references, although a woman, she is listed before Aquila, which may indicate either that she is of a higher status or that she is a prominent missionary. Second, it is clear that she is a full partner with Aquila in teaching the basics of the faith, as the example of instructing Apollos, an educated man himself, reveals. "In a rare and un-usual portrayal in Acts, we see a woman exercising decisive leadership and sustained intellectual engagement and instruction with a male."[13] Finally, in his letter to the Romans, Paul greets Prisca and Aquila as coworkers, using the Greek word *synergos* (Rom. 16:3), which he uses elsewhere to refer both to important colleagues and to less well-known participants in the early Christian missionary movement.[14] Some Bibles translate *synergos* as "helpers" (King James Version) or interpret the passage in verb form—"who work with me in Christ" (New Revised Standard Version)—which masks the stature that Prisca and Aquila have as Paul's coworkers.

Other Greek words Paul uses to describe women leaders in the church are equally illuminating. One example is *diakonos*, which at that point in the church's history meant minister; another is *prostatis* (the feminine form of *prostates*), which meant patron or benefactor. Although Paul commends the *diakonos* Phoebe, "a benefactor of many and of myself as well," to the Roman church (Rom. 16:1), translators are loathe to say that Phoebe is a minister. Some render *diakonos* as servant; others present it as deaconess, placing her in a church office for women that did not exist for another two centuries; still others depict her as a helper, leader, or "special servant" to the church; some even say that she is a deacon, although that literal approach is also misleading. Phoebe undoubtedly has a position of some standing in the Christian missionary movement, since Paul calls her a *sister*, a *minister* of the church at Cenchreae, and a *patron* of the church and of himself (in Greek, *adelphē, diakonos, prostatis* [Rom. 16:1–2]).[15]

When Paul says that Andronicus and Junia, a missionary couple like Prisca and Aquila, "are prominent among the apostles" (Rom. 16:7), still more difficulties arise for androcentric translators. Because some interpreters could not believe that a woman was an apostle, they have tried to make Junia a man, grammatically speaking. The fact that there are no instances of a man with this name in late antiquity, and that the female name Junia is well attested epigraphically, makes this a challenging position to defend. Moreover, early Christian male theologians had no doubt that Junia was a woman. John Chrysostom (347–407) praised her, saying, "How great the wisdom of this woman must have been that she was even deemed worthy of the title of apostle."[16] The earliest English translations of the Bible kept her female—Junia, or sometimes Julia—

and the King James Version always presented her as the feminine Junia. But thanks to Martin Luther in the sixteenth century and subsequent interpreters, she changed gender and became the male Junias.[17] It is only in recent translations, such as the New American Bible, the New Revised Standard Version, and the New Living Translation, that her proper gender is restored.

For feminist theologians, Paul definitely has a mixed reputation, given his conflicting and contradictory statements about women and their place in the church. From radical equality (no longer male and female) to women's subordination (Christ is the head of every man, and the husband is the head of his wife), Paul's pronouncements about women can be used, and have been used, to justify a range of opinions. As the Christian theologian Georgia Harkness observes, a number of Paul's statements are repeatedly cited to bar women from ordination, and "have doomed women to subordination and exclusion from leadership in both church and society."[18] The irony is that Paul did allow women to speak in the churches. These texts have taken on a life of their own, however, "not because of some historical accident, but rather because of their critical position in the history of the dominant religious tradition in the West."[19]

House Churches: The Center of Christian Life and Practice

The basic unit of organization in the Pauline missions was the home, where people gathered on the Lord's Day (Sunday) for a common meal in remembrance of Jesus.[20] The New Testament mentions a number of women leaders of these house churches (Philem. 2; 1 Cor. 16:19; Rom. 16:5; Col. 4:15; Acts 16:14–15, 40). The household functioned at the intersection between the public and private spheres for early Christians, providing the arena for conversion, especially when believers and non-believers lived in the same home. Because women were charged with managing the household, they gained prestige by hosting church meetings in their homes. "Scholars now recognize that because so much important activity took place in a sphere traditionally associated with women, possibilities for women's involvement in leadership roles must have been greatly increased."[21]

The clear involvement of women in directing and running house churches may at first appear to be an anomaly, given the fact that women in the ancient world seem to have had limited options. Feminist historians, classicists, and theologians have challenged that stereotype. Although wives in Athens were completely under the control of their husbands, the *hetairai* of Corinth were somewhat independent, well-educated courtesans, and Spartan women had relatively great freedom and the ability to own property. The Roman matron "apparently enjoyed a greater degree of freedom than in any other ancient civilization," but she remained under the power of the father (*patria potestas*), the life-and-death rule by the male head of the household.[22] Jewish women also took positions of responsibility in late antiquity. Funerary epitaphs and dedicatory inscriptions reveal that Jewish women held a range of religious offices from the first through sixth centuries, "such as ruler of the synagogue, mother of the synagogue, elder, and priest."[23] In reality, women in the ancient world did not lead entirely circumscribed lives, since as managers of the household they supervised employees, administered financial resources, and even ran profitable businesses from the home.

Yet the extent to which women could engage in these activities outside the home remained limited by the social and cultural norms regarding what was believed to be the proper domain of the two sexes. Men belonged in the public sphere—the courts, the marketplace, the government—where they maintained the reputation of themselves and their families by acting honorably. Women belonged in the private sphere—the home—where they, too, maintained the family's honor by protecting their chastity. "A woman's reputation rested on her sexuality, on a public demonstration that she was sexually exclusive," writes Karen Jo Torjesen, professor at Claremont Graduate University. "The process of achieving honor—challenge, competition, public identity—

contradicted what a woman as an embodiment of femaleness should signify, namely, submission, passivity, timidity, and sexual restraint."[24] This honor-shame system based on gender duties dominated the ancient Mediterranean world, and still exists today within some cultures.

It is easy to see why participation of women in public religious assemblies might create problems within a culture that believed that a woman's place was in the home, and why female-led house churches might be troublesome, especially if they were spreading false teachings. The New Testament letters of 1 Timothy, 2 Timothy, and Titus were composed by an author or authors known by scholars as "deutero-Paul" (second Paul), writing under Paul's name in the second century to tackle exactly this problem.[25] The author of 1 Timothy advises, "Have nothing to do with profane myths and old wives' tales" (1 Tim. 4:7). The second letter to Timothy also expresses concern about false teaching and predicts that people will have "itching ears" and "will accumulate for themselves teachers to suit their own desires, and will turn away from listening to the truth, and wander away to myths" (2 Tim. 4:3–4). What are these false teachings? In the letter to Titus, the author complains of those who advise circumcision; in both 1 and 2 Timothy the teaching is probably a form of Gnosticism because of the reference to myths and "old wives' tales." First Timothy also indicates that some are urging celibacy upon church members, especially upon young women—married and unmarried alike—and young widows.

These false teachings were undoubtedly spreading through the house churches. Each house church was relatively independent, with the congregation coming together weekly for prayer and confession of faith, for reading of scripture and its interpretation, for teaching and preaching to give spiritual or moral instruction, and for sharing of the Lord's Supper, which began as a common meal and developed into a ritual commemoration of Jesus's death.[26] Baptisms may have been conducted in "living water," that is, streams or rivers, or in ritual baths.[27] Women were engaged in all of these activities and rituals. "The house church, by virtue of its location, provided equal opportunities for women, because traditionally the house was considered women's proper sphere, and women were not excluded from activities in it."[28]

The house churches seem to threaten the author(s) of the Pastoral Letters. Women should not teach, but rather must "learn in silence with full submission. I permit no woman to teach or to have authority over a man; she is to keep silent" (1 Tim. 2:11–12). There is a hierarchical arrangement of responsibility in this post-Pauline situation, with specific qualifications required of bishops, deacons, elders, and widows. An order of widows described in 1 Timothy 5:3–16 states that women must be at least sixty years old and married only once; a woman must "be well attested for her good works, as one who has brought up children, shown hospitality, washed the saints' feet, helped the afflicted, and devoted herself to doing good in every way."

These various orders developed in the first and second centuries for three important reasons. First, an institutional and hierarchical ministry had supplanted the charismatic ministry of the missionary period. The Pauline "participatory structure was gradually replaced by patriarchal office and cultic ministry."[29] Second, the canon of scripture was in flux, which meant that Gnostic and apocryphal texts were just as authoritative as the texts that eventually entered the New Testament canon. Finally, because Jesus had not returned, the radical egalitarianism of his early followers was virtually banished by conformity to social norms and expectations. This meant that Christian women needed to conduct themselves appropriately and not call negative attention to themselves by being gadabouts or busybodies (1 Tim. 5:13). "It seems that what outsiders are saying about early Christian women is being internalized and transformed into a teaching about the behaviour of women."[30]

One practice particularly at odds with cultural expectations was the adoption of chastity as a lifestyle. Chastity means abstaining from all sexual relations, not just extramarital ones, and has the advantage of suggesting "womanly virtue"; celibacy also means abstinence, while continence merely indicates self-restraint.[31] The Pastoral Letters are critical of the unmarried lifestyle because it challenges the prevailing Greco-

Roman understanding of marriage as the foundation of a stable social order. One apocryphal text, the *Acts of Paul and Thecla*, may have actually prompted the composition of the Pastoral Letters.[32] In this very popular tale, a young woman named Thecla dedicates herself to chastity after she hears Paul preaching. She rejects her fiancé and is brought before the authorities for punishment. But acts of God and the intercession of females—and an obliging lioness in an arena—protect her from the many tribulations she undergoes. Thecla's main transgression is that, as a single female, she rejects the patriarchal order of the household and enters the public sphere of men to preach and teach.[33]

The Pastoral Letters, in contrast, recommend that young "widows" marry quickly. In the New Testament, *khēra* (widow) can mean a woman with a dead husband, a woman living without a husband—that is, separated from a husband—or a woman who is destitute, miserable, or living in solitude.[34] The early Christian martyr Ignatius of Antioch (d. ca. 117) concludes his letter to the Smyrnaeans with a salutation to "the virgins who are called widows." Thus, 1 Timothy 5:11–14 actually announces a new prohibition on the adoption of chastity by young women. The Pastorals try to defuse mounting tensions between church and empire, since "remaining unmarried was readily interpreted as a challenge to the order of the household."[35]

Widows constituted a well-recognized church office. Writing in the early third century, Tertullian explicitly mentioned an "order of widows" and described their duties as "educators of children . . . readily aiding all others with counsel and comfort."[36] That is to say, they taught and they performed pastoral duties. But another third-century work, the *Didascalia Apostolorum* (*Teachings of the Apostles*), explicitly prohibited widows from teaching and said that their work was to pray and "to supplicate the Lord God."[37] Widows were considered to be "the altar of God," both the location where sacrifices were brought and the sacrifice itself, through their life and work. By interceding for the church and by providing a living reminder of Christ's example, "the widow was an effective agent in a spiritual transaction within the Christian community."[38]

By the third century, a separate order of women—deaconesses (*diakonissai*)—developed in the Eastern Church, that is, the church in the eastern Mediterranean, North Africa, and Asia. Deaconesses ministered to women participating in the baptism ritual, since baptizands were naked. They also provided services to women in their homes, when it would have been inappropriate to send a male deacon.[39] The Western Church did not have an order of deaconesses until the fifth century, when the order of widows was dismantled by the rise of the imperial church. In the Middle Ages, monasteries of unmarried women superseded both orders.

Church of the Martyrs

Despite the efforts of Christians to be model citizens, their secret practices, their independent women, and their disavowal of civic duties—namely, their refusal to participate in community religious rituals—brought the wrath of public and imperial opinion upon them. "When the worship of gods and the emperor's genius [his divine part worthy of veneration] assured the immortals' favor, Christians were blamed for natural disasters because they alienated the gods and caused them to withhold their pleasure and benefaction from mortals."[40] Because Christians pledged allegiance to Christ instead of Caesar, they were deemed unpatriotic. This treasonous behavior took them to the arena, where they faced fiendish torturers, professionally trained gladiators, and wild animals.

Initially, persecution was not widespread but was ordered by individual officials and limited to particular locations: Rome and cities in North Africa and elsewhere. Pliny the Younger, governor of Pontus-Bithynia (r. 111–113)[41] in the Eastern Mediterranean, describes the torture of two female slaves who were called *ministrae* (Latin for the Greek *diakonoi*) in order to learn the truth about the heresy called Christianity that was spreading in the area. "I found nothing else but a depraved and excessive superstition," he reported to the Emperor Trajan.[42] The martyr Blandina fell victim to the localized persecutions in Lyon in Gaul around 177, where Christians faced charges of cannibalism and orgies. Her courage and power, even after her entire body was broken and torn, inspired her fellow sufferers.

The Passion of Saints Perpetua and Felicitas describes the martyrdom of two women in the Carthaginian persecution of 203. Perpetua is a well-born woman, married and with a newborn son, who spurns her father's pleas to renounce Christianity. Felicitas is a pregnant slave who wants an early delivery so that she might die with the other Christians rather than later with a group of criminals; this happens, thanks to the prayers of Felicitas's fellow Christians. The martyrology presents four visions that Perpetua has, during the last of which she sees herself as a man in physical conflict with an Egyptian, whom she interprets to be the devil. She and Felicitas refuse to be dressed as priestesses to the goddess Ceres, and when they walk into the arena in simple tunics, the crowd is repulsed to see that one of the women has just given birth. Wild heifers trample the women, but they remain alive, and Perpetua rearranges her dress and her hair before helping Felicitas get up. They are then put to the sword, but the gladiator commissioned with executing Perpetua botches his first attempt, and she has to guide the sword to her own throat in order to die.[43]

Stephanie Cobb's examination of martyrdom, *Dying to Be Men*, argues that through martyrdom, Christian women and men become more masculine than Roman citizens because they embody the manly virtues of restraint, rationality, and power.[44] It is the mob in the galleries who cannot master their passions, and the torturers themselves who lack self-control and are defeated by the strength of the weak: old men, slaves, women, and youths. "Even Christian *women* were manlier than their male persecutors."[45] Although the martyr accounts masculinize the women, they feminize them as well, noting their attire, their children and families, and their naked bodies.

The number of martyrs killed in the first three centuries of the Common Era is estimated to be between one thousand and ten thousand;

those who were moved by the accounts of martyrs are numbered in the hundreds of thousands. These narratives were written to prepare future martyrs for what they would face in the arena and to gain converts for the church. The spectacles served as a sacred "theater of suffering, attended by a watching cosmos."[46] Few Christians attended these exhibitions, hearing the stories of sacrifice and courage in homes and churches instead. They retold the events in aboveground cemeteries and underground tombs, called catacombs, for the church of the martyrs was also a cult of the dead, led primarily by women.

We have the earliest example of female responsibility for the dead in the women disciples going to the tomb of Jesus to anoint his body. In later centuries women held all-night prayer vigils for those who had died; they met and prayed in cemeteries, bringing gifts of food for the dead until the imperial church banned the practice. Saint Ambrose, bishop of Milan (ca. 340/4–397), chastised Saint Augustine's mother, Saint Monica of Thagaste (331–387), for taking food offerings to graves. Women mourned the dead, cared for their bodies, and, in the era of persecutions, gathered the bones of the martyrs. Romans viewed Christians with horror "because they eagerly revered and treasured the remains of the martyrs' bodies."[47] Churches were constructed on the sites of the martyrs' sacrifices, and if that were not possible, then relics—that is, bones—of the saints were encased below the church altar. In the third century, Roman women who collected and traded in the bones of the martyrs were "religious and economic agents, commodity brokers in the spiritual marketplace that was the newly Christian city of Rome."[48] These female protectors (*patronae*) laid the foundation for Rome's cult of the saints by financing the construction of churches, monasteries, hospitals, guesthouses, cemeteries, and shrines to martyrs.

The Cult of Virginity

Official persecution ceased when Christianity became a legal religion in the Roman Empire with Emperor Constantine's Edict of Milan (313).

Martyrs nevertheless continued to be revered. Church leaders encouraged veneration of their relics and pilgrimages to the holy sites where their deaths occurred, and feast days commemorated their lives. But without being able to endure pain or to sacrifice one's life for God—without suffering like Jesus—how could one be a perfect Christian? In an age of social acceptance, Christians transformed martyrdom into asceticism. One might not be able to die in the arena, but one could die to one's own egotistic desires and ambitions. This renunciation required denying oneself food, clothing, shelter, and most importantly, sex.

Chastity had been an ideal for Christians from the very beginning. Jesus said, "There are eunuchs who have made themselves eunuchs for the kingdom of heaven" (Matt. 19:12). Paul observed that unmarried women and men were more concerned about "the affairs of the Lord" than married couples, who are "anxious about the affairs of the world" (1 Cor. 7:32–35). A number of groups interpreted these statements as advocating a celibate lifestyle. Sexual renunciation was foreign to Jewish tradition, which considered marriage to be the natural state for humans, although there are a few historical exceptions. But Greco-Roman culture prized self-control, rather than self-indulgence, and ascetic schools of philosophy predate the Christian era.

Ascetic communities of women probably existed as early as the second century. Letters from Saints Ignatius of Antioch and Clement of Rome (d. 101) refer to young women who may have taken a vow of chastity, and 1 Timothy 5:16 may also refer to such a community. A number of second- and third-century apocryphal Acts portray women's perspectives on female chastity, suggesting that there may have been communities of single women, subsidized perhaps by a wealthy patroness.[49] In the third century, a movement called the New Prophecy arose, in which two women, Priscilla and Maximilla, and a man, Montanus, channeled messages from the Holy Spirit and advocated a chaste lifestyle in expectation of the imminent return of Jesus.[50] And though Christian histories of asceticism usually begin with the desert hermit Antony, "there were single women living together in Christian community before Antony," since he left his sister with "well-known and faithful virgins" to begin his career around 270.[51]

It is primarily with the end of the persecutions, however, that Christian leaders promoted a cult of virginity. Neoplatonic Greco-Roman culture contributed to the view that the body was inferior to the mind and that women incarnated this inferiority. At the same time, sex differentiation existed on a continuum between masculinity and femininity; "male" and "female" were fluid identities that could be ascribed to either gender.[52] One way for a woman to become manly was through martyrdom; another way was through asceticism and the renunciation of everything that makes a woman female.

The theologians of this era shared the Greco-Roman dualistic worldview and its misogynistic evaluation of women. They unconsciously seemed to reject the Jewish anthropology, accepted by both Jesus and Paul, in which body and soul exist together as a unit. Most theologians of the Eastern Church continued to marry and value family life because they did not equate sin with sexuality.[53] "For the Western Fathers, like Augustine [however], sex and sin became inextricably entwined for reasons that were personal and peculiar to the time and place but which had no real warranty from the New Testament."[54] Augustine's doctrine of original sin—that is, the belief that all humans inherit sin from Adam through conception, and thus are ontologically evil—made sexual intercourse a guilty pleasure. Virginity resolved this problem by eliminating sin and sex in a single stroke.

Asceticism required the destruction of women's, and men's, bodies by severe practices of mortification, which included fasting to the point of anorexia; wearing sackcloth or goatskin, or going naked, any of which would be highly uncomfortable; not bathing, which produced lice and body odor; and physically punishing the body with objects. A number of ascetics entombed themselves in tiny cells with no doors and a single window. Numerous sinner-turned-saint tales arose to inspire the faithful. Saint Pelagia of Antioch (fl. ca. 300?)[55] began her life as a voluptuous harlot, repented and fled to Jerusalem, and died many years later as the presumably male hermit called Pelagius, "an emaciated figure with sunken eyes," no longer recognizable as a woman.[56] Mary of Egypt (d. ca. 421?), another prostitute who experienced forgiveness, went into the Jordanian desert at the heavenly behest of the Virgin Mary. "Mary's hagiographer characterizes her independence, piety, and extreme asceticism by providing her with emaciated flesh, withered breasts, short hair, and sun-blackened skin."[57]

In her book *Sacred Fictions*, Lynda Coon identifies a "theology of the cosmetic" in the patristic writers, by which she means an ideology that results in the progressive annihilation of women's clothing, hair, and bodies, and a corresponding exaltation of men's clothing, hair, and bodies. We see the theology of the cosmetic as early as the New Testament, when women are instructed on hats, hair, clothing, and jewelry (1 Cor. 11:4–7, 13–15; 1 Tim. 2:9). In the early third century, Tertullian's treatise *On the Veiling of Virgins* (*De virginibus velandis*) recommends that women expiate for Eve's sin by wearing penitential garb. By the fourth century, Saint Jerome, "a master of cosmetic rhetoric," lauds the mortifications that the widow Paula of Jerusalem has performed on her body and face. "Asceticism reduces Paula's body to a skeletal state in the service of reversing Eve's fall from grace."[58]

In spite of the denigration of the female body and spirit these "sacred fictions" promoted, feminist theologians nonetheless argue that chaste women found autonomy and fulfillment in a life set apart from men. "Chastity leads to autonomy, freedom from the oppressive authority of husband and political ruler," declares Virginia Burrus, professor of early church history at Drew University. She argues that a negative attitude toward marriage might indicate a healthy dislike of the patriarchal subjugation of women.[59] "Christian women of the patristic era who renounced traditional sexual and domestic roles did indeed find new worlds open to them, worlds of scholarship and contemplation, pilgrimage and charitable endeavor," writes Elizabeth Clark, professor of religion at Duke University.[60] She points out that some upper-class women did enjoy a scholarly life, learning Greek, if they were living in the Western Roman Empire, and Hebrew with which to read the scriptures. Daily activities for women living in religious communities revolved around worship, study of religious—especially ascetic—literature, and copying scripture.[61] Yet, as Clark also notes, this path to freedom was limited to a few wealthy women.

The End of Church Leadership

Women made up the majority of church members throughout the Roman Empire: they officiated at cults for the saints; presided over a "table ministry" at house churches;[62] established semipublic churches, which met in houses specially purchased for worship gatherings; funded monasteries; and provided financial support to individuals, both male and female. Well into the fourth century, women served as church leaders in almost every conceivable capacity.

The decriminalization of Christianity by Constantine, however, marked several changes that would eventually bar women from church administration. First, it became possible to construct public churches, including large structures modeled on pagan basilicas. Public worship would prevent women from conducting services in mixed company. Second, church office, rather than charismatic leadership, was emphasized. Theologians had contended for episcopal supervision beginning in the second century, arguing from the principle of "one God" to "the emerging institution of the 'one bishop' as monarch ('sole ruler') of the church."[63] The office of bishop became increasingly monarchical from the third to the fourth centuries, and church architecture changed to reflect this: the bishop was now seated on a cathedra, or throne, on a raised dais in front of the congregation.[64] The *Apostolic Constitutions* (*Constitutiones Apostolorum*), a fourth-century revision of the *Didascalia Apostolorum*, calls the bishops "high priests" who are above presbyters, deacons, lectors, cantors, porters (men who functioned like today's custodians), deaconesses, widows, virgins, and orphans, reiterating at the end of the list that "the high priest is above all these."[65] Widows must be obedient to the teaching of the bishop "as if to God."[66]

Third, Pope Damasus (p. 366–384) helped to centralize the Catholic Church in Rome at the expense of female sponsors and patrons. He created new, male martyrs for veneration and accordingly built many new churches and remodeled old churches originally constructed through female patronage. He continued the push for papal primacy, asserting that the bishop of Rome was the most important of all bishops. He emphasized Saints Peter and Paul and made Rome the "apostolic see," that is, a bishop's "seat" of authority founded by a disciple of Jesus.[67] "Damasus' deliberate invocation of glorious Rome threw into shadow the cults of venerated female martyrs and the patronage of powerful women."[68]

Conclusions

The history of Christianity has usually been written through the careful examination of texts, which explains why the male, hierarchical church is seen as normative for early Christianity. Since women left few writings, it is difficult to chronicle their activities. Inscriptions, epigraphs, and artifacts tell part of the story. Reading between the lines of texts written by men tells another part.

The emphasis of previous scholarship on texts has erased the memory of the actual contribution that women made to the expansion of Christianity. It is the hundreds of thousands of unnamed women, not a few dozen male writers or martyred female saints, who caused the conversion of an empire. According to the sociologist Rodney Stark, these women married pagan men, remaking their households into centers of Christian education and worship. They did not practice female infanticide or abortion, the norm in Roman society, and as a result, had more children—especially more girl children—with whom to propagate the faith.[69] The high fertility rate of Christian women expanded the faith further, providing a source of marriageable Christians to pagans. Stark also outlines the gender profile of individuals who became Christian, observing that ancient as well as modern sources indicate that women more than men seemed drawn to Christianity. It was the marriage and motherhood of ordinary women, not the chastity of wealthy women, that changed the Greco-Roman world.

Yet elite religion continued to exert an influence over women and men, with chastity valued above marriage. In the Middle Ages, widows and virgins entered the cloister in new monastic orders as nuns, where they labored as scholars, administrators, and mystics. They also entered a new world—continental Europe—as missionaries, evangelizing and teaching those to whom the gospel was unknown. And they continued to do what they had done from the beginning: to care for the least and the last.

FIGURE 4.1. *Joan of Arc*, by Dante Gabriel Rossetti. Reproduced under Creative Commons License.

4

Saints, Seers, and Scholars in the Middle Ages

Christianity spread outward from Palestine, beginning as a renewal movement within Judaism and becoming a separate Gentile religion within a few hundred years. By the end of the first century, Christianity had penetrated to Rome, the capital of the empire, and to the Arabian Peninsula (see Gal. 1:17). A century later, Christian communities existed throughout the Mediterranean: across North Africa, through Asia Minor, and along the southern edge of what is now Europe. Scriptures originally written in Greek were translated into Latin, Syriac (a form of Aramaic), and Coptic, the language of ancient Egypt. By the end of the third century, Christianity extended from Syria into Persia, and north to what is now Armenia and Georgia. From Persia, missionaries entered India and China. Christian missionaries arrived in Ethiopia in the fourth century, and the first Ethiopian bishop—Abba Salama—was consecrated in 346.[1] This geographical reach explains the diversity found in the religion, both then and now.

A clear division ran between the Eastern and Western Churches from the very beginning, due to the geography of the Roman Empire. Those from Rome spoke Latin and inherited Greco-Roman philosophy and culture. Those from Byzantium—the Greek city that became Constantinople under the Emperor Constantine I in 330 and is now Istanbul, Turkey—spoke Greek, and while they too inherited much from Greco-Roman civilization, they also bore the influence of societies from the East, especially Persia. These differences were exacerbated by the division of the empire among Constantine's sons. The Western Empire, with its capital in Rome, fell to Germanic invaders before the end of the fifth century. The Eastern Empire, in contrast, endured for another millennium, surviving the Muslim conquest of the seventh century, the

European Christian crusades of the twelfth and thirteenth centuries, and collapsing only in 1453 following the invasion of the Ottoman Turks.

The churches of the East were called Orthodox, or Eastern Orthodox, and diverged from the Roman, or Catholic, churches in large and small ways.[2] Theological differences were apparent quite early in various Trinitarian debates and discussions about the nature of the Son of God. As time progressed, the Eastern Church emphasized the salvific work of the incarnation (the enfleshment of the Son of God through Jesus), while the Western Church emphasized the atonement (the sacrificial death of Jesus). Rather than recognizing the pope, the bishop of Rome, as the head of all churches, Orthodox Christianity accepted national patriarchs who made decisions for independent, or autocephalous, churches. This is why we see today churches named after specific countries: the Ukrainian Orthodox Church, the Greek Orthodox Church, the Serbian Orthodox Church, and so on.

Just as the Eastern and Western Churches had distinct profiles, so too did the women who lived in their discrete locales. Women in the West tended to have more legal rights and greater opportunities to act in public. Women in the East, on the other hand, lived lives circumscribed by the household and were strictly controlled by their male relatives, not just husbands but also fathers, brothers, and uncles. Relatively few were literate, and there is no evidence that girls attended schools.[3] Despite these drawbacks, women were far from unimportant in Eastern Christianity, especially during the Middle Ages.

The concept of the Middle Ages was invented during the European Renaissance, a time during which individuals saw themselves returning to the golden age of classical civilization. The Middle Ages were sandwiched in between these two glorious eras in the minds of cultured citizens of the fifteenth and sixteenth centuries. Today scholars generally consider the millennium between 400 and 1400 to roughly constitute the medieval period, which is usually divided into the early, high, and late Middle Ages. Each epoch saw a shift in the status of women, sometimes for the better, sometimes for the worse. What is clear throughout the millennium is that women, East and West, contributed to the expansion of Christianity, the reform of the faith, and the enhancement of a mystical theology with Christ at the center.

Piety and Power in Byzantium

The Empress Helena (ca. 248–ca. 330), mother of the Roman Emperor Constantine I (r. 306–334), established a pattern that subsequent empresses in the East tried to emulate. She financed large-scale searches in Jerusalem and Bethlehem in quest of historical sites from the life of Jesus. According to one legend, she identified the true cross of Jesus because it miraculously healed a sick woman.[4] Although she did not inaugurate the cult of relics, she ushered in reverence for, and proliferation of, pieces of the cross on which Jesus was crucified.

Saint Helena's primary importance lies in the fact that she was the first Christian imperial patron; that is, she used the empire's treasury to pay for numerous excavations and to fund the construction of more than thirty churches in the Holy Land as well as churches in Rome.[5] Succeeding empresses continued to erect religious structures—churches, monasteries, mausoleums—throughout the empire, so much so that by the tenth century, constructing churches was a regular service provided by empresses. "Within the structures of Byzantine society, building a church, a poorhouse, even a palace, appears to have been one of the few very public gestures open to women."[6]

Wealthy women as well as empresses shaped Byzantine Christianity, not only through financial patronage but also through their advocacy of a form of piety unique to Orthodox Christianity: the veneration of icons. An icon is an image or visual representation, usually of Christ, the Virgin Mary, angels, or saints. It can be a painting on wood, a fresco on a wall, a mosaic on a ceiling, or a woven tapestry. Icons became integral to religious life and liturgy in Eastern Christianity. Thus when iconoclastic, or image-smashing, emperors prohibited their use and destroyed them in what are called the Iconoclast Controversies (730–787 and 813–843), public opposition to imperial policy led to widespread rioting and consequent military intervention.

Two women helped decisively to legitimize the use of images by Christians. Empress Irene of Athens (r. 797–802) called together the seventh and last ecumenical council, which concluded the first period of iconoclasm. The bishops meeting in Nicaea in 787 declared that "the honor which is paid to the image passes on to that which the image represents, and he who reveres the image reveres in it the subject represented."[7] Another empress, Theodora II (r. 842–855), ended the second iconoclast period. She reportedly used an icon to cure her husband, Emperor Theophilos, of an illness, and though he was healed, he himself remained an iconoclast. When he died in 842, she became empress regent, and the next year called together a church council that returned the use of icons to the churches and expelled all iconoclastic clergy.

"The exact role of women in this historic triumph is unsatisfactorily documented," observes Judith Herrin, professor emerita of Byzantine studies at King's College London. "But from their positions on the throne and in the streets of the capital, they clearly played a militant part."[8] Women and monks appear to have strongly supported the use of icons, quite possibly for the same reason: One could honor an icon in the privacy of the home or the monastery. Women were involved in the production of icons as both patrons and manufacturers. Reports of devotion to images include a legend about an incident in 726 when women rioted outside the imperial palace after Emperor Leo III ordered removal of the Christ icon from the entrance gate.[9] Yet accounts of such dedication may simply indicate attempts to discredit the movement of iconophiles (those who favored icons) by associating it with a marginalized group, namely, women.[10]

Nevertheless, the prevailing view is that the religiosity of women in Byzantium required the use of icons, because private daily devotions "played a vital role in the lives of Byzantine women, who for the most part led a secluded existence in their homes."[11] This seclusion explains the need for deaconesses, who were ordained clergy charged with instructional, pastoral, and social service duties directed at women. The majority of deaconesses were either monastics or widows, though some were the wives of bishops, priests, or deacons.[12] Laywomen did attend services in village churches, but in urban areas they tended to practice their religion at home, except when entire communities publicly exercised their faith during weekly processions, occasional festivals, and special vigils.

No wonder, then, that Byzantine women's piety focused on personal devotions, with women praying with equal fervor to the Mother of God, to Jesus Christ, and to the saints. They would visit shrines of saints, or of living holy women and holy men, for relief of problems such as infertility, failure to lactate, or uterine bleeding. Some pregnant women wore protective amulets inscribed with prayers or images on their arms, while others wore pendants depicting female saints as intercessors for safe pregnancy and childbirth.

If Pachomius of Egypt (c. 290–346) can be said to be the father of cenobitic (communal) monasticism for men, his sister Maria (fl. 4th cent.) is the mother of women's communal monasticism. She founded the first cenobitic monastery at Tabenna, an island in the Nile River, which "indicates that women's communities were developed from the start of the movement alongside men's."[13] Monastic institutions burgeoned in Byzantium in the ninth through twelfth centuries, thanks to individual and family patronage, with small monastic churches replacing large imperial public churches.[14] A register of all monastic institutions in Constantinople covering the first eleven centuries of the city's history reveals that more than one-fifth—77 out of 347—of all monasteries were female.[15]

Most convents were located in Constantinople, chiefly because wealthy women established them as refuges for themselves or their families.[16] Generally fifty nuns lived in each convent, with twenty responsible for basic housekeeping and thirty responsible for observing the *Horologion*, or Daily Office, which is the reading of scripture and the recitation of prayers and psalms scheduled eight times throughout the day and night. Like their sisters in the West, they performed acts of charity, working in hospitals and hospices, running old age homes, and caring for the dead. Unlike their Western counterparts, however, the nuns of Byzantium "rarely engaged in the copying or illumination of manuscripts, or the composition of hymns, saints' lives, theological treatises or historical chronicles."[17] Nevertheless, literate nuns were encouraged to teach their sisters to read in order to sing the chants, maintain accounts, and work in the library. A final difference is that "the highest achievement of a Byzantine nun was to renounce or transcend her femininity,"[18] especially in the eyes of the men writing about them. The brother of Saint Macrina (ca. 330–379/380)—founder of one of the earliest groups of female ascetics East or West—describes her masculine virtues in his biography, *Life of Macrina*. He wonders whether Macrina should even be called a woman, "for I do not know if it is appropriate to apply a name drawn from nature to one who has risen above nature."[19]

The Power of the Intellect

Fewer than a half dozen texts written by women in the Eastern Church between the ninth and the fifteenth centuries remain. "Compared to their sisters in the West, the women of Byzantium were extremely silent, one might even say mute."[20] In contrast, an abundance of literature—letters, sermons, poems, plays, instruction manuals, community rules, mystical writings, and more—reveals a rich intellectual culture that women helped to develop during that same period in the Western Church. This remarkable flowering came despite increasingly repressive efforts by ecclesiastical authorities to control, and then to exclude, women from religious life.

Christianity had spread as far north as the British Isles under Emperor Constantine I, but its Celtic and Germanic forms differed from their Roman and Byzantine counterparts. Far from the centers of empire, ethnic churches developed with distinct personalities. As in the era of early Christianity, during which time women disciples and apostles participated fully in the life of the church, these far-flung outposts included women in various leadership positions. Missionaries, abbesses, noblewomen, and others helped to extend Christianity to all corners of Europe, a region dominated by diverse tribal peoples.

Although it is somewhat of an exaggeration to say that the Irish saved civilization,[21] it is true that Irish male and female religious introduced Celtic Christianity to England, Scotland, and continental Europe. Celtic Christianity was both harsher and softer than Roman, or Latin, Christianity. Irish monastics practiced severe austerities and withdrew to windswept, isolated hermitages. They developed what are called "penitentiaries," little books that list specific sins and the penances required to make restitution for the sins. At the same time, they practiced a communal Christianity in which women and men lived and worked together, side by side. They designed their own liturgies and practices, and maintained their unique customs until the Synod of Whitby (663, possibly 664) attempted to bring Celtic churches into conformity with Roman practices. Complete compliance did not occur until the eleventh century.

In an era during which few were literate, the Irish women and men religious devoted themselves to learning: they mastered Hebrew, Greek, and Latin, and they copied religious texts in elegant illuminated manuscripts. Irish missionaries took their love of learning, as well as their relative egalitarianism, wherever they went. This is most evident in the establishment of double monasteries in England and the Continent. Female and male religious houses existed adjacent to one another and had the advantage of sharing work and worship. "In these monasteries the nuns did not live like parasites on the monks. They were required to perform manual labor."[22] Their duties included cooking, cleaning, serving, sewing, brewing, fishing, and fire building, while men worked in the fields to produce food for the monastery. Usually under the direction of an abbess, or "mother"—undoubtedly an educated woman of the nobility—these double monasteries became intellectual centers that emphasized education and enlightenment through study of scripture and the writings of early church theologians. One of the most important of these abbesses was Saint Hilda (614–680), who established Whitby Abbey, a significant center of learning in the north of England. A number of her male students went on to become bishops, being well-prepared in both biblical studies and ethics at her abbey.[23]

In the eighth century, thirty nuns from Wimbourne Abbey in England embarked on the dangerous journey to the Continent to establish schools and monasteries in Germany. The religious houses that these women founded became known as intellectual centers, and the women themselves gained reputations for wisdom and knowledge. Saint Walburga (ca. 710–779), recognized for her medical acumen, became abbess of the double monastery in Heidenheim. Saint Leoba (d. 782) became the abbess of Tauberbishofsheim, which she administered with a moderate hand, allowing the sisters to rest after lunch and prohibiting late-night vigils because "lack of sleep dulled the mind."[24] Moreover, "she committed to memory everything she read and asked the nuns to read to her while she was napping."[25] Leoba maintained a warm and collegial relationship with Saint Boniface (ca. 675–754), who entrusted her with the supervision of biblical studies and church law at the monasteries at which they worked.[26]

The close attachment of Leoba and Boniface was not atypical at the time. Women and men worked as partners in the early medieval period just as they had in the early church. Similarly, women of wealth and power supported religious endeavors. Queens and princesses in particular maintained friendships with clerics, even appointing bishops and abbots, and influencing religious policies.[27] They also practiced "domestic proselytization," converting households, families, and entire nations. Saint Clotilda (ca. 470–544), queen of the Franks, repeatedly entreated her husband, King Clovis (ca. 465–511), to "recognize the true God" and reject his pagan deities. After he won a battle by calling upon Clotilda's God, Clovis finally agreed to be baptized.

The religious life of the peasantry, in contrast to that of the nobility, centered on the parish church. There a strict division by gender was maintained, with women standing on the north, or left-hand, side of the church, and men standing on the south side. Yet women supported these churches by cleaning the building; raising funds through sales; washing and mending church linen; baking bread for communion; and housing traveling craftsmen hired to make repairs. They gave their children religious instruction until the age of seven and sometimes beyond. Like their sisters in Byzantium, they prayed to saints and the Virgin Mary for help in pregnancy and childbirth. Similarly, they were excluded from the sanctuary for forty days after giving birth, at which time they underwent a purification ceremony that involved prayers and blessings.[28]

It is clear that religious life offered many opportunities for women in the sixth and seventh centuries, although these openings were limited to wealthy women who could afford a dowry or an endowment to a nunnery for their care and support. Lay sisters frequently performed the housework while the aristocrats prayed, studied, copied manuscripts in scriptoria, and taught girls and boys the seven liberal arts: the *trivium* (grammar, rhetoric, and logic) and the *quadrivium* (arithmetic, geometry, music, and astronomy). Women religious also sewed, elaborately embroidering altar cloths, vestments for priests, and coverings for sacred objects. The most important task, though, was the Daily Office, which recalled the nuns to mindfulness of God and their vocation.

The abbess played a pivotal role in the life of the monastery. Ordained just as other clergy at the time by virtue of her consecration and her taking of the cup of wine from the bishop, the abbess performed "an important and influential ministry."[29] With responsibility for the spiritual life of her charges, she heard confessions, provided penance, and conducted last rites at death for both women and men in the double monasteries. She preached and interpreted scripture, and served communion. She administered the finances of large landholdings, negotiating with local nobility over water rights and property boundaries. She conferred with bishops and popes, setting policies or protesting them. This is all to say that the abbess wielded great power, at least for a time.

Reactionary Reforms

The institutional church and its male hierarchy reasserted its power over women in a series of reforms in the ninth, tenth, and eleventh centuries. It began with the Carolingian Reform under Emperor Charles the Great (r. 771–814)—better known as Charlemagne—who wanted to create an educated class of clergy. Prior to that time, priests had little more education than the laity whom they instructed. Charlemagne required that each cathedral institute schools to create an educated cadre of young men who could enter professions requiring literacy, primarily the priesthood. Whereas monasteries taught children of both sexes, the cathedral schools would teach boys alone.

The second reform came from the monastery of Cluny, located in the Burgundy region of France. Odo of Cluny (ca. 879–944) favored a return to strict enforcement of the Rule of Saint Benedict, the operating guidelines that most monastic organizations had used ever since Saint Benedict of Nursia (fl. first half of 6th cent.) devised them. Benedict's rule specified everything from the clothes monks should wear to the food they could eat. Some orders had grown rather lax in their observance, and the Cluniac reformers sought to enforce the rule to the letter. But this model specifically excluded women. "Rather than seeing nuns as partners in the spiritual enterprise of shedding gender," writes the medieval historian Jo Ann McNamara (1931–2009), "the Cluniac monks equated manliness with self-control, producing a rhetoric dominated by the implication that women were simply not capable of conforming to the demanding Benedictine rule."[30] Most importantly, the Cluniac order received special exemption from episcopal or papal control, while women's orders were denied this freedom and the immunity from outside interference.[31] In reality, episcopal oversight and control increased over female religious houses.

The cult of the Virgin Mary, emphasized in both the Carolingian and Cluniac Reforms, valorized female virginity over spiritual equality, and thus made protection of virgins a priority. This meant the enclosure, or cloistering, of nuns who had once been a highly visible presence during the era of missions and education. A spiritual meritocracy, first articulated by Saint Jerome, divided women into three orders of importance: "virgins would be rewarded a hundred times their deserts; widows, sixty times; and wives, thirty times."[32] Defending one's virginity, even to the point of death, was the sole means of salvation for those who had dedicated themselves to the virginal life. The dramas by Hrotsvitha of Gandersheim (ca. 935–ca. 1000/1003) rework the classical plays of Terence (ca. 195–ca. 159? BCE) and make them Christian morality tales in which women choose death rather than dishonor. Hrotsvitha dedicated her five plays to the abbess of Gandersheim, Gerberga (fl. 10th cent.), "testifying to the heroic chastity that, in her view, characterized true womanhood."[33] Nuns escaped violation through various forms of self-martyrdom—in other words, suicide—and it is possible that the expression "to cut off your nose to spite your face" may have originated in some of the desperate measures sisters took in defense of virginity.[34]

The third reform came under Pope Gregory VII (p. 1073–1085) and further eroded women's participation in church leadership. Although the apparent intent was to purify the church by requiring clerical celibacy, the actual purpose was to assert church independence from secular nobility by ensuring that priests did not have children who might inherit property.[35] As a consequence of this power struggle, women were excluded from every level of church governance and lost the variety of ministries in which they had served for centuries. In addition, a theology of the sacraments began to be clarified and systematized. This laid the groundwork for the development of canon law in the twelfth century, which redefined the concept of ordination, limiting it to a class of people—men—and to a particular function—service at the altar. All of these developments help to explain how the powers of abbesses, and even abbots, were arrogated by priests in less than a hundred years.[36]

Innovations in Women's Religious Life

Female participation in monastic life generally declined as a result of the alterations made in ecclesiastical structures during the three centuries of reactionary reforms. This changed during the Twelfth-Century Renaissance, however, when the effects of an agrarian revolution and technological innovation improved the standard of living for most people in Europe and brought about a flowering of art, culture, and education. Barred from attending the newly incorporated universities in Paris, Oxford, Salamanca, and elsewhere, women nonetheless forged their own centers of learning. Discouraged from affiliating with the new men's religious orders, women nonetheless formed their own communities. Excluded from ordained ministries, women nonetheless continued to provide the services of clergy well into the thirteenth century.

Two twelfth-century abbesses stand out. Heloise (d. mid-1160s), abbess and cofounder of a monastery called the Paraclete, acquired goods, properties, and benefactions for the nunnery through personal persuasion and the force of her character; she enjoyed the favor of popes and kings during her thirty-five-year tenure.[37] Her *Problemata* directed a number of questions about contradictions that appear in the Bible to her husband and mentor, Peter Abelard (ca. 1079–ca. 1142). She also sought a rule for organizing the monastery that would be "suitable for women," given the fact that the Rule of Saint Benedict was written for men. As she reasonably pointed out, "How can women be concerned with what is written there about cowls, drawers or scapulars? Or indeed, with tunics or woolen garments worn next to the skin, when the monthly purging of their superfluous humours must avoid such things?"[38]

Saint Hildegard of Bingen (1098–1179) was another remarkable abbess, moving her community from a double monastery and taking the community's endowment along with her, over the objections of the abbot. A prolific writer—although scholars believe she dictated all of her writings—Hildegard authored letters, plays, summaries of doctrine, medical treatises, and scientific expositions. She also composed the first chants for women's choirs. Her creation-centered spirituality, the product of a series of visions she experienced, greatly inspired twentieth-century Christians looking for an environmentally sensitive expression of their faith.

The mendicant movements inaugurated in the late twelfth and early thirteenth centuries by Saint Francis of Assisi (ca. 1182–1226), from Italy, and Saint Dominic (1170–1221), from Spain, encouraged the development of complementary orders and movements in which women sought to live a life in service to the poor. In Italy, the tertiaries, or members of the third orders, were generally affiliated with the Franciscans and Dominicans but lived as laywomen following a modified rule. The tertiaries were actively engaged in charitable endeavors, as were the *beatas* in Spain. Saint Clare of Assisi (1193/94–1253), a close companion of Saint Francis, founded the Order of Poor Ladies to serve the destitute and underprivileged. The first woman to write a monastic rule specifically for women, Clare created a nonhierarchical, relatively democratic structure in which most decisions would be made by a consensus of all sisters and in which abbesses would be advised by a council of eight or more experienced sisters; this was in contrast to Benedictine abbesses, who wielded absolute control over their communities.[39]

The most significant innovation of the period was the rise of independent laywomen's groups, particularly in the Low Countries (Belgium and the Netherlands), France, and the Rhineland of Germany. Called the Beguines, these groups of laywomen organized religious communities called beguinages, which consisted of convents of a dozen women; or entire villages, called courts, of hundreds or more.[40] Women who became Beguines took a vow of chastity, but could leave the group to marry; they could maintain their own property, and needed to do so at times in order to support their community; and they traveled freely within cities seeing to their three worldly duties of charity, manual work, and teaching.[41] "The [B]eguine was a new creature, living in a pious community but free to leave at any time; not answerable to any man; self-determined and self-supporting."[42]

Beguines shared a number of characteristics despite the diversity of location and the independence of each convent or court, since they had no overarching rule or hierarchical structure.[43] They did have leaders, or superiors of their convents and courts, however, whom they called "Marthas," after the New Testament figure (Luke 10:38–42).[44] They were committed to a life of material simplicity, in the face of economic growth and urban expansion. They tended to reject marriage, arguing for continence among married people and protecting young women who fled forced or arranged marriages. They made escape possible by providing opportunities for single women to support themselves. Manual work was both a social and spiritual task for the Beguines, who modeled their lives after the New Testament apostles, who worked for a living. Most were employed in the textile industry, but they labored in many other occupations as well.

Although their commitment resided in charitable rather than scholastic endeavors, several Beguines contributed to the emergence of vernacular literature, that is, writings in the spoken language of the people. Beatrice of Nazareth (ca. 1200–1268), a visionary and mystic who grew up as a Beguine before she became a Cistercian nun, wrote the earliest known extant Dutch prose, *Seven Manners of Loving*.[45] This short treatise describes different types of love the soul feels for God. In erotically charged language, Beatrice declares that in the soul's "violent desire and excruciating impatience, she wishes to be delivered in order to be with Christ."[46] Hadewijch of Antwerp (fl. 1230–1250) wrote in the vernacular of Old Flemish. Like Beatrice, she emphasizes the soul's pursuit of divine love. "Those who in that high knowledge / Of naked Love, / Speechless Love, / Strive to go ever deeper, / Find that their lack / Always increases," she writes in one of her mystical poems.[47]

Finally, Mechthild of Magdeburg (d. 1282/1287) received a series of visions around 1230, which she wrote down in Middle Low German some twenty years later. *The Flowing Light of the Godhead* transcends easy classification, for it contains dialogues, poetry, prose, sermons, autobiography, and more, all in a single work.[48] Like Hadewijch and

Beatrice—and like many other male and female mystics—Mechthild writes in nuptial metaphors, that is, in the imagery of sexual intercourse, reflecting the influence of contemporary troubadours and the language of courtly love: "Then the Most Beloved goes toward the Most Beautiful in the hidden chambers of the invisible Deity. There she finds the couch and the pleasure of Love, and God awaiting her in a superhuman fashion."[49] According to Sara S. Poor, professor of German at Princeton University, "Mechthild, Hadewijch, and Beatrice stand at the beginning of what historians now term a new era characterized by the rise of vernacular theology."[50] Thus, they were important for Western culture in general, as well as for Christianity in particular.

Still another Beguine, Marguerite Porete (d. 1310), wrote in the Old French vernacular, but her theological treatise, *The Mirror of Simple Souls*, was condemned and publicly burned in her presence. Marguerite saved a copy and tried to promote it to respected scholars, but the work continued to be considered heretical and, since she had already been warned once, Marguerite was executed on 31 May 1310. Part of the problem was her assertion that the perfect soul did not need the mediation of priests, since it "neither desires nor despises poverty nor tribulation, neither mass nor sermon, neither fast nor prayer, and gives to Nature all that is necessary, without remorse of conscience."[51] In short, the soul does not need the church, but only God.

The Beguines and other independent women's lay groups were always viewed with suspicion because they moved outside male control, answerable primarily to themselves and to their patrons. Despite a number of setbacks, most communities of Beguines continued to flourish as independent entities well into the fourteenth and fifteenth centuries, with some surviving into the twentieth.

The Humanization of Jesus

The earthly man of Nazareth served as the model for those wishing to live a simple life in *imitatio Christi* (the imitation of Christ), which helped to humanize Jesus. The idea of the real presence—that Christ is materially present in every particle of bread and drop of wine consecrated for communion—also contributed to the humanization of the Son of God. Known as transubstantiation, Jesus's actual presence in the eucharistic elements led to greater ceremony in the celebration of the Mass and much greater importance of the priest. The practice of elevating the consecrated Host, that is, raising the bread for all the congregation to see, became for some Christians more important than consuming the Host: It meant seeing Jesus in the flesh, literally broken for humanity.

Women religious contributed to the process of humanizing Jesus by relating to him as females. In their visions they saw themselves nursing the baby Jesus, responding to him as a spouse or lover, and sharing in the sufferings of his last week on earth. Their piety focused on his flesh, "both flesh as body and flesh as food," according to Carolyn Walker Bynum, an American medievalist.[52] This meant that fasting, on the one hand, and the Eucharist, on the other, became constitutive components for the religious life of nuns.

"Food was an obsessive and overpowering concern in the lives and writings of religious women between the twelfth and fifteenth century," Bynum asserts.[53] Legends circulated that some women could live on the Eucharist alone and had ceased to excrete due to their fasting. The eucharistic elements actually became God, and consuming God was a powerful metaphor in the medieval mind. Fasting, in contrast, was a way to share in the sufferings of Christ, and was also a form of service, redeeming individuals from purgatory, the way station before reaching the heaven of blessedness spent with God.

Angela of Foligno (1248–1309), a Franciscan tertiary, presents a vivid example of the way eating, fasting, and taking the Eucharist structured the religious life of someone who utterly identified with Christ's sufferings. Angela's piety was absorbed in the physicality of Christ's body and her own, as demonstrated on the occasion when she stripped naked in the church of Foligno and pointed to each body part as she promised that it would no longer sin.[54] In one of her visions she saw monks enter Christ's bleeding side, and emerge from it with their lips red from drinking his blood.[55] "Blood and drinking were her dominant images for encounter with God."[56]

For some mystics, Jesus was not only human, he was also female. "God, like woman, fed his children from his own body, and if God did not make his children from his own flesh, he saved them by taking for himself a body from their humanity."[57] Themes such as childbearing, lactation, sexual surrender, and ecstasy are found in the texts of both female and male religious. These occur not simply because of the humanization of Jesus but also because of a shift in theological emphases: from atonement and judgment to creation and incarnation.[58] Female characteristics best reflected this theological change in concepts about God.

Although Cistercian monks writing in the twelfth century were among the first to call Jesus Mother,[59] the most notable proponent of a theology in which the second person of the Trinity is female was Julian of Norwich (1342–1415/1423). An anchoress living in a cell attached to a church in England, Julian received mystical "showings" of God when she was ill in 1373. These showings revealed to her that the Trinity has three attributes: fatherhood, motherhood, and lordship.

> We see that Jesus is the true Mother of our nature, for he made us. He is our Mother, too, by grace, because he took our created nature upon himself. All the lovely deeds and tender services that beloved motherhood implies are appropriate to the Second Person.[60]

The visions of women like Julian of Norwich, Angela of Foligno, and others may seem curious or even bizarre to twenty-first-century readers. Yet their mystical encounters with the divine were valued as superior to book learning or "word-based human knowledge."[61] Scholasticism, a rational and logical approach to theology that attempted to reconcile Christian theology with Aristotelian and Neoplatonic philosophies, came under increasing scrutiny at the end of the Middle Ages. Mystical theology, an experiential form of knowledge, gained traction as scholastics became increasingly skeptical about the use of human language and logic for perceiving the divine. Those living in the Middle Ages believed that theology and religious experience were intimately related, thus "theological understanding appears to be essential for the occurrence of a religious experience and the interpretation of it."[62] Medieval women visionaries made important contributions to this debate about the ways to know God.

Conclusions

Far from being a period of darkness and decay, the European Middle Ages witnessed a variety of innovations and developments, both in women's religious lives and in the larger scope of Christian theology. At the same time, they point to the coming radical transformations in culture and in Christianity, namely, the Renaissance and the Reformations.[63] Three women of the later Middle Ages point to the future.

Saint Catherine of Siena (1347–1380) was a Dominican tertiary who led an active life as a teacher, theologian, mystic, and adviser to secular and ecclesiastical authorities. She worked as a peacemaker to return the papacy back to Rome from Avignon, France, where it had been since Pope Clement V (p. 1305–1314) moved it there in 1309. She succeeded in persuading Pope Gregory XI (p. 1370–1378) to do exactly that in 1377. She died, however, before the Great Western Schism—in which there were three rival claimants to the papacy—ended. Division within the church, and efforts to restrict the powers of the pope, would continue and would serve as an impetus to the Reformations.

Saint Joan of Arc (ca. 1412–1431) began hearing voices of the saints when she was twelve, and when she was seventeen, she aggressively led French forces to victory against the English during the Hundred Years' War. When the English captured her in 1430, they initially charged her with sorcery and seventy other crimes, but in the end reduced all charges to about a dozen, which included wearing men's clothing and maintaining that she talked with God. Joan signed a confession, but recanted a few days later, donning her male attire and telling judges that the voices continued to speak to her. Judged to be a relapsed heretic, she was burned at the stake. Joan personifies the hundreds of thousands of women put to death as heretics and witches in the coming centuries.

Finally, the French-Italian Christine de Pisan (1364–1430?) foreshadows what will become Renaissance humanism. Best known today for her literary debates and her vigorous defense of women, she is praised "as the first woman to attack the medieval tradition of clerkly [clerical] misogyny for its portrayal of the female sex as intrinsically sinful and immoral."[64] Her *Book of the City of Ladies* (*Le livre de la cité des dames*) argues that if women were neither denied an education nor kept at home raising children, they too would rise intellectually, and she provides sterling examples of women who did just that. Not only does de Pisan's work prefigure subsequent humanism, it heralds a new genre in Christian literature: the defense of women against the misogyny of men.

FIGURE 5.1. Engraving of Queen Elizabeth I, by Crispin van de Passe, after Isaac Oliver. Reproduced under Creative Commons License.

5

Women Reformed, Women Resistant

The dramatic social, cultural, economic, political, and religious changes that occurred in sixteenth-century Europe had their origins in developments of the late medieval period. The invention of the printing press made books and other reading materials readily accessible to large audiences. Women produced texts and read them—by the hundreds of thousands. The upsurge in humanism, which turned scholars to the classical texts of antiquity as sources of knowledge and inspiration, created an interest in original sources, including the Bible. Christian humanists such as Saint Thomas More (1478–1535) taught their daughters the classical languages so that they might enter into more intellectually equal partnerships with future spouses.[1] Technological advances improved agricultural productivity, which in turn spurred population growth, especially in urban areas. Notwithstanding their exclusion by many guilds, women contributed to the new mercantile economy, as owners and householders as well as laborers. In England, for instance, they dominated the brewing and silk-making guilds. Queens and noblewomen, and kings and noblemen—from small principalities to emerging nation-states—wielded a secular power that challenged the religious authority of the papacy. In addition, European adventurers began to claim the lands of the Americas for their respective monarchs to explore and exploit.

Finally, throughout the fifteenth century, the Christian church saw several efforts to reform a corrupt ecclesiastical structure, which had been dominated by different political factions and used for their own ends. The Council of Constance (1414–1418) and the Council of Basel (1431–1449) sought a more conciliar form of church governance that would place the pope under the jurisdiction of a congress of bishops. At the same time, other proposals sought to make changes in the liturgy, such as introducing translations of the Latin Vulgate Bible, so that lay-people might better understand the scriptures.

A movement supporting vernacular editions of the Bible began in England in the late fourteenth century and continued well into the sixteenth. Derisively called Lollards, or "mumblers," these individuals circulated books of the New Testament in English. Women members hosted secret meetings at which passages of scripture or liturgy, such as the Lord's Prayer, were memorized in the English language so that they could be shared with others. They celebrated communion in their homes, believing that the bread and the wine remained bread and wine after consecration; they refused to pay tithes, the taxes that supported the church; and they believed that priests were no better than layper-sons. Women made up a significant portion of this movement, repre-senting one-third of the seventy-four people examined for the heresy of Lollardy at Coventry in 1511 and 1512.[2]

Although the Protestant Reformation is usually dated to 1517—when an Augustinian monk named Martin Luther (1483–1546) posted ninety-five complaints against practices of the Catholic Church—it could have started at any time. We could say it began with John Wyc-lif (ca. 1330–1384), who was the inspiration for the Lollards, or with the Lollards themselves, who went to the stake as heretics in the early sixteenth century. Or it could have begun with a Peasants' War in Ger-many (1525–1526), in which poor rural people rose up against their wealthy landlords because they believed that the day proclaimed by the gospel—the last shall be first, and the first shall be last (Mark 10:31)—had arrived. It could be said to have commenced in 1525, when Conrad Grebel (ca. 1498–1526), a Swiss minister, baptized—or rather rebaptized—two adult men because they did not believe that the New Testament supported infant baptism. Or perhaps it all began in 1536, when a French reformer named John Calvin (1509–1564) fled to Ge-neva, Switzerland, to establish a godly city in which church and state would merge.

There were many who criticized the practices of the Catholic Church. Though most used scripture as their primary warrant, not all reformers were alike. Indeed, we can speak of five Reformations: the Lutheran (primarily German, but spreading to Scandinavian countries); the Calvinistic (also known as Reformed Theology, beginning in Switzerland, but spreading to the Netherlands, France, and the British Isles); the Radical Reformation (beginning in Switzerland and establishing various groups throughout Europe, including what today is known as Eastern Europe); the English Reformation; and the Catholic Reformation (frequently called the Counter-Reformation, occurring in Catholic countries with Catholic monarchs). At the same time, it is possible to speak of a single Reformation in which a number of doctrines, such as soteriology, ecclesiology, sacramentology, and anthropology, were revisited.

Not only did these changes profoundly affect the status of women in society, but women themselves generated much of the change. Exemplary women, from the lowest classes to royalty, shaped the future of what would split into Protestant Christianity and Roman Catholic Christianity. Eastern Orthodox Christianity would continue on its own trajectory, living in uneasy harmony with Muslim rule. In the West, a spirit of freedom encouraged women's participation in a variety of Protestant movements and led to the development of new religious orders in Catholicism. Women began to publish their works for wider audiences, and some writings directly challenged the subservient status of women both in society and in the church.

Religious and secular authorities attempted to roll back the social equality that accompanied the spiritual equality found in the Bible. Dissidents were arrested, imprisoned, tortured, and executed. It was not a great leap from searching out heretics bent on destroying the true faith, to destroying witches, who, along with their consort Satan, were also determined to bring down Christendom, in the eyes of their persecutors.

Despite the reign of terror, or perhaps spurred on by it, new breeds of churchwomen arose. Educated and intellectual, some defended their right to study and speak as equals. Others created new religious orders, mixing the active life of social service with the contemplative life of prayer and meditation. Thus, some women reformed the church, while others resisted their "re-formation."

Marriage versus Chastity

Reformers especially targeted the tradition that exalted virginity. Antichurch and anticlergy sentiment fueled resentment toward monks, and especially nuns, who tended to come from the upper classes. Yet it was the monastic vows themselves that Martin Luther and others found objectionable. The reformer believed that "everything not necessary for salvation must be free," and since the monastic vows of poverty, chastity, and obedience constricted freedom, they could not lead to salvation.[3] Moreover, he thought that monks and nuns believed that their prayers and sacrifices, their self-renunciation, would provide the means of salvation. But since humans were hopeless sinners, according to Luther, there was absolutely nothing they could contribute to their own salvation: Only having faith in God, through hearing the scriptures—the Word of God—would bring that about. This pessimistic anthropology contrasted with the relatively optimistic anthropology of medieval Catholicism, which taught that faith working through love—that is, through acts of charity—effected salvation through the grace of God. Catholics and Lutherans today have said that they are in basic agreement on a soteriology of justification by faith; yet Catholics, and probably most Christians, also believe that the fruits of faith are good works, and that Christians must therefore act as well as believe.

The antipathy of the reformers to the celibate life led to the valorization of marriage. Although God's first commandment was the decree for male and female to procreate (Gen. 1:28), the disobedience of Eve led to the institution of marriage in order to restrain sexual impulses, in the reformers' eyes. They believed that "Women's purpose in life is procreation, companionship to man, [and] management of the household."[4] To be a wife and mother became a vocation, a religious calling for women, just as devotion to the virgin life had once been for Catholic women religious. The supreme exemplar was the wife of the evangelical minister. "The pastor's wife acting out a totally new 'semi-spiritual' function—an appealing substitute for loss of the 'sacral' role of the cloistered celibate woman—did indeed become a role model for other women in the wider community."[5]

In the first decade of the Reformation, when former monks and former nuns married, and the doctrinal and political situation was unstable, married women were important participants. Luther's wife, Katherine von Bora (1499–1552), bore six children, and managed a household that protected fugitive Protestants, sheltered evangelical students, and fed far more than the nuclear family. Katherine Schütz Zell (1499–1572), the wife of Matthew Zell (1477–1548), a former priest and evangelical reformer in Strasbourg, also managed a household full of children, reformers, and refugees, sometimes lodging eighty or more for weeks.[6] A prolific writer, she composed hymns, sermons, letters, and treatises, including an interpretation of the Lord's Prayer. Defending her work against one critic, she admitted that "I have never mounted the pulpit, but I have done more than any minister in visiting those in misery."[7]

Feminist historians argue that the exaltation of marriage had a devastating effect on women in a number of significant ways. The primary one was that the family—now considered the kingdom of God in miniature—fell under the absolute patriarchal control of the husband, father, and master. Disobeying one's husband was tantamount to disobeying God. Whereas women once sought the confessional and the spiritual advice of a male outside the home, now wives were supposed to admit their faults to their husbands.

The religiously inspired limitation of women's tasks to *Kinder, Küche, Kirche* (children, kitchen, church) had widespread effects in secular society. Where women had once been highly visible agents in business and labor, they now became invisible, thanks to legislation instituted by local governments. Guilds encouraged restrictions on widows' rights and imposed wage controls that paid women less for the same work done by men. Marriage courts regulated domestic life, making it more difficult to get a divorce. In some cities, rape was downgraded from a crime of violence to just one among several sexual offences, including fornication and seduction.[8] City councils banned public begging and criminalized poverty by incarcerating the poor who could not, or would not, work. Religious vocations were eliminated with the compulsory closure of hundreds of monasteries and convents, which forced women into marriage, the workforce, and poverty. Women nevertheless resisted these restraints, both in new egalitarian communities of women and men and as women living under vows in Catholic communities.

Radical Reform

The churches of Germany that followed Luther's call to focus on "scripture alone" and to abandon traditional practices continued to look very Catholic, retaining both the physical characteristics of their churches—such as organs, stained glass windows, and statuary—and a belief that Christ was present in the elements (sometimes referred to as consubstantiation) if not actually the substance of the elements (transubstantiation, the Catholic doctrine). Praying to the saints or believing in any sacraments other than baptism and Holy Communion, however, was forbidden. The Calvinists in Switzerland went further, removing or destroying anything that might be construed as idolatry: windows, statues, and organs were smashed, while priestly vestments and nuns' habits were torn apart. Meanwhile the pulpit was physically elevated within the church sanctuary so that the congregation could better see and hear the preacher, because it was only through receiving the Word of God that people might be saved.

Even these changes were not enough for the activists of the Radical Reformation. Some who believed that the New Testament sanctioned baptism only for adult believers undertook rebaptism, denying that being baptized as infants counted for salvation. Called Anabaptists, or rebaptizers, these reformers faced capital punishment for practicing their belief; generally they were executed by being put in a sack and drowned. According to the radicals, other reformers had not gone far enough in eliminating accretions of tradition that obscured what they believed was the purity of apostolic Christianity, namely, sharing possessions and sharing leadership.

Some radicals moved to areas where they could create communities set apart in which to practice their faith. They rejected Catholicism's hierarchical ecclesiology; and although Luther promoted the idea of the "priesthood of all believers" in which all Christians could read and interpret the Bible for themselves, Lutherans and other reformers maintained a clergy class. In contrast, Moravians, Brethren, Mennonites, Hutterites, and others believed that the church comprised believers who were called out of the world. This ecclesiology dictated withdrawal in order to live a truly godly life. Moreover, the radical reformers expected the imminent return of Jesus on earth, and thus their eschatology also dictated their abandonment of the world.

The Moravians, for example, withdrew from their Slavic homeland to the estate of Nicholaus Ludwig Count von Zinzendorf (1700–1760) in Saxony, the easternmost state in Germany, where they established communities in which men and women had separate but equal jurisdiction. Single men, single women, and widows each lived in communal groups called choirs, while married couples and families maintained their own homes. Just as men managed the male choirs, women supervisors administered the female choirs through teaching, preaching, counseling, and managing their affairs. Moravian women "began to enjoy an exceptional measure of equality, assumed leadership roles, and voiced their insights and experiences in written and oral testimonies."[9] Sources indicate that women preached to other women, and criticisms leveled at the Moravians claimed that they also preached in mixed gatherings. Reformers repeatedly used Paul's injunction for women to keep silent in the churches to prevent women from speaking in public, and Zinzendorf initially accepted this view. But his encounter with a Quaker woman preacher in 1736, coupled with his continued study of the New

Testament, prompted him to conclude that Paul was speaking to a specific situation, rather than making a universal mandate.[10]

The most egalitarian of the radical groups was the Society of Friends, better known as the Quakers. Beginning in the 1650s, lower-class, rural women evangelists swept down from the north of England to London and the south, publicly preaching the message of their charismatic leader, George Fox (1624–1691): An inner light exists in all humans. This inner light was implanted by the Holy Spirit, and illuminated human understanding of scripture, tradition, and reason. The indwelling Holy Spirit caused women and men to tremble and shake in ecstatic experiences, which led outsiders to apply the name Quaker to them. The spiritual equality manifested in the idea of the inner light dictated a social equality that prevented women from curtseying, and men from removing their hats, to apparent superiors. Not only charismatic preachers, Quaker women prophets also created a system of charity, established networks of communications, cared for prisoners, provided safe houses for those who were persecuted, and negotiated with magistrates.[11] Margaret Fell (1614–1702), a wealthy widow who married George Fox in 1669, organized and directed "an informal but effective international postal system," in which her home served as a clearinghouse for all correspondence between Quakers, including those in prison, those in missions, and those in hiding.[12]

As Quakerism moved into a second generation, it became more established and less charismatic. Margaret Fell led the successful effort to organize a separate women's Friends Meeting rather than be silenced in a joint meeting. These women's meetings adjudicated the affairs of women, provided assistance to women and children in need, and screened potential marriage partners, to the shame of men who had to submit to the oversight of women. "In establishing a formal, collective identity for women as women . . . the meeting system was unique within Protestantism."[13]

While Quakers faced oppression in England and the American colonies for their nonconformity to religious practices, the most persecuted sect of the radical reformers remained the Anabaptists, who were executed by the hundreds on the Continent. Mennonites, Amish, and Hutterites today are the descendants of sixteenth-century Anabaptists. Although they preached a spiritual equality between men and women, these groups maintained strict patriarchal households. Forbidden to preach, teach, or baptize, women nevertheless spread the message by donating property and wealth to establish new churches. In 1660 Thieleman van Braght, a Dutchman, wrote *Martyrs' Mirror* (*De Martaelerspiegel*), which detailed the ordeals that the first generation of Anabaptist men and women suffered in the early sixteenth century. Of the nine hundred martyrs listed, almost a third were women. The women were tortured and executed, but the cruelest agony was being stripped naked in front of their tormentors.[14] Women could have avoided execution if they recanted, but they chose not to.

Monarchs and Martyrs

The diversity and motives of the people involved in the religious changes of the sixteenth century are additional factors for describing a plurality of Reformations. Martin Luther and John Calvin began their careers in theology, and their scholarship and academic study of the Bible led them to a doctrinal break from Catholicism. They had the support of the nobility and other secular authorities who wanted to shatter the power of the papacy. The Radical Reformers tended to emerge from the working and poorer classes, although wealthy persons joined and financially supported the movements. In contrast, the English Reformation started at the top, when King Henry VIII (r. 1509–1547) persuaded the Parliament to make the monarch the head of the church in England. Henry's church was Catholic in all other respects—doctrine, liturgy, worship—although the king did confiscate monastic lands and shut down convents in order to redistribute their wealth to his friends. "Eventually every house was closed and the nuns turned out without their dowries to seek shelter from their families or live as best they could on meager pensions."[15]

These annuities came from the confiscation of the nuns' communal and private properties.

Rulers across Europe dictated the religion of their areas, as the French phrase captured it: *une fois, une lois, un roi* (one faith, one law, one king). Nowhere was this more apparent than in England, where the religious landscape changed with each new monarch. Under Henry VIII's successor, Edward VI (r. 1547–1553), the church became more Protestant with the adoption of the English-language Book of Common Prayer, written by the archbishop of Canterbury Thomas Cranmer (1489–1556). This new book of worship retained many Catholic elements, such as the doctrine of transubstantiation and the ritual of purification designed for postpartum women. It also allowed women to baptize infants who had died in childbirth. Under Mary I (r. 1553–1558), however, the Protestant churches reverted to Roman Catholicism; priests had to separate from their wives, and wealthy Protestants fled to the Continent. The majority of Protestants martyred under the reign of "Bloody Mary" were too poor to flee. About a fifth of them were women.[16]

With the ascension of Elizabeth I (r. 1558–1603) to the throne, England returned to Protestantism, but a different kind from its European varieties. The Act of Uniformity, passed within the first year of her reign, required everyone to attend church and to use Cranmer's prayer book, now revised to reflect Protestant rather than Catholic dogma: Christ was present symbolically, rather than literally, in the communion elements. At the same time, the worship service looked very Catholic. Priests wore vestments, the creeds and prayers were the same, and an episcopal system oversaw local parish churches. Elizabeth wanted uniformity of practice, but did not dictate uniformity of belief, though like her half-sister Mary, she executed dissenters. Monarchs across Europe had the power, and used it, to enforce either Protestant or Catholic practice, but none molded a Protestant denomination so decisively as did Elizabeth.

Royal preferences led to religious wars and the pursuit of dissenters, but they also led to religious toleration. Marguerite of Navarre (1492–1549), for example, protected reformers and attempted to reorganize her own faith by encouraging vernacular translations of the Bible, even though she was a French Catholic. "She would not come out flatfootedly for either side, but would curb the violence of both."[17] Her many mystical writings reflect the spirit of both Renaissance humanism and Reformation spirituality. Her daughter, Jeanne d'Albret (1528–1572), took a more militant stance and "was the acknowledged leader of the French Protestant cause."[18] As queen of Navarre, Jeanne issued an edict on religious liberty in 1564 that protected the Huguenots, that is, the French Protestants. "Wake up. Read the signs of the times," she wrote to one of her opponents. "In the judgment of God your consciences will be your everlasting executioners."[19] Although her son Henry IV converted to Catholicism in order to become king of France, he issued the Edict of Nantes in 1598, granting the Huguenots civil and religious liberty, and restoring freedom of religion to Catholics in areas where it had been suppressed.

Toleration, however, was frequently seen as compromising God's Word. Religious rebellion, therefore, could not be permitted since it destabilized society by attacking theological, secular, and royal dominion. Those who did not conform were deemed heretics and punished accordingly. Two martyrs to religious freedom from colonial America illustrate the temper of the times. The civil and religious magistrates of Boston put Anne Hutchinson (1591–1643), a midwife and prophet, on trial for holding meetings in her home to discuss the previous week's sermons, "that hath been condemned by the general assembly as a thing not tolerable nor comely in the sight of God nor fitting for your sex."[20] The Puritan hierarchy exiled Hutchinson from the city because she would not cease prophesying in public. She founded a settlement in Rhode Island, which granted religious toleration, but was killed shortly thereafter in an Indian raid. Mary Dyer (1611–1660), a Quaker prophet and a friend of Anne Hutchinson, defied the city of Boston's restrictions on preaching Quakerism, which put her at risk for increasingly harsh punishments: having an ear cut off, having the tongue bored through with a hot iron, or being hanged.[21] But Dyer continued to preach the inner light in Boston, and although she received one reprieve while standing on the gallows with two Quaker men who were hanged, another arrest resulted in her execution. Drummers marched along with her to the scaffold, drowning out anything she might say to those who had assembled on Boston Common to witness her death.

The Persecution of Women

It was a short step from stifling dissent to rooting out heresy, and thence to searching out witches. Authorities had already set the stage by limiting the participation of women in public. Poverty was feminized, and charity—once the province of female religious activity—was masculinized, that is, turned over to secular jurisdiction to be administered by men.[22] Since Protestants believed that God's providence determined everything that happened to an individual, they also thought that poverty was the punishment for sin; thus, they criminalized poverty by outlawing almsgiving and begging. If poor people could not find employment, they were confined to workhouses. Poor women, who once relied upon the charity of neighbors, lost their support system.

Coupled with these changes was the widespread desire among both Catholic and Protestant reformers to monopolize all entry to the supernatural. "To use any of the forbidden arts and rituals or to consult with those who did with expectations of success was at least implicit witchcraft, for they had no efficacy in nature and no warrant in Scripture."[23] But villagers relied on the good magic implemented by healers, diviners, and blessers (those who gave blessings) to solve a multitude of everyday problems. They also believed in malevolent and harmful magic (*maleficium*) perpetrated by angry or hostile neighbors. It took Catholic inquisitors and Protestant preachers to "diabolize" the magic and link it to the devil.[24] "As popular religion turned away from the monastic image of celibate women as brides of Christ, the fearful vision of the witch as Satan's sexual partner arose in its place."[25]

Scholars have explained the ferocious persecution of rival mediators of supernatural power in a number of different ways: as an elite movement against peasants, as a widespread obsession with evil, as cultural evangelization, and as the monopolization of religious power. The persecutions occurred in waves, beginning in Italy and Spain in the late fifteenth and early sixteenth centuries, rolling through continental Europe and the British Isles in the mid- to late sixteenth century, before hitting Northern and Eastern Europe in the seventeenth century.[26] Estimates of the number who died range from fifty thousand to hundreds of thousands, with the highest number of deaths concentrated in Germany.[27] The vast majority of those who were executed were women, especially poor elderly women. There was a proliferation of instruction manuals written by Catholic and Protestant clerics to guide readers in the signs of witchcraft and the diabolism that accompanied it; there were also training manuals on how to extract confessions via torture. The best-known of these handbooks—the *Malleus maleficarum* (Hammer of Female Witches)—was published frequently from the fifteenth century on. But skeptics of the idea of diabolism and critics of the criminalization of witchcraft were also writing and publishing attacks against the abuse.

The Salem witch trials of the Massachusetts colony in 1692 happened at the tail end of the hysteria that had swept through Europe. Most of those accused were women; especially vulnerable were postmenopausal women who were property owners, or stood to inherit land or wealth, or who were insufficiently deferential to patriarchal norms.[28] An impartial review of the documents reveals outright fabrication of accusations, fraud in creation of evidence, and inconsistencies in testimony.[29] Although a number of prominent persons opposed the official prosecutions, ministers and magistrates who believed that witches were terrorizing the people of Salem Village and Essex County persuaded the governor of Massachusetts to allow the trials to proceed. Nineteen people were hanged, several died in prison, and one man was crushed to death by stones because he refused to cooperate with authorities.

The craze stopped in the colonies and in Europe as suddenly as it started. Some scholars have argued that the spirit of Enlightenment rationalism dampened the religious enthusiasm that fueled and justified the savagery. But the Enlightenment did not immediately undermine the prevailing view of women as inferior, weak, and feebleminded. It would take women themselves to voice that challenge.

Women Defending Women

The eighteenth century concluded with the publication of Mary Wollstonecraft's *Vindication of the Rights of Woman* (1792).[30] Wollstonecraft was an atheist daughter of freethinking parents, and her ringing defense of women's equality usually is seen as the first clear manifestation of feminism in Western history, and perhaps it is. Yet a number of precursors had already argued in religious tracts for the right of women to study, to teach, and to speak and preach in public, based on the demonstration of women's equal intellectual ability. While Christine de Pisan in the fifteenth century highlighted the accomplishments of great women from the past, several other Catholic and Protestant women writing in the seventeenth century also deserve mention as additional antecedents to the nonreligious Wollstonecraft.

Anna Maria van Schurman (1607–1678), a Dutch Calvinist "widely regarded as the most learned woman of her day in Europe," wrote a number of treatises and letters that made the case for teaching women how to read and, more broadly, for women's scholarship.[31] She knew Hebrew, Greek, Chaldean (Neo-Aramaic), Arabic, and Syriac well enough to use competently in her biblical exegesis, and she wrote an Ethiopic grammar.[32] Most European scholars thought she was an exception to the idea that women were intellectually inferior, but van Schurman argued strongly, if politely, that educational opportunities should be extended to everyone. "Since wisdom is so much an ornament of the human races that it ought by right to be extended to one and all," she wrote in one letter, "I do not see why the most beautiful adornment of all by far is not fitting for a maiden."[33]

The Mexican Hieronymite nun Sor Juana Inés de la Cruz (1651–1695)—called the "First Feminist of America"[34]—was a self-taught scholar who gained fame as a popular poet and dramatist in Spain's Golden Age of literature. Her collection of books, music, and instruments—both scientific and musical—was one of the largest in colonial Mexico, and portraits show her dwarfed by a library of books. Sor Juana entered the Convent of San Jerónimo (Saint Jerome) in Mexico City, rather than marry, because she wanted to pursue of life of scholarship. "I study because I must," she declared.[35] In *The Answer* (*La respuesta*), she contended that everyone, including women, needed to study logic, rhetoric, physics, and natural science in order to understand theology. Because Christ's divine mind was the storehouse of wisdom, all believers must pursue wisdom in order to know Christ. To counter the criticism of her theological writings, Sor Juana provided examples of women from church history and the Bible who spoke and wrote publicly.

The Quaker Margaret Fell was the first woman to publish a defense of female preaching.[36] Quakers had long agreed that women could prophesy: under the compulsion of the Holy Spirit no one could deny its inspiration. But debate existed in Quakerism, especially in its second generation, about whether or not women could preach, that is, address a mixed assembly through a sermon that was carefully constructed, and thus not a spontaneous outburst of the Spirit. *Womens Speaking Justified, Proved and Allowed by the Scriptures* (1667) mined the Old and New Testaments for examples of women who preached.[37] Fell addressed 1 Corinthians 14:34 and the deutero-Pauline verses in 1 Timothy 2:11, since they continued to be used to silence women in church. She pointed out that Paul would be contradicting himself and scripture if he had meant that no women could ever speak. She reminded her readers that Paul said that Christians are under the Spirit of God and not the Law. Many of the arguments Margaret Fell broached four hundred years ago are used by those who support the ordination of women to the preaching ministry today.

The Catholic Reformation: New Religious Fervor

The Council of Trent, which met in Italy from 1545 to 1563, clarified and solidified Catholic teaching on the nature of the church, the sacraments, and other doctrinal matters. The council reaffirmed the prohibition on priestly marriage and support for the Latin Vulgate translation of the Bible, and reasserted the primacy of the pope. Many changes occurred even before the council met, with new missionary orders arising for male and female religious, who felt called to respond to the challenge of Protestant evangelism. In addition, Catholic women continued to practice their faith—sometimes clandestinely, sometimes under assault—in what Jo Ann McNamara calls the matriarchal phase of Catholic Christianity.[38] In some regions only in the convent did women continue to attend Mass. In other areas, nuns would sing loudly, chant the psalms, or recite the rosary when they were forced to listen to Protestant sermons. In still other locales, laywomen held services in their homes or refused to attend compulsory Protestant services, saying their prayers in the Latin they had learned in girlhood. Catholic women were visible partisans in the religion wars that wracked sixteenth- and seventeenth-century Europe, but they moved in two distinct directions: Some turned inward as nuns to the mystical path of contemplation, while others turned outward as laywomen to the larger mission field of Europe and the New World.

One of the greatest of the sixteenth-century mystics was Saint Teresa of Avila (1515–1582). Her erudition as one of four female doctors of the church is evident in her numerous books, manuals, and commentaries.[39] The daughter and granddaughter of Jewish converts to Christianity, also known as *conversos*, she boldly challenged the Inquisition by protecting other *conversas* in an exceedingly strict order of cloistered nuns. Her mystical path of mental prayer was also at odds with the Inquisition. As her vocation evolved, her writings "began to address more forcefully the misogynist and antimystical biases of her day,"[40] though it is unclear whether this was her actual intent. Nevertheless, she vehemently defended women's right to write—Sor Juana pointed to Teresa as one of her exemplars—by arguing for a theory of divine inspiration that allowed her to compose literally thousands of pages during a time of inquisitorial scrutiny.

Teresa wanted to unite the active and contemplative aspects of religious life in her reformed order of Carmelite nuns. She turned to the figures of Martha and Mary as described in Luke's gospel (10:38–42) as her models. "Believe me, Martha and Mary need to come together to offer hospitality to Christ," she wrote in her mystical text, *The Interior Castle* (*El castillo interior*). "How can Mary, seated constantly at [Jesus's] feet, give him anything unless her sister helps her?"[41] In her autobiography, Teresa says that the soul is both active and contemplative at the same time: "It tends to works of charity and to business affairs that have to do with its state of life and to reading."[42] No one aspiring to be Mary, the contemplative, can succeed "before having worked with Martha."[43]

The contemplative impulse could also be seen in the New World with Peru's first saint, Rose of Lima (1586–1617), best known for the excruciating punishments she inflicted on herself. A Dominican tertiary who lived at home throughout her career as a holy woman, "she was particularly revered for her care of the sick and poor and for miraculous cures of Indians and African slaves as well as her protecting the city of Lima from earthquakes and the attack of pirates through the power of her prayers."[44] Like the medieval mystics, Rose used her sufferings as the means to sanctity. In some respects, her religiosity hearkened back to a previous era.

In contrast, other women adopted a new type of religiosity. The Italian Saint Angela Merici (1474–1540), for example, established an order of laywomen whose purpose was to teach the poor outside the convent. Called the Company of Saint Ursula—after the legendary fourth/fifth-century virgin martyr Ursula of Cologne—the movement spread out from Italy to evangelize the French peasantry and, eventually, the native peoples of New France, that is, Canada. The Ursulines were "domestic saints," living at home but vowing never to marry. "The presence of a young unmarried woman . . . was no longer a dishonor; rather, it signaled that family's holiness."[45] But the company clashed with local bishops, especially in France, who did not like laywomen teaching, and possibly preaching, in public. Although the Ursulines were forced back to the cloister, they continued to teach inside the convent.

Saint Louise de Marillac (1591–1660) was a *dévote*, a type of French-Catholic-Puritan who eschewed parties, dancing, gaming, and other frivolous activities. Working with Saint Vincent de Paul (1581–1660), she organized rural young women to work with the urban poor. Funded by wealthy Ladies of Charity, these Daughters of Charity enlisted the poor to care for their own neighbors.[46] Pairs of lay "daughters" would live together in community, nursing the sick, teaching children, and supporting themselves through some kind of paid labor. They successfully resisted efforts to be cloistered by simply pronouncing promises to be renewed annually, rather than taking solemn vows, considered indissoluble. Some women followed a modified version of the Daughters of Charity, calling themselves *filles séculières* (secular daughters).[47] They acted essentially as independent contractors, as did, for example, Saint Marguerite Bourgeoys (1620–1700), who organized a school in Montreal, Canada, through a contract with the civil government. Bourgeoys defied all attempts to enclose her *filles séculières*, and in 1698 the bishop of Montreal finally accepted the secular status of the Congregation of Notre Dame, whose members traveled throughout New France as teachers.

A final group of noteworthy lay sisters were the so-called Jesuitesses of Mary Ward's Institute of the Blessed Virgin Mary. After receiving a humanist education in Yorkshire, England, Mary Ward (1585–1645) established a lay religious group of women dedicated to female education that worked underground in London during the suppression of the

Catholic Church. Ward wanted to model the institute after the Jesuits, a new missionary order of men founded by Saint Ignatius of Loyola (1491–1556). Without benefit or approval from either the Jesuits or the pope, Ward and her company of Englishwomen opened free public schools for the poor throughout the European continent. But critics accused the women of scandalous behavior, and the pope condemned and imprisoned Ward as a heretic. Though the institute gained papal recognition after Ward's death, not until 1909—when six thousand sisters were teaching seventy thousand young girls at more than two hundred schools—was the community allowed to recognize Mary Ward as their founder.[48]

Conclusions

The era of the Reformations simultaneously saw reform and resistance in the activities of women within Christianity. The spread of Christianity at this time through small house churches, cell groups—or conventicles, as they were called—occurred through the efforts of women. Martyrdom cut across gender lines, especially when it came to the execution of those accused of witchcraft. Some Catholic women continued to choose virginity over marriage, although they expressed it in different kinds of religious orders.

At the same time, the turn to the authority of experience, coupled with the stirrings of rationalism, opened new doors for women. Unless Christians were to deny the power of the Holy Spirit, women could prophesy; unless they were to deny the need for evangelization, women could teach and preach, but only to women and children; unless they were to deny the elemental equality of male and female stated at the very beginning of creation (Gen. 1:27), women might claim a right to education, to labor, and to privileges once reserved to men. Women demonstrated their courage as martyrs and missionaries in the expansion of Christianity beyond the bounds of Europe. In the nineteenth century, they would take Christianity even further.

FIGURE 6.1. *Saint Kateri Tekakwitha*, by Julie Lonneman. © Julie Lonneman. Courtesy of Trinity Stores, www.trinitystores.com.

6

Spirit-Filled Women in the Nineteenth Century

The Reformation's turn to the authority of scripture in the sixteenth century and the Enlightenment's turn to the authority of reason in the seventeenth and eighteenth centuries found a parallel move in the nineteenth century: a turn to the authority of the Holy Spirit. Each of these shifts dramatically altered the religious landscape, not only of Europe but of the rest of the world. Moreover, each move had the potential to erode the foundations of patriarchal Christianity, though in different ways. The reliance upon scripture rather than tradition—the teachings of the church that had been handed down for centuries—offered biblical examples of strong women who led armies, prophesied with wisdom and power, served as disciples of Jesus, and worked as ministers in the early church. The reliance upon reason undermined scriptural foundations. Although educated writers of the Enlightenment continued to argue that women were inferior to men, they no longer claimed that such inferiority was sanctioned or created by God. Moreover, women could assert their equality through arguments based on reason. The reliance upon the Holy Spirit—the faith placed in divine inspiration outside scripture and reason—empowered women to testify and witness to their faith both inside and outside the home. More than anything else, the perceived experience of the Holy Spirit impelled women to act and gave them the confidence to challenge societal norms. Denying the call of God and the movement of the Spirit in their hearts would be to turn their backs on God, regardless of what scripture, tradition, or reason might say about women speaking out in church.

The mechanical processes of industrialization, which had revolutionized the economies of Europe and the United States, were the backdrop for the emotionalism of Spirit-filled religion. "The shift from the farmland to the cities, from the fields to the factories, resulted in profound disruptions in gender roles and family life."[1] Whereas women once contributed in concrete ways to the family's economic survival—providing necessary labor in an agricultural environment or in a metropolitan artisan household—they were now pushed out of the workforce and into the home. There they had two primary duties: to make life pleasant for their husbands and to raise their children. Men, who once defined their masculinity through physical labor, now dirtied their hands by working in the public sphere of business and industry. Meanwhile, women were elevated on the pedestal of "True Womanhood," which in reality meant being confined to the domestic, or private, sphere.[2] Working-class women continued to toil in factories, while slaves, former slaves, and farmwives contributed to the family enterprise with their sweat. But after the mid-nineteenth century, the new urban, middle-class white woman was supposed to find meaning and fulfillment entirely in the home.

Nevertheless, women of all classes rejected the new enforced domesticity and found their calling as evangelists, missionaries, community organizers, and successful fundraisers. They traveled the world, preaching the gospel at home and abroad. They led reform movements to improve the condition of women and children by providing education, health care, and social services. They established new forms of Christianity that exist to this day. In short, they returned to the public sphere and made it their home. "The True Woman evolved into the New Woman," active and yet conflicted about her activism.[3]

Missions to Native and Immigrant Americans

The earliest female missionaries from Europe to the New World were Catholic sisters. Nuns accompanied the friars in the footsteps of the conquistadors and helped to establish the first school system in Mexico City. "By 1534 there were eight schools where Native Indian girls learned reading, writing, and arithmetic along with European household skills."[4] But the convents of Central and South America generally catered to the families of the colonizers. More than a fifth of the white female population of Peru was cloistered by the middle of the seventeenth century.[5] Segregated convents, in which native, black, and creole sisters lived apart from each other, also multiplied, such as the Convent of Corpus Christi, founded in Mexico City in 1724 for Aztec noblewomen. Yet sisters also attempted to serve the native peoples; and a laywoman, Jeanne Mance (1606–1673), and the Hospitalières de Saint Joseph established the Hôtel Dieu of Montreal to care for Indians as well as settlers. Marie of the Incarnation (1599–1672), a French Ursuline nun who founded the Ursuline Order in Canada, wrote an Algonquin dictionary and an Iroquois catechism.[6]

In spite of these positive strides, Indian resistance to missionary activity gave Canada the reputation of being the land of martyrdom.[7] The first Native American saint, Kateri Tekakwitha (ca. 1656–1680), was something of an exception.[8] A Mohawk Indian, she saw her parents die in one of the many smallpox epidemics that ravaged the tribes of North America. She herself survived with a scar-darkened face, which, according to legend, became clear and bright shortly after she died. Her Catholic Christianity spiritually matured with a confraternity of native women in the village of Kahnawake, a self-governing Iroquois hamlet. A number of young women observed severe austerities, including flogging each other and immersing themselves in icy streams, and Kateri participated in these and other penances. These punishing activities compromised her already poor health, and she died at age twenty-four. Popular devotion kept her alive in the hearts of indigenous peoples for centuries. In the twentieth century, Kateri Conferences drew hundreds of scholars and devotees to international convocations year after year. Kateri Circles, which are local devotional groups, have attracted Native American women for decades. "A lot of people say that in praying to her, she has answered their prayers," according to one Pueblo woman.[9] It was no surprise, then, when—following her elevation to sainthood in 2012 by Pope Benedict XVI (p. 2005–2013)—hundreds of Native American women from a variety of tribal nations traveled to Rome for the canonization ceremony.

Another missionary success story comes from the Tlingit peoples in Sitka, Alaska, who were particularly receptive to Russian Orthodox missionaries. Some Orthodox traditions seemed parallel to native ceremonies. The Indians "must have been impressed with the elaborate ceremony [of baptism], which involved immersion in water, reminiscent of the Tlingit purification rituals (i.e., bathing in the ice-cold water of the ocean) engaged in by boys and young men to strengthen the mind and body and thus to secure good fortune or blessing (*laxeitl*)."[10] Baptism established a bond between godparents and neophytes, which replicated Tlingit habits of reciprocity and gift-giving. Even after America's purchase of Alaska, when Presbyterian missionaries attempted to Americanize natives through mission schools, Tlingit women continued to practice and promote the customs they had learned from Russian Orthodox priests one or two generations earlier. "Orthodox canon law, Russian and Creole folk traditions, and indigenous beliefs about the rules of conduct for Orthodox women became so intertwined that eventually most Tlingit could not distinguish them from each other."[11]

But as often as not, mission projects failed. Marcus Whitman (1802–1847), a medical missionary, and his wife, Narcissa Prentiss Whitman (1808–1847), were killed during an Indian uprising. The Presbyterian missionaries failed to convert a single Cayuse Indian in the twenty-one years they lived at the Waiilatpu mission in what is now part of Washington state. Although Narcissa had tried to establish both a day school and a boarding school, she learned, as did her Catholic counterparts, that it was easier to teach the children of white settlers. Part of the problem undoubtedly was her failure to learn the Nez Perce language, but another part was her contempt for native women, whom she viewed as lazy and dirty. "Narcissa, like most whites, viewed cultural transfer as a one-way process."[12] Missionaries wanted the so-called heathen to conform to Western ideas of civilization, which—either tacitly or explicitly stated—required the destruction of Indian civilization.

Because of ~~Indian~~ _{Native} resistance to this process of cultural suicide, missionaries found themselves ministering to other transplants. This was especially true for the nuns who arrived in the United States in the nineteenth century. At first, the sisters were unwelcome interlopers in the new nation, where Protestant feeling ran high against Catholics, especially nuns, who were visible targets in their attire. In 1834 an angry mob set fire to an Ursuline convent in Charlestown, Massachusetts. Protestants elsewhere insulted sisters and threw mud at those who appeared in public. Consequently, nuns took to wearing secular dress outside the cloister and donned special robes at night in case they needed to leave their quarters quickly.

The Civil War changed popular attitudes toward nuns, however, since one out of five served as a nurse on the battlefield. Many non-Catholics also used the services of Catholic hospitals and orphanages run by the sisters. By 1900, there were almost four times as many nuns as priests in the United States; there were also 3,811 parochial schools—most of them run by sisters—and 663 Catholic girls' academies, as opposed to 102 academies for boys.[13] While this tremendous growth came as a result of the waves of immigrants arriving from Europe, the beginnings of Catholic education can be traced to Saint Elizabeth Bayley Seton (1774–1821), the first saint to be born in the United States. Seton, a convert to Catholicism, had established the earliest parochial school, the initial orphanage, and the original Catholic religious community of women in the United States in the early nineteenth century.[14] The distinctive habit of Seton's Sisters of Charity—a black dress, a shoulder cape, and a white hat tied under the chin—became a well-respected sign of service among Protestant Americans who had a historic distrust and dislike of Catholics.

Revivalism and the Quest for Holiness

Although most U.S. history textbooks today describe a First Great Awakening (1730s–1740s) in colonial America, and a Second Great Awakening

(1797–1840) in the period of the early republic, it is probably more accurate to say that a number of religious revivals occurred throughout the eighteenth and nineteenth centuries.[15] These revivals generated renewed energy and enthusiasm for religion and fostered a rededication of the Christian's life to God. While the earliest revivals saw a surge in the participation of women in the administrative and organizational life of the church, later revivals actually featured female leaders and evangelists who felt called by the Holy Spirit. Many women who testified to their conversion experience, who exhorted others to come to Christ, or who themselves preached sermons, found their inspiration at camp meetings. Hundreds, and sometimes thousands, of people pitched tents at these weeklong religious retreats held out in the open. Revivals in churches and urban auditoriums also brought in the penitent, who would sing, pray, listen, and hope for the conviction of sin—a feeling that one's personal failings are utterly hateful in the sight of God—which would lead to the assurance of forgiveness that would bring them closer to Christ.

These revivals generated a desire among believers to be holy. The experience of regeneration could not stop at the altar of the camp meeting; rather, it had to be carried out in everyday life. But what was holiness? And could anyone truly achieve it, since the doctrine of original sin taught that humans were incorrigible sinners? The Methodist movement, begun in the eighteenth century, offered a practical way to be holy. John Wesley (1703–1791), a minister in the Church of England and the founder of Methodism, believed that salvation was a two-step process. First, people were justified by their faith, through the grace of God. A second blessing—sanctification by the Holy Spirit—then occurred. This process of sanctification eventually induced a Christian to become perfect in love, that is, holy. While Wesley believed this would probably happen over the course of a lifetime, he did not rule out the possibility of complete sanctification occurring sooner.

There were several ways to pursue the path of Christian perfection, including performing daily devotions, writing in a spiritual journal each day, and examining one's conscience every evening. Wesley learned this practical approach from his mother, Susanna Annesley Wesley (1669–1742). "[Susanna] was a 'methodist' long before her son was—indeed, long before the critical term was coined."[16] Her popular Sunday Society, at which she read from the Anglican Book of Common Prayer and spoke "freely and affectionately," attracted more than two hundred followers, although it also drew the criticism of her husband.[17] These weekly meetings, along with Susanna's strict rules for conducting personal devotions, formed the core practices of the Holiness clubs that Wesley later put forth at Oxford University. Because of the methodical approach to perfection, group members were called Methodists, although they remained members of the Church of England in the initial decades of the movement.

Initially Wesley was reluctant to let women preach in the new movement, but again Susanna Wesley paved the way by encouraging him to utilize lay preachers, that is, those who were not ordained ministers, especially women. He grudgingly let Sarah Crosby (1729–1804) lead Methodist class meetings, but advised her not to discuss scripture for more than four or five minutes, lest it appear she was preaching. Eventually, though, he gave permission to Crosby and a number of other women to preach sermons, justifying the practice on the grounds that Methodism was an "extraordinary dispensation" of the providence of God that allowed for exceptions.[18] "In Mr. Wesley's Methodism, women became preachers, group leaders, founders of schools, active visitors and callers, benefactresses, [and] models of Christian life for male and female alike."[19]

The quest for Christian perfection, or holiness in this life, was revolutionized in the United States by two women who grew up in a strict Methodist family: Sarah Worrall Lankford (1806–1896) and Phoebe Worrall Palmer (1807–1874). After experiencing what she said was "the assurance of entire sanctification," Sarah organized a prayer known as the Tuesday Meeting for the Promotion of Holiness, which met for sixty years. Initially open only to women, it ultimately attracted seminarians, clergymen, and theologians. Palmer became the more famous spokesperson for holiness, however, leading revivals and camp meetings in the United States, Canada, and England, and substantially redefining the concept of holiness through her many books.[20] According to Palmer, a Christian could experience complete sanctification immediately, bypassing the long period of spiritual growth anticipated by Wesley. The way to holiness required two steps on the part of the believer: faith in Christ's promise of sanctification, and consecration of one's life to Christ by symbolically laying one's all on the altar.[21] But what did "one's all" mean? Some interpreted this very broadly to include home, family, friends, possessions, and time, while others understood this narrowly to mean husband, fashion, and reputation. In either case, "giving God first place undermined the belief that women should devote their lives wholly to their families."[22]

The Holiness movement, which grew out of Methodism, opened the door wider for women preachers and evangelists. A number of breakaway groups believed that Methodism, by then the largest denomination in the United States, had diluted the requirements of true holiness, both personal, such as dressing modestly or avoiding alcohol; and social, such as opposing slavery or helping the poor. Moreover, Holiness churches ordained women to be pastors of churches. With a few exceptions, Methodist churches in the nineteenth century did not.

One of the most visible denominations that has survived from the Holiness tradition is the Salvation Army, a church created to help the poor that was cofounded by William Booth (1829–1912) and Catherine Mumford Booth (1829–1890). Growing up in England and the United States in a Methodist, working-class household, Catherine learned John Wesley's doctrine of sanctification at an early age, and as a young woman encountered Phoebe Palmer's books on holiness. In fact, Catherine wrote a tract—first titled *Female Teaching* and later *Female Ministry*—defending Phoebe Palmer's right to preach to mixed groups.[23] She herself did not preach until 1860, when she could no longer resist her heartfelt sense that God was telling her to speak publicly in church. What followed was a twenty-eight-year career as a popular preacher and a leader of the Salvation Army. "From the very beginning the Army was organized on a quasi-military model, with women having total equality in service and status."[24]

of course, it was .... *(handwritten annotation)*

Yet the first responsibility of women officers, regardless of rank, was to care for their families. "The home ultimately represented a female officer's highest calling because she bore the primary responsibility for raising her children to follow God."[25] Thus, the contributions of Catherine Booth to full inclusion of women in the life of the church are somewhat ambiguous.

Foreign Missions — don't do this! *(handwritten annotation)*

An enlargement in educational opportunities for girls in Europe and the United States in the nineteenth century created a cohort of highly qualified women who were excluded from working in the public, or masculine, sphere of society. They therefore used their organizational skills in the churches, the only semipublic domain then open to Protestant women. Prior to the 1850s, women contributed financially and logistically to male-run missionary societies, both home missions, targeting Native Americans, African Americans, and the poor; and foreign missions, targeting Africa and Asia (South America was ceded to the Catholics). Women's involvement in these organizations, and their participation in various reform movements, such as the abolition of slavery or the promotion of purity, provided the background for the establishment of their own, female-led boards of missions. The first, the interdenominational Woman's Union Missionary Society (WUMS), emerged in 1861; within fifteen years, the mainline denominations in the United States—Congregational, Baptist, Presbyterian, Methodist— all had women's boards "that selected single women as missionaries and raised money for their support."[26] The creation of women's boards of missions dramatically changed the gender profile of Protestant missionaries in the field. In 1910, for example, the number of women missionaries in India exceeded the number of male missionaries.[27]

As were the missions to Native Americans, the missions to Africans and Asians were largely efforts to convert people to Western civilization as well as to Christianity. "Missionaries came to represent both the best and the worst of the civilizing mission itself."[28] Christianity and com-

leave them alone! (handwritten annotation)

merce seemed to work in tandem wherever the missionaries went; at the same time, missionaries also served as the conscience of the colonizers, speaking out at times against exploitation of the local people. Female missionaries became aware of social problems affecting women in other parts of the worlds, like arranged marriages, concubinage, maternal death, and infanticide of girls. While they worked to solve these problems directly, they also saw education for girls as a more permanent solution. Three women stand out in this regard.

Isabella Thoburn (1840–1901) "devoted her whole life to the cause of female education in India."[29] The very first single woman appointed by the newly formed Women's Foreign Missionary Society of the Methodist Episcopal Church, she arrived in Lucknow, India, in 1870. There she opened a primary school for girls with six students in a mud-walled room in the local bazaar. In 1886, with financial support from the mother of one of the graduates of the school, she inaugurated college classes with three students. The Women's Christian College, as it was called, was the first such institution in all of Asia.[30] Thoburn believed "that if India were to progress and her women be emancipated, it was necessary to educate and train women who could be leaders."[31] In 2011 the Isabella Thoburn College, renamed in 1901 after Thoburn's death, celebrated the 125th anniversary of its founding.

The Methodist Women's Foreign Missionary Society also sent another single woman to India the same year that Thoburn went. Clara Swain (1834–1910) "was an archetype of the professional medical missionary of the late nineteenth century,"[32] the first such female to be stationed in India. In 1870, Dr. Swain began her service as a staff physician at the Methodist hospital in Bareilly. There she taught courses in medicine to Indian women and provided medical care to the women and children of the city. She soon obtained a land grant to build a women's hospital and dispensary, which she directed until she was retained in 1885 by the Rajah of Khetri State to supervise a new women's clinic. She worked there for ten years before traveling to the Middle East for a time, finally returning to the United States for the last decade of her life.

FIGURE 6.2. Maria Fearing. Courtesy of Alabama Department of Archives and History, Montgomery, Alabama.

African American missionaries felt a special obligation to Africa, believing it was the responsibility of black Americans to save Africa for Christianity. The Southern Presbyterian Church assigned five black women to the Presbyterian Congo Mission between 1894 and 1941. All of the women were born in Alabama and had attended black colleges in the South, where they heard the message of God's providential design: Africans had been enslaved so that former slaves could return to Africa to save them.[33] Maria Fearing (1838–1937) grew up in slavery, and did not have any formal schooling until after Emancipation in 1863. Although she taught school for many years, she continued to feel drawn to the mission field. When the Presbyterian mission committee rejected her application to go to Congo, the fifty-six-year-old sold her house, took her life savings along with $100 pledged by the women of the Congregational church in Talladega, Alabama, and finally received permission to go—once she agreed to pay all of her expenses. Fearing quickly learned the local language and soon began offering religious instruction at the mission station in Luebo, Congo. The mission committee then agreed to support her by providing food at first, then labor, then a salary, and finally by giving her an appointment as a regularly stationed missionary. Known as *mamu wa mptutu* (the mother from far away), she "believed that her major duty in Africa was to improve the lives of women and children."[34] She took in orphaned and kidnapped girls, and by the time she left Congo in 1915, one hundred lived under her care in the Pantops Home for Girls at Luebo.

Reform Movements

"Woman working for woman" was the slogan of the women's missionary societies, though children were included in their mandate for care. This might also have served as the motto for the social reform movements that arose out of the nineteenth-century revivals in Europe and the United States. Churchwomen provided social services like rent and food assistance, clothing, bedding, medicine, heating fuel, and other necessities to the poor. They set up rescue homes for prostitutes and orphanages for children. They revolutionized society by pushing for legislative changes that would provide a living wage, reduce prostitution, promote equal rights, and end slavery. The church and its outreach ministries served as the training ground, and even the breeding ground, for women's activism. The first women's rights convention held in the United States, for instance, met at a Wesleyan Holiness church in Seneca Falls, New York, in 1848.[35]

One of the largest, if not *the* largest, women's reform efforts was the temperance movement, which first called for moderation in alcohol consumption, and then complete prohibition. Alcoholism had not been seen as a serious problem prior to the nineteenth century. Low-alcohol-content wine and beer were often more available than clean drinking water. But actual alcohol consumption seemed to escalate as poverty burgeoned in the new, factory-driven economy. In addition, whereas alcohol had once been consumed primarily in the home, taverns and saloons became the venue for drinking as a social, rather than dietary, occasion. These bars were the province of ordinary men, but the only women who frequented them were prostitutes or others of low repute. Thus, the movement to limit drinking, especially by closing bars, was a female incursion into male territory, often a literal invasion, when women demonstrated at bars to prevent the selling or buying of liquor. The Woman's Crusade, for example, was a temperance movement organized by midwestern Protestant women against the sale of alcohol. Though it was short-lived, running only from 1873 to 1875, it succeeded in reducing alcohol consumption in twenty states. By April 1874, more than a thousand saloons had been temporarily shut down.[36]

It took a national organization, the Woman's Christian Temperance Union (WCTU), founded in 1874 during the Woman's Crusade, to activate women across the United States and eventually around the world. The movement was not really or only about alcohol. It was concerned with what women saw as the problems of male irresponsibility, failure to provide for their families, and domestic violence. "Temperance was an attractive issue for women because men's drinking symbolized so many of the injustices that women felt, and also because men's drinking posed many real problems for women in late-nineteenth-century America."[37]

The driving force behind the WCTU in its first two decades was Frances Willard (1839–1898). For a time she taught at the college level—and was dean of the Women's College at Northwestern University—before she became an evangelist with the revivalist D. L. Moody. She found her calling with the WCTU, and served as its president from 1879 until her death in 1898. Although the WCTU emphasized temperance, Willard expanded its agenda to encompass many issues, including women's right to vote. Her aim was the "Christianization of society," and she worked with religious, labor, charitable, and political groups to achieve this goal.[38] Christianization could be seen in the Chicago WCTU chapter, which sponsored "two day nurseries, two Sunday schools, an industrial school, a mission to shelter four thousand destitute or homeless women per year, a free medical dispensary that treated sixteen hundred people that year, a lodging house for men, and a low-cost restaurant."[39] An international WCTU was established under Willard's tenure, and by the time of its fourth meeting, the organization had more than two million women members worldwide.

Recruiters for the international WCTU found fertile ground among Japanese female Christians, who had already established schools for girls and young women with the help of American missionaries. In 1886, seven churchwomen founded the Tokyo Fujin Kyofukai (literally, the Tokyo Women's Custom-Correcting Society; or, more loosely, the Tokyo Women's Reform Society).[40] They selected a name that did not mention either Christianity or temperance: in the former instance, because of Japanese animosity to Christianity, despite the turn toward Western culture during the Meiji Restoration of 1868–1912; in the second, because for Japanese women, temperance was not the most important worry—discriminatory marriage laws were.

The group's founding mothers—Kajiko Yajima (1833–1925), the wife of an alcoholic Christian minister, and Toyujuo Sasaki (1853–1901), the wife of a Christian doctor, by whom she had her first child out of wedlock—initially disagreed on whether the group's focus should be on temperance or women's rights. Ultimately "the two women agreed to work together for the 'correction' of feudalistic customs that subjugated Japan to the West and women to men."[41] Combating the geisha system, eliminating prostitution, rescuing pleasure women, and elevating the status of wives above that of concubines were their primary issues of concern. Yajima and Sasaki spoke to mixed groups and published articles on women's right to speak. Sasaki translated many WCTU articles from English into Japanese and maintained a correspondence with Frances Willard. In addition to supporting education for poor women, the successful fundraising efforts of the Tokyo Women's Reform Society resulted in the donation of money for the construction of the WCTU's temperance building in Chicago.

Efforts to improve the condition of women in India were occurring under the leadership of Pandita Ramabai (1858–1922) at the same time. A highly educated Hindu, Ramabai converted to Christianity during a trip to England. A two-year speaking tour in the United States brought her both fame and fortune as she described the horrors of widowhood in India.[42] When she returned to India, she established a nonsectarian widows' home, the Sharada Sadan (Home of Learning) in Pune, formerly known as Poona. During a devastating famine in the Central Provinces and Gujarat in 1896, she conducted a massive rescue effort, housing hundreds of victims on land she had recently purchased. Then she opened a new, explicitly Christian institution—the Mukti Sadan (Home of Salvation), which later on became the Mukti Mission. She also established the Kripa Sadan (Home of Mercy), a rescue home for sexually victimized women, which included housing for blind women, who received education in Braille and were taught useful crafts. Ramabai built a "female kingdom" in which all the tasks—including income-generating activities and management of the facilities—were done by women. "It had been Ramabai's cherished dream to develop self-reliance in, and provide an alternative shelter for, women whose homes were their 'social universe' but often an oppressive one."[43] Unfortunately, the more popular Ramabai became among Christian women of the West, the more isolated she became from Hindu nationalists and reformers in India, especially because she served as the primary conduit for foreign aid directed at Indian women. The WCTU provided ongoing support for Ramabai's projects, and Frances Willard was a personal friend. The Indian reformer died at age sixty-four, having just completed a translation of the Bible from the original Hebrew and Greek into her native language, Marathi.

Sectarian Religions

In contrast to the reformers who sought to purify society, a number of women wanted to purify Christianity, forming a number of distinctive sectarian churches within Christianity. "Large numbers of women turned to new forms of religious expression to meet their rising awareness of themselves and the world."[44] Some of these expressions of Christian thought advanced the idea of the Motherhood of God. Others reintroduced practices of early Christianity, such as prophesying and speaking in tongues, to create denominations that have come to dominate global Christianity in recent decades. Three groups—the Shakers, the Mormons, and the Christian Scientists—deserve mention in regard to the Motherhood of God, while two groups—the Seventh-day Adventists and Pentecostal Christians—are notable for attracting millions of adherents today.

In 1758 Ann Lee (1736/42?–1784), a young, uneducated mill worker, joined the United Society of Believers in Christ's Second Appearing, in Manchester, England. The group became known as the Shakers because of their ecstatic dancing. Recognized as a prophet by members of the group, Lee delivered a message of total sexual abstinence—based on her belief that the sin of Adam and Eve was sexual—to the New England colonies in 1774. She died in 1784 after suffering violent beatings as she preached the message of Christ's imminent return. But the Shaker movement survived, thanks to the organizational efforts of Lee's successors. The co-leaders Joseph Meacham (1742–1796) and Lucy Wright (1760–1821) fashioned Shaker theology and organization to create communal, self-sustaining farms based on gender parity. "Integral to Meacham's organizational plan was the idea that the millennial Church must be led by parallel male and female leadership, representing the dual spiritual parentage of Christ as Father and Mother."[45] Jesus of Nazareth was viewed as the father, while Ann Lee was seen as the mother in Christ, who gave women freedom from bondage to men, but who also gave men freedom from their sinful natures. By living a pure and holy life, the Shakers were preparing themselves for Christ's return, a belief that was built upon the eschatological expectation that the end of the present age was near.

In 1796 Lucy Wright was selected over a male as First Elder to head the Shakers, which she did for more than two decades until her death. Better educated and more maternal than Ann Lee, Wright supervised the greatest period of expansion of the movement from New England into Kentucky, Ohio, and Indiana, mediating conflicts between the growing Shaker communities. She formulated the unique Shaker worship style, wrote songs and hymns, and choreographed dances and marches.[46] Her letters and comments to the various settlements are warm and friendly, as evidenced by her fashion advice to the male Shakers: "A few years ago they had their trousers almost as tight as their skin, but now they resemble meal bags. I want to have Believers avoid these extremes and keep a proper medium, entirely regardless of the vain fashions of the world."[47]

Unlike the Shakers, the Church of Jesus Christ of Latter-day Saints—the official name for the Mormon church—has a patriarchal hierarchy in which gender complementarity rather than gender equality is the norm. Yet Joseph Smith's (1806–1844) revelation of a material Father God in heaven logically led to the idea of a material Mother God. "All of the evidence, though mostly circumstantial, demonstrates that this idea of God, the Mother in Heaven, originated with Joseph Smith and that it was part of the alternative image of God that he taught at Nauvoo[, Illinois]."[48] In the nineteenth century, this Heavenly Mother played a more prominent part than she does in contemporary Mormonism, but twentieth-century feminist Mormons attempted to recapture the notion of the Motherhood of God. Since the highest heaven for Mormonism is designed for married couples, women are essential to salvation, although on earth they maintain a traditionally gendered role.

A final new denomination within nineteenth-century Christianity that posits the Motherhood of God is that of the Church of Christ, Scientist, also known as the Christian Science Church. Founded by Mary Baker Eddy (1821–1910), Christian Science teaches that human understanding of God and of reality is flawed. Reality, like God, is spiritual rather than material, and so evil and sickness do not exist. Rather, they are errors of perception.[49] According to Eddy, the feminine quality of love, rather than the masculine qualities of intelligence and truth, best impart the idea of the divine. In addition, God has a dual nature, male and female, and consequently the term "Father-Mother God" appears throughout Eddy's writings. "Mrs. Eddy felt that her womanhood was essential to the very nature of her mission; for she and her followers believed that it had been given to her to reveal the Motherhood of God."[50]

Christian Science once claimed more than a quarter million members, according to the last reported figures from 1936. Unofficial estimates range from 100,000 to 400,000 today. In the nineteenth century, the Shakers had two dozen thriving communities in the United States, with more than six thousand members at their zenith. Today Shakerism exists in museums and monuments rather than in membership. The Church of Jesus Christ of Latter-day Saints has grown into a religion with more than 14.1 million members worldwide, according to figures from 2010, although active members may account for only 5 million, or 35 percent, of that total. Two other movements spearheaded by women, however, have become major forces in global Christianity: Seventh-day Adventism, with 17.5 million adherents claimed in 2011; and Pentecostalism, with more than 250 million adherents.

Many nineteenth-century Christians believed that Jesus was going to return to earth in the near future. William Miller (1782–1849), one of the prophets of Christ's Second Coming, predicted that Jesus would come in the year 1843; when Christ failed to appear, new dates were set, the last date being 22 October 1844. Hundreds, if not thousands, of Christians sold their possessions in anticipation of Christ's arrival, or advent. Most of William Miller's followers, known as Millerites, fell away after they experienced the Great Disappointment, but one woman's ongoing revelations revived expectations of the advent. Ellen Gould Harmon, who married James White, is best known as Ellen G. White (1827–1915), the cofounder of the Seventh-day Adventist Church. A small group of Adventists accepted the direction of White and her husband, guided by her visions. It was not until 1860, however, when the group named themselves Seventh-day Adventists—accepting the scriptural requirement of observing the Sabbath—that the group began to grow. In the early days of the denomination, White created schools and promoted education, formulated programs in diet and health, including vegetarianism, sponsored health care institutions, and oversaw the publishing arm and organizational structure of the denomination.[51] "The unquestioned acceptance of her visions and their divine origins became basic to Seventh-Day Adventist orthodoxy."[52] Her voluminous writings continue to serve as a type of scripture for Adventists today.

The origins of Pentecostalism are usually traced to the Azusa Street Revival in Los Angeles, led by William Seymour (1870–1922) in 1906. Historians have neglected the extent to which women led the revival, however. Pentecostalism is a highly ecstatic form of Christianity in which people are filled with the Holy Spirit and begin to speak in tongues as they did in the New Testament (Acts 2:4). They may speak in glossolalia—an unknown spiritual language—or in xenolalia—an existing language unknown to the speaker. Although Charles Parham (1873–1929) is credited with the idea that speaking in tongues indicates baptism by the Holy Spirit, it was actually his cook, an African American Holiness preacher named Lucy Farrow (1851–1911), who introduced both Parham and Seymour to glossolalia. Parham sent Farrow to help Seymour in his evangelistic ministries in Los Angeles, which had been fairly unsuccessful. Farrow had the gift of impartation—that is, enabling others to experience the Holy Spirit—and within a few days of her arrival, the revival took off. "Her stirring testimonies of her own Holy Spirit baptism added fire to the fever pitch that the meetings had already reached."[53] While there were many women leaders at Azusa Street, Farrow stands out for her spiritual leadership, especially among African American women. Within a few months of the commencement of the revival, Farrow embarked on a preaching tour around the United States, including many states in the South. She also evangelized people in Johnsonville, Liberia, where she reportedly received the Holy Spirit in Kru dialect and could preach in that language.[54]

The sight of white men kneeling in church before black women in order to receive the Holy Spirit shattered all sorts of cultural fault lines in the early twentieth century, and Pentecostalism today reflects the economic, racial, and ethnic diversity with which it started. Its larger denominations, however, have retreated from their historical commitment to gender equality. This is why some women founded their own Pentecostal churches. Aimee Semple McPherson's (1890–1944) Foursquare Church is one example of this. She became the first religious broadcaster in history after creating KFSG radio station at her Angelus Temple in Los Angeles to facilitate her transmission of the Christian Gospel. McPherson gave sermons and messages that drew thousands to Angelus Temple, and millions listened to her radio broadcasts. Although she fell from grace after publicity emerged about a sexual liaison, she continued a successful ministry to the poor and disaffected until her death, and the Foursquare denomination exists with both female and male pastors to this day.

Conclusions

The nineteenth century saw an uptick in the number of women taking the initiative in Christianity, both within the mainstream denominations and outside them in sectarian branches. The inspiration and call of the

Holy Spirit could not be denied, women argued, and, overcoming centuries of scriptural warrant against women speaking in churches, the Holy Spirit won. A changing economy also modified the gendered division of religious and social responsibilities by creating a middle class that provided sufficient leisure for some women to become social activists.

The twentieth century would continue to witness the claims of women for full participation in and recognition by the churches, from top to bottom. Every denomination would hear the call for women's ordination. At the same time, a countermovement of female religious conservatives would echo the concerns of the nineteenth-century purity crusades, namely, home, family, and sexual morality.

FIGURE 7.1. The Reverend Gwynn Freund, vicar of St. Mary's in the Valley Episcopal Church, Ramona, California. Photo by author.

7

Churchwomen on the Margins and in the Mainstream

Women in the twentieth century became more visible and vocal in the public sphere than ever before. Increased communications, coupled with information distribution, demonstrated the extent to which women were involved in every aspect of society. This expansion of access to the media and to the public sphere meant that women leaders faced the kind of scrutiny previously reserved for male politicians, priests, and celebrities. And like these individuals, women also sometimes exhibited feet of clay. The Nobel laureate Mother Teresa (1910–1997), whose noteworthy mission to the poor of Kolkata, formerly Calcutta, India, will undoubtedly earn her sainthood in the near future, nevertheless experienced a crisis of faith for decades;[1] more significantly, she failed to use the many millions of dollars donated to the Missionaries of Charity to provide even a modicum of health or hospice care for those in her charge.[2] Simone Weil (1909–1943), a convert to Catholicism and one of the century's foremost Christian mystics, renounced her Jewish heritage in the most cruel and disparaging terms. Although she was a member of the French Resistance during World War II, "her unwavering dedication to the victims of social and military oppression" collided with her "desire to obliterate her Jewishness," which she explicitly and repeatedly renounced.[3]

Paradox marked the lack of true equality that women experienced in their daily lives. Despite remarkable gains made throughout the twentieth century—which ranged from winning the right to vote to gaining access to the workplace—most women in the world remained second-class citizens. This was no less true of women in many Christian organizations as in other religious and secular institutions. Even though women worked throughout the century in the vanguard of social and political movements to secure changes that would improve the living conditions of themselves and others, many were denied that same equality and justice in their own churches.

In the Western Hemisphere the century began with the Social Gospel, a crusade waged by liberal Protestants and Catholics who sought to "Christianize" the social order by bringing about legislative change to improve the lives of poor people. African American churchwomen contributed to the Social Gospel movement as well as to the civil rights movement in the United States, an undertaking that gave birth to the womanist critique of male sexism and white female racism. The secular feminist activism of the 1960s and 1970s played out in the churches as a struggle for women's ordination, successful in most mainline Protestant denominations, but to this day unsuccessful in the Orthodox and Roman Catholic churches.

The radical shift in social mores that occurred in the nations of the West in the 1960s and 1970s sparked a counterrevolution of conservative Christian women in the 1980s and 1990s. A cadre of politically active women worked during the last decades of the twentieth century on what they considered a pro-family agenda that focused on the issues of abortion and homosexuality. Meanwhile, the influence of indigenous female leadership grew throughout the global South and Asia. Although Christian women suffered and were martyred for their faith, they also overcame their sufferings to lead mass movements for peace and reconciliation.

The Social Gospel

In the nineteenth century and early twentieth century, the Industrial Revolution and the changes wrought by a manufacturing economy created a large underclass of factory workers that included women and children. Poverty, once hidden in the countryside, became starkly visible in the tenements and slums of large industrial cities. Both liberal and conservative Christians sought to help those suffering from hunger, homelessness, and illness, albeit in different ways.

Conservatives evangelized individuals mired in sin whose dependence on alcohol, drugs, prostitution, and other vices prevented them from flourishing. Liberals challenged a sinful economic system in which employees worked twelve-hour days, six or seven days a week, in unsafe and unsanitary conditions. The liberals' "Social Gospel" proclaimed "the brotherhood of man under the fatherhood of God," that is, the ultimate unity and equality of all people under the protection and guidance of a Christian deity. Two women embody the spirit of uplift and reform inherent in the Social Gospel.

Dorothy Day (1897–1980) is widely known "as social critic, protestor, and dissenter, as anarchist, pacifist, and Communist become Catholic, as advocacy journalist and editor of the *Catholic Worker* newspaper, [and] as founder of numerous houses of hospitality for the homeless."[4] She self-consciously tried to follow the model of Jesus, performing every-day works of mercy, which she described as "feeding the hungry, giving drink to the thirsty, clothing the naked, sheltering the homeless, visiting the sick, ransoming the prisoner, and burying the dead," as commanded in Jesus's parable of the Last Judgment (Matt. 25:31–46).[5] Juxtaposing the words "Catholic" and "Worker" in the newspaper she established during the Great Depression in 1933 startled many who wanted to disassociate religion and labor, but for Day and her coworkers, the two were an inseparable part of their mission. Those who were part of the Catholic Worker movement advocated for legislative changes to help workers and the poor, but also provided direct services to those hurt by economic dislocation. Above all, they shared a commitment to voluntary poverty, which Day believed was required of Christians: "At least we can avoid being comfortable through the exploitation of others," she wrote. "Giving liberates the individual not only spiritually but materially."[6] The houses of hospitality she and others founded during the Great Depression still exist today, with volunteers serving in more than two hundred communities in the United States and abroad.

Nannie Helen Burroughs (1879–1961) worked as a youth pastor, a janitor, a bookkeeper, and an editorial assistant before beginning her career in 1900 with the Woman's Convention of the National Baptist Convention (NBC), the nation's oldest and largest denomination of African American Christians. As corresponding secretary—that is, director—for the Woman's Convention, she proposed and instituted the National Training School for Women and Girls, established in 1909, in order "to train women for missionary work, teaching Scripture, homemaking, domestic service, and general industrial work."[7] An African American herself, Burroughs wanted to raise the status of domestic help by professionalizing their work. She directed the renamed school—now the National Trade and Professional School for Women and Girls—which offered courses in interior design, shorthand, bookkeeping, Latin, English, and black history, in addition to home economics.

Burroughs connected middle-class women belonging to social clubs with female industrial workers, advocating the unionization of domestic workers and founding the National Association of Wage Earners in 1921. In 1934 she launched the *Worker*, a devotional and informational quarterly aimed at women's missionary societies. As she admitted at the time, "We realize that financial conditions are not altogether favorable to launch a magazine, but *our church women need it. God will, therefore, make it possible* for us to meet this definite need."[8] She turned to scripture in all of her writings, believing that God was directing her work every step of the way, since religion was "an everyday practice and not just a Sunday-go-to-meeting performance."[9] Burroughs's religious beliefs anticipated the spirituality of the African American women who struggled for civil rights later in the twentieth century.

Civil Rights and Women's Rights

A profound and abiding faith in the God of justice, coupled with the belief that Jesus was a fellow sufferer who knew of the daily crucifixion that African Americans experienced under slavery and in a segregated society, drove churchwomen to fight for the survival of their communities. Because of the racism of the nation's dominant society and its

isn't this the point of Jesus?, this is written like it's silly notion.

institutions, black religion in general could never be otherworldly: it had to oppose the powers on earth. Thus, "from the period of slavery through modern times, many Black religious women in the United States practiced racial uplift and social responsibility as a means of fulfilling what they understood as their duty to God."[10]

Two ways African American women fulfilled this duty was through testifying and witnessing, according to Rosetta E. Ross, professor of religious studies at Spelman College. "For slaves, to testify was both an acknowledgment of God's work and the act of refuting the circumstance of bondage," she writes.[11] Testifying meant speaking truthfully to others about one's own experiences, including one's interactions with God. Witnessing meant hearing the testimony, certifying its truth, and living out the reality of God's presence in everyday life. "Witnessing and testifying both anticipate a response from persons, frequently functioning to encourage others to act or to persevere."[12]

This dialectical process can be seen in the ways African American churchwomen fought racial oppression in the United States. Nannie Helen Burroughs sought to improve the lives of black women by providing education and opportunities for advancement. Ida B. Wells-Barnett (1862–1931) launched social reform movements from her Sunday school class. Her national crusade against lynching even led her to clash with Frances Willard, president of the Woman's Christian Temperance Union (WCTU). Willard chose to remain silent on the issue of race rather than alienate the ladies of the all-white southern chapters of the WCTU, and Wells-Barnett publicly criticized her for this.[13] as she should

African American churchwomen used the Bible as their moral and spiritual compass to regulate both personal and social conduct. They believed they were required to change society if it did not measure up to the biblical commandment to care for "the least of these my brothers and sisters." Victoria Way DeLee (1925–2010), for example, felt called by God to work for school desegregation and voting rights for African Americans and poor people in Dorchester County, South Carolina. Her lifelong career grew out of her commitment to personal holiness and her conviction that the central message of Christianity was to help those who cannot help themselves.[14]

The Bible was not the only source of religious authority, however. Human experience, traditions taught by church and community, and the insights of the social sciences and humanities also informed the spiritual lives of black churchwomen.[15] Thus, leaders like Ella Josephine Baker (1903–1986), whose mother and grandfather instilled in her a deep sense of human equality and the dignity of all persons through their religious instruction and involvement, eventually moved into a type of "radical humanism" or a "positive theological humanism."[16] Called the mother and midwife of the civil rights movement,[17] Baker worked with church groups throughout her life, serving as a field organizer for the National Association for the Advancement of Colored People; organizing a prayer pilgrimage at the Lincoln Memorial in 1957; helping to create and direct the Southern Christian Leadership Conference, best known for its direction by Martin Luther King Jr.; founding the Student Nonviolent Coordinating Committee; and working with myriad persons and groups to craft a truly democratic society. She never attained full recognition for her work, though, perhaps because she was not an ordained clergy member.[18]

The failure to achieve respect within the black churches, especially from male leaders, coupled with white feminists' claim to represent the experience of all women, led to the development of womanist theology by African American feminist theologians. The black churches have both sustained and suppressed their female members.[19] They helped slaves retain their humanity and served as the locus of protest against segregation after Emancipation. At the same time, black churchwomen "have given the most and . . . gotten the least."[20] Womanist theologians seek to correct this imbalance of power in all churches—black, white, and ethnic.

The Quest for Ordination

Although churchwomen had been at the forefront of most twentieth-century reform movements, it was not until the secular women's movements of the 1960s and 1970s that they turned their attention to reform of the churches. A major issue concerned the ordination of women, that is, the conferring of priestly or ministerial orders upon them as clergy. Historically there had been two ordination tracks open to women. Deaconesses in the early centuries of Christianity worked primarily with other women, preparing them for baptism, counseling them in their homes, and caring for the dying and the dead. The order of deaconesses was never strong in the Western Church, but the Eastern Church maintained the order well into the high Middle Ages. At that time arguments against menstruating women touching the eucharistic elements, approaching the altar area, or even entering the church began to be revived, and the order declined throughout the period of the Ottoman Empire (1301–1922).[21] In the nineteenth century, however, Orthodox Christianity saw the revival of deaconess orders in Russia, Georgia, and Greece. In addition, new Protestant orders of deaconesses in Europe and the United States ran hospitals, educational institutions, settlement houses, and other programs that served the disadvantaged, especially women. The deaconess movement was so widespread that "by the mid-nineteenth century, deaconess institutions had become the primary source for trained nurses on the continent and in England."[22]

But ordained deaconesses could never become clergywomen, and they tended to operate in church-related endeavors, rather than in churches themselves. In contrast, women ordained as deacons, rather than as deaconesses, can, in theory, become pulpit or sacramental ministers. Deacons are ordained to some tasks, such as counseling, teaching, or preaching, but they are excluded from performing most sacramental duties, including blessing the elements of the Eucharist, although Roman Catholic deacons may officiate at baptisms and marriages. In many Protestant denominations and in the Catholic and Orthodox traditions, ordination as a deacon is the first step to being ordained an elder, a clergy member who can perform all of the sacraments.[23] Evidence shows that the abbesses of the Middle Ages conducted most, if not all, of the duties of priests, and that Catholic sisters who worked in the mission field were also called upon to fulfill some sacerdotal (priestly) duties. Moreover, women were ordained in times of political crisis, when male priests were lacking. Ludmila Javorova (b. 1932) and several other women, for example, were secretly ordained Roman Catholic priests when Christians in Czechoslovakia suffered repression under communist rule. But until the twentieth century, the ordination of women as priests or ministers was rare in all churches. Thus ordination has come to symbolize the extent of, and commitment to, full equality and participation of women in Christianity.

Although women in the nineteenth century preached in Protestant churches, evangelized at revivals, taught in Sunday schools, and lectured in auditoriums, only a few were ordained to serve as pastors in churches. The path to this type of ministry was especially difficult, since theology schools did not admit women. Antoinette Brown Blackwell (1825–1921) was denied formal admission to the Theology Program at Oberlin College, and though she completed the courses in 1850, the faculty would not award her a degree until 1878. Nevertheless, in 1853 the Congregational church that she served in upstate New York voted to ordain her. Olympia Brown Willis (1835–1926), who endured ridicule and harassment from the male students at St. Lawrence College—the only seminary to accept her into a theology program—was the first woman ordained by a denomination rather than by a congregation, when the Northern Universalist Association called her to a parish, also in upstate New York. The Methodist Episcopal Church (MEC) granted a preaching license to Anna Howard Shaw (1847–1919), who graduated first in her class from Boston University, but denied her ordination. When the Protestant Methodist Church ordained her in 1880—the first white female Methodist to be ordained—the MEC revoked her license and those of other licensed women preachers. In 1895 Julia Foote (1823–1901) became the first black woman to be ordained a deacon in the African Methodist Episcopal Zion Church, which ordained Mary Small (1850–1945) as the very first woman elder in 1898; Foote was ordained an elder a year later.[24]

Being an ordained minister was a lonely profession for women, ill-paid and fraught with conflict. To ameliorate these problems and to mentor other clergywomen, two Unitarian pastors, Mary Augusta Safford (1851–1927) and Eleanor Gordon (1852–1942), created the Iowa Sisterhood. They successfully organized their first church in Hamilton, Iowa, in 1879, and were then sent to Humboldt, Iowa, where Safford was ordained in 1880.[25] There they recruited and trained other women, and when Safford and Gordon moved to a new church further west, they gave responsibility for the Unitarian church in Humboldt to two biological sisters they had been preparing for ministry. The many clergywomen in the Iowa Sisterhood worked in pairs, and during its height in the 1880s and 1890s they erected twenty church buildings with the aid of their parishioners.[26] The sisterhood included ministers not only in Iowa but throughout the Upper Midwest. Highly successful, the clergywomen nonetheless faced criticism from the more conservative Unitarian establishment on the East Coast, and by the end of the century many had left the ministry to work in reform movements.

"Contrary to the glowing expectations of their predecessors," writes Georgia Harkness, "the opportunities for women ministers did not increase in the twentieth century, but in its early decades began to decline."[27] One reason for the decline was that seminaries steered women into religious education—that is, Sunday school—rather than pastoral ministry. Another reason was the shift from prophetic to priestly church leadership, which led to the masculinization of the pastorate.[28] For example, Pentecostal denominations such as the Assemblies of God and the Church of God in Christ, which had first welcomed women ministers, began to discourage them as the denominations became more institutionalized.

Harkness (1891–1974) herself was a case of ordained ministry deferred. After earning a PhD in philosophy from Boston University in

1923, she taught courses in religion and philosophy at several colleges. When in 1940 she joined the faculty of Garrett-Evangelical Theological Seminary, she became the first woman ever to teach at a seminary in the United States. Although she was ordained an elder in the Methodist Church in 1926, she and other female elders lacked annual conference membership, which in Methodism meant they could not be appointed to a church. But in 1956 the church voted to admit all qualified applicants for ordination into conference membership, regardless of gender, and Harkness finally achieved the goal she had sought since the 1920s.

Other churches in the United States followed suit, thanks to the feminist activism of the 1960s. By 1965, about seventy Protestant denominations had begun to ordain women.[29] Although the Anglican Church in England and the Episcopal Church in the United States had ordained women as deacons and deaconesses throughout the nineteenth and twentieth centuries, both groups resisted the tide toward the ordination of women as priests. After making several attempts to gain legitimate ordination in the Episcopal Church, eleven women deacons were ordained as priests by three retired bishops on 29 July 1974, the feast day for Mary and Martha. More irregular ordinations followed, until the Episcopal Church's 1976 General Convention formally approved ordination of women to the priesthood. In 1988, the first woman Episcopal bishop, and the first female bishop in all of Anglicanism—Barbara Harris (b. 1930)—was elected in the United States. It was not until 1992, however, that the Church of England approved the ordination of women as priests, and in 2013 Anglicans appointed the first female bishop, the Reverend Pat Story, in the United Kingdom and Ireland.

The two largest branches of Christianity that do not ordain women remain the Orthodox Church and the Roman Catholic Church. A strong move among Orthodox theologians to promote the ordination of women deacons began in the mid-twentieth century. In 1952 the Church of Greece instituted a school for lay deaconesses, which led to the establishment of a graduate-level college for women church leaders.[30] In

1988 an ecumenical council comprising representatives of all Orthodox Churches met to discuss "The Place of Woman in the Orthodox Church and the Question of the Ordination of Women."[31] Although none of the representatives could imagine women serving as elders or bishops, the council did unanimously advocate restoration of the order of women deacons, with full ordination to that function. Yet the difference between what is known as the officiating priesthood (those who preside over the sacraments) and the diaconal priesthood (those who serve in other forms of ministry) would still exclude women from becoming Orthodox priests. Moreover, the pronouncements of official church bodies have not yet been realized at the congregational level. To encourage female activism, an international Orthodox women's journal called *MaryMartha* was published by the World Council of Churches between 1991 and 1998 to promote women's full participation in the life of Orthodoxy, especially ordination to the diaconate. *MaryMartha* has been superseded by *St. Nina Quarterly*, a journal published by the Women's Orthodox Ministries and Education Network (WOMEN), which also advocates ordination of women.[32]

In the Roman Catholic Church, the struggle for women's ordination has been particularly intense, in part because the possibility of change seemed promising in the 1960s and 1970s. It began with Pope John XXIII (p. 1958–1963), who called Vatican Council II (1962–1965), a worldwide ecumenical meeting of Roman Catholic church leadership. Although women were invited late to the proceedings and were not allowed to speak or vote at the sessions, the council adopted a number of constitutions, or official policy statements, that signaled a more open attitude toward women and their influence in the Church. This resulted in a tremendous upturn in women's participation in parish councils (52 percent), as eucharistic ministers (60 percent), and as lectors (readers of scripture, 50 percent), according to a 1985 study of U.S. Catholic parishes.[33] Other signs of changing times included the presence of altar girls assisting at Mass, officially approved in 1994; the Women's Ordination Conference, first convened in 1975 to advocate for ordination; and a

pontifical commission studying women's ordination that found nothing in scripture that would preclude the practice.[34]

Yet a series of statements issued by the popes who succeeded John XXIII and by other Vatican officials all but extinguished the possibility of official women's ordination. Under the auspices of Pope Paul VI (p. 1963–1978), the Congregation for the Doctrine of the Faith (CDF—the theological watchdog for the Vatican) issued a statement in 1976. The CDF declared in *Inter insigniores* (*Among the More Noteworthy*) that the church could not admit women as priests because the priest was acting in the "person of Christ" when celebrating the Eucharist, and Christ was a man. In 1994, repeating an argument made in *Inter insigniores*, Pope John Paul II (p. 1978–2005) claimed in *Ordinatio sacerdotalis* (*Priestly Ordination*) that the church could not confer priesthood on women because Christ had not included any among the twelve "apostles" he called to help him in his ministry.

Somewhat ironically, a worldwide shortage of priests has required Roman Catholic bishops to appoint women and laymen as parish administrators or pastoral associates in order to keep parishes without priests open. These administrators act as chaplains, counselors, business managers, homilists, human resources directors, and pastors. As of 2005, there were 30,632 lay ministers working in paid positions: 64 percent were laywomen, 20 percent were laymen, and 16 percent were women religious; that is to say, 80 percent were women.[35] Although the title of pastor is usually reserved for priests, most parishioners call their female administrator pastor, while they see the priest as a sacramental minister.[36]

Since 2002, women in Europe and the United States have sought ordination, and dozens have received it from consecrated Roman Catholic bishops. This means that Catholic female priests are serving in what is known as apostolic succession: they have received the laying on of hands by those who received it in a presumably unbroken line from the apostles. Although the official Roman Catholic Church does not recognize these ordinations as valid, "Womenpriests" serve as sacramental ministers in

Catholic congregations around the world and belong to a movement called Roman Catholic Womenpriests.[37] Tension exists within the Catholic women's ordination movement, however, with some calling for reform of the church prior to any ordinations; while others, like Roman Catholic Womenpriests, embracing ordination as a first step toward greater reform. Despite the fact that the Roman Catholic Church has excommunicated the Catholic women who have been ordained, their numbers are growing, according to the Roman Catholic Womenpriests website.[38]

Conservative Christian Activism

At the opposite end of the spectrum from the Roman Catholic Womenpriests are Fundamentalist Christians who believe in a male-only pastorate. Fundamentalism arose as a religious movement in the 1920s in the United States in reaction to the women who had achieved power both in society and in the home, according to Betty DeBerg, professor of religion at the University of Northern Iowa. She claims that the Fundamentalists' arguments "about Christian doctrine or biblical interpretation were simply rhetorical tactics used to strengthen their case for maintaining Victorian gender roles well into post-Victorian times."[39] Margaret Lamberts Bendroth, executive director for the Congregational Library in Boston, adopts the opposite view, arguing that "During the 1920s [F]undamentalist men began to take on the role as guardians of orthodoxy and women lost their standing as the morally superior sex, becoming not just morally but psychologically inferior to men."[40] Both scholars would agree, however, that gender issues helped to fashion the masculine religiosity—sometimes called "muscular Christianity"—in which men reassumed authority over morals and religious leadership.

It is difficult to define Fundamentalism, which is a strict form of Calvinist Christianity that accepts the literal truth of the Bible and its inerrancy, that is, its freedom from all error. In contrast, Evangelical Christianity, as the name suggests, focuses on evangelizing the unsaved and on developing a personal relationship with Jesus. Together Fundamentalist and Evangelical Christians—two categories that frequently overlap—created a distinctive subculture "that came together in the late 1970s and 1980s in North America in an effort to reshape the world according to their understanding of the Bible."[41] For these conservative Christians, the heterosexual family is the primary locus for living a godly life, where the husband and wife live by God-given mandates in a complementary, rather than equal, relationship.

Nowhere is antagonism to sex equality more apparent than in the Fundamentalist takeover of the Southern Baptist Convention (SBC). In 1984 the denomination took a step away from the equality it once espoused when it adopted a statement that limited ordained ministry to men. The statement says that the apostle Paul "excludes women from pastoral leadership (1 Tim. 2:12) to preserve a submission God requires[,] because the man was first in creation and the woman was first in the Edenic fall."[42] Humanity's sinfulness is due to Eve's disobedience, from which women can never be redeemed. This new policy ostracized the Baptist member congregations that employed some 175 ordained clergywomen.

In response to the Fundamentalist tilt at the national Southern Baptist Convention, women formed Women in Ministry, SBC. The group met regularly just prior to each national SBC convocation in order to advocate for ordained women's ministry, and in 1995 changed its name to Baptist Women in Ministry to extend its reach. Although a number of Southern Baptist clergywomen lost their jobs or found it difficult to get church placements after 1984, female enrollment in Baptist theology programs continued to climb. Fifty-five percent of ordained women in the SBC received ordination after their official exclusion from the denomination, and as of 1999, approximately 1,225 were serving as SBC clergy, mostly as chaplains and counselors, either on church staff or in an agency job.[43]

In 2000, the Southern Baptist Convention revised its "Baptist Faith and Message" statement to emphasize its exclusion of women as ministers: "While both men and women are gifted for service in the church, the office of pastor is limited to men as qualified by Scripture."[44] With the concerted effort in the SBC to discourage congregations from ordaining women, the movement to ordain Baptist women clergy shifted to moderate-to-progressive Baptist associations in the southern United States, such as the Cooperative Baptist Fellowship, the Alliance of Baptists, the Baptist General Association of Virginia, and the Baptist General Convention of Texas. Within these bodies, there was a 33 percent boost in women's pulpit ministry between 2005 and 2010.[45]

The repudiation of women's ordination by the Southern Baptist Convention was just one example of a rejection of societal changes in the 1960s and 1970s. Women had not only left the home to enter the marketplace, they were increasingly visible in positions of leadership. Artificial means of contraception—in two words, birth control—allowed women, rather than men, to choose whether or not to bear children. The U.S. Supreme Court's 1973 decision *Roe v. Wade* legalized nonviable fetal abortion, a procedure that conservatives believed was murder. It appeared to conservatives that the family, the basic unit of Christian society, was under attack.

Theological developments also disturbed conservative Christians. New translations of the Bible—the Word of God—proffered gender-neutral language, substituting "brothers and sisters" for "brothers," interpreting the pronoun "He" as the proper noun "God," and using "Our Parent" instead of "Our Father" in the Lord's Prayer. Ordained women ministers exercised clout over both laymen and laywomen, and female faculty instructed male seminarians in the rudiments of the faith. A "Re-Imagining Conference" convened by women in mainline Christian denominations in 1993 challenged the very notion of a patriarchal deity, with liturgies that paid homage to divine Sophia, a feminine image for God. A proposed constitutional amendment—the Equal Rights Amendment, passed by Congress in 1972 and sent to the states for ratification by 1982—explicitly gave women equal rights under the law in the United States, but also energized religious conservatives, who succeeded in thwarting its ratification.

Conservative churchwomen (including all Fundamentalists and some—though not all—Evangelicals) believe that secular feminists have helped to destroy the nuclear family by denigrating and abandoning woman's natural calling as homemaker and mother. At the same time, many if not most of these women work outside the home, as Colleen McDannell's examination of the Focus on the Family organization, led by Dr. James Dobson, suggests.[46] Moreover, enclaves of Christian female leadership—in Bible study, homeschooling, women-only retreats and courses, charitable and mission endeavors, and other women-centered and women-directed programs—exist throughout the conservative Christian subculture and in almost every Fundamentalist or Evangelical congregation. In addition, while women have volunteered in a number of conservative political programs led by men, such as the pro-life/anti-abortion movements Operation Rescue and Missionaries to the Preborn, they also have founded their own organizations.

Beverly LaHaye (b. 1930), known for offering Christian marriage seminars with her husband, Tim LaHaye (b. 1926), established Concerned Women for America (CWA) in 1979 "to contest feminist claims of representing women."[47] The mission of CWA is to promote and protect biblical values, "*first through prayer*, then education and finally by influencing our society—thereby reversing the decline in moral values in our nation."[48] Its core issues include sanctity of life, family values, education, religious liberty, national sovereignty, sexual exploitation, and support for the state of Israel.[49] Restated less ambiguously, the CWA opposes abortion, same-sex marriage, the United Nations, human trafficking, and prostitution; it wholeheartedly supports the state of Israel; promotes abstinence-only sex education; and seeks to redefine obscenity to include forms of artistic expression that it considers pornographic. With its 500,000 grassroots members, 30 national staff members, and an $8 million annual budget, CWA has successfully lobbied at the local, state, and national levels to pursue this agenda.[50]

"Feminism doesn't speak to Christian women because we know we are equal where it counts, in the eyes of the Lord," says Wendi Kaiser

sure,

(b. 1953), cofounder of Jesus People USA.[51] She and her husband, Glenn Kaiser (b. 1953), live collectively in a Christian commune that serves the poor and homeless of Chicago. Jesus People USA also sponsors Cornerstone, the nation's largest Christian rock festival, where devout teenagers find an alternative, and hip, way of being Christians and feminists. "They teach these young people that a repackaged version of the fundamentals of feminism—self-respect, pride and equality in the sight of God—is part of the core doctrines of their faith."[52] Wendi Kaiser feels that women today are less respected than they were in the past because secular feminists have failed to address the fact that "there are only twenty-four hours in a day and women have to be breadwinners, spiritual leaders and parents."[53]

sorry but ew

To ameliorate this and other problems, many conservatives have written self-help books designed to teach women how to be better wives, mothers, and Christians. *The Total Woman*, by Marabel Morgan (b. 1937), was a 1973 best seller that offered spicy sex tips, like greeting your husband at the door wearing baby-doll pajamas and white boots. "Eat by candlelight," she advised, "you'll light his candle!"[54] Morgan's primary advice, however, was to let the husband be the boss and to submit to him in all things. Beverly LaHaye proffered similar advice in *The Spirit-Controlled Woman*, first published in 1976, observing that "most men cannot stand to be dominated by a woman in the home," adding that "there can only be one head of a family . . . and that head should be the husband."[55]

used by LulaRoe founders! they're mormons

These exhortations to submission need to be understood within the proper framework, according to several feminist scholars. In her study of participants in the charismatic Women Aglow movement, R. Marie Griffith finds that "Conservative evangelical women who believe that their true liberation is found in voluntary submission to divine authority consider this a bold surrender, an act of assuming the crucial role God has called women to play in the making of history."[56] These women see themselves surrendering to God's will in their lives, rather than submitting to the dictates of their husbands. Brenda Brasher's ethnographic research

ahh gross

on Calvary Chapel and Hope Chapel congregations in Southern California reveals that "Though [F]undamentalist women insistently claimed that the proper relationship between a woman and her husband is one of submission, they consistently declare that this submission is done out of obedience to God not men and is supposed to be mutual, a relational norm observed by both spouses rather than the capitulation of one to the other."[57] Nevertheless, not all Evangelical women accept the idea of submission to male authority, as Julie Ingersoll's research on conservative Christian women seeking ordination demonstrates. Ingersoll identifies a number of "biblical feminists," who argue for gender equality using the same Bible, but different passages, that the Fundamentalists use.[58]

Much of the literature written by conservative churchwomen is inspirational and evangelistic. Joni Eareckson Tada's (b. 1949) description of her faith journey, recounted in *Joni* (pronounced Johnny), tells the story of her coming to grips with quadriplegia.[59] Initially she learned to sketch holding a pencil or brush in her teeth, but her memoir became a best seller, and her determination—which she credits to the unfailing presence of God—led her into an evangelistic ministry to the disabled. Today her organization, Joni and Friends, offers a wide variety of services to the disabled, all with the purpose of helping people and spreading the gospel.

Another Evangelical classic is Corrie ten Boom's memoir *The Hiding Place* (*De schuilplaats*), which ranks tenth in the all-time Christian best seller list.[60] Ten Boom (1892–1983) and her family of Dutch Reformed Christians hid Jews in their house and rescued dozens of others in Haarlem during the Nazi occupation of the Netherlands during World War II. *The Hiding Place* dramatically portrays the dangers that ten Boom faced, including being sent with her sister Betsie to a concentration camp. Although Betsie died in Ravensbrück, Corrie was released and traveled the world for the rest of her life as a Christian evangelist, preaching a message of forgiveness through Christ.

Ten Boom is memorialized at Yad Vashem in Israel as one of the Righteous Gentiles of the Shoah, but she has received little attention from Holocaust scholars. "Ten Boom's Christianization of the Holocaust has limited the appeal of her story among scholars of the *Shoah* in particular and Jewish audiences in general."[61] The message that Evangelical Christians draw from ten Boom's life is not so much the need to rescue individuals facing persecution, but rather the need to practice the Christian virtues of faith, courage, witness, and forgiveness.

The Majority Christians

The majority of Christians living throughout Asia and the Southern Hemisphere—where the number of Christians far exceeds that of Europe and the United States and Canada—share many of the values of conservative Christians in Westernized nations, such as opposition to abortion and homosexuality. Christian women in South America and Africa are critically engaged in the improvement of society, although their involvement in ordained ministry and church leadership has met with mixed responses, as in the Northern Hemisphere. Christianity can be a source of either empowerment or enslavement for women: It can free them to participate fully in church and society, or it can restrict them to gender-defined responsibilities. Three illustrations show the liberating effects of female Christian activists.

Protestant theological students in Indonesia have used a number of strategies for resisting the limitations of a patriarchal society. "Despite indigenous and government-supported gender ideologies and Western Christian theologies that do not espouse gender equality, aspiring women Christian leaders became convinced of the value of gender equality and pursued it."[62] Their protest against institutional criticism included study, preaching, and pastoral counseling, and those living in monasteries led daily communal prayer. "In following their religious callings, their practices modeled a new gender ideology of choice and purpose for other women."[63] Indonesian female seminarians have become role models for each other as graduate students and for women in the communities that they serve as educators and pastors.

Similarly, the Filipina sisters of the Missionary Benedictine order in Manila are unique examples of feminists in Philippine society. In the 1960s and 1970s, the nuns taught skills of responsible wifehood and motherhood. "Now, however, the Missionary Benedictines are educating their charges to be independent, self-confident, activist, and concerned with women's rights in the Philippine context."[64] Women's studies classes are required in the curriculum of Saint Scholastica's College, where the nuns teach, and it is the only college in the Philippines to accept single mothers. The sisters see consciousness-raising seminars, counseling sessions on marriage and sexuality, and other "pro-woman" undertakings—a term some Filipina activists prefer to "feminist"—as religious duties, since God requires working for social justice and caring for the poor.

Churchwomen have also been involved in a number of peace-making and peace-building ventures, because "civilians, particularly women and children, account for the vast majority of those affected by armed conflict."[65] Along with two other women, Leymah Gbowee (b. 1972) won the Nobel Peace Prize in 2011 for nonviolent organizing to end the civil war in Liberia. Gbowee belonged to St. Peter's Lutheran Church in Monrovia, where she was a social worker for the Lutheran World Federation's Trauma Healing and Reconciliation Program. When she began to counsel female security personnel, she learned she had a talent for helping women to discuss the traumas they had experienced.

One night she had a dream in which she heard a voice say, "Gather the women to pray for peace!"[66] This was the start of weekly prayer meetings, which soon included Muslim as well as Christian women. The movement for peace in war-torn Liberia grew, and women organized demonstrations, picket lines, and even a sex strike. Gbowee believes that "God's hands were under our effort and I saw daily how right it had been to begin the work by mobilizing at the bottom."[67] The women's actions emboldened others and, after several years, brought all parties in the Liberian conflict to the negotiating table. Ellen Johnson Sirleaf (b. 1938), one of the other Nobel laureates, was elected president of Liberia on 17 March 2006, and Gbowee went on to obtain a master's degree in conflict transformation from Eastern Mennonite University in Harrisonburg, Virginia, in 2007. She lives in Accra, Ghana, and continues to work for peace in Africa.

Conclusions

Peace and reconciliation efforts during the twentieth and twenty-first centuries have not come without suffering or martyrdom. In 1980, during the civil war in El Salvador, three Catholic religious sisters and a lay missionary were raped and murdered. The killings of these four American churchwomen raised public awareness in the United States of the larger issue of human rights violations perpetrated by government-sponsored death squads. As a result of public outrage, much of it coming from church groups, U.S. policy toward El Salvador changed, with the U.S. Congress demanding that military aid to the nation be linked to progress in human rights.[68]

Nor has social change come without conflict in the churches themselves. In 2012, during the papacy of Pope Benedict XVI, the Congregation for the Doctrine of the Faith issued a "doctrinal assessment" that chastised American Catholic sisters for being more concerned about peace and justice than about abortion and same-sex marriage. The CDF claimed that the Leadership Conference of Women Religious (LCWR)—a group representing most of the fifty-seven thousand Catholic sisters in the United States—was a hotbed of radical feminism, and appointed an archbishop delegate to implement changes that would bring LCWR practices in line with Vatican priorities. Pope Francis (p. 2013–present) expressed agreement with the findings of the assessment, and though LCWR officers have met with Vatican officials in Rome and with the archbishop delegate, it remains to be seen how the American sisters will respond to the Vatican effort to alter their organization.

Although women make up ever growing numbers of seminarians preparing for the ordained ministry, "to have a theological degree does not ensure that one will preach, or be ordained, or even enter a religious vocation as a profession."[69] Moreover, once in the pastorate, clergywomen encounter problems their male counterparts do not experience. A 2003 survey on clergywomen and sexual harassment in the United Methodist Church in the United States reported that 56 percent of respondents received sexual comments, 48 percent experienced unwelcome touching, 42 percent felt publicly humiliated, and 41 percent felt fear in the work environment.[70] Some parishioners advised their female ministers to wear makeup in order to look more professional; others advised the women *not* to wear makeup because it made them look like sluts.

Nevertheless the church is changing as a new generation of feminist theologians investigates the classic doctrines, especially those relating to sin and salvation. Contemporary feminists are attempting to reconstruct Christian dogma by reading scripture and tradition through the lenses of feminist theory. They also are examining church teachings in light of the Christian encounter with globalization and the extreme disparities between the rich and the poor.

A noticeable element in the new theology is a rejection of essentializing ideas about women: they are neither victims nor viragos, neither helpless nor heroic. Sarah Coakley is a good example of a feminist theologian today who attempts to recover the theology of *kenosis*—the self-emptying of Jesus Christ described in Philippians 2:5–11—despite the fact that, historically, women have been asked to sacrifice themselves in what appears to be a very similar way. But Coakley sees self-emptying as a way to be vulnerable to God and to therefore resist the powers of global capitalism that are causing such severe social problems around the world. She sees the feminist denial of any form of spiritual, rather than material, vulnerability to be mimicking the masculinist styles of power that lead to abuse.[71]

Mary Grey, whose book *Sacred Longings* explores the ways Christians can resist the destructive forces of globalization, turns to a theology of *kenosis* as well. The Catholic theologian sees in "the image of the self-emptying, kenotic God . . . a direct challenge to the idolatry of money."[72] The way to resist force is not by force, she argues, but by compassion, love, empathy, and insight. The cross is the symbol of innocent suffering, in which nature as well as humanity is crucified. The Eucharist, therefore, is an act of solidarity with the suffering earth and suffering people. And while suffering "is built into the very fabric of creation," resurrection and hope are present as well, she writes.[73]

Deanna Thompson also proposes a new theology of the cross, attempting to "cross the divide" between Martin Luther and contemporary feminism. Thompson accepts her Lutheran heritage that "never lets me forget my chronic predisposition to sin, the inevitability of suffering, and God's saving work through the cross and resurrection of Christ."[74] At the same time, she protests the harm that Christianity has done to women. She finds parallels in Luther's critique of abusive ecclesiastical institutions and today's feminist theology, with the theology of the cross serving as the judgment and condemnation of all types of sin, social as well as personal. Thompson argues that the crucified Christ confronts us in our own wrongdoing, namely, our crucifixion of others, contending that women can simultaneously be victims and victimizers.

Like Thompson, Serene Jones is in dialogue with historic Christian teachings, which she believes serve as a regulatory function for Christians, providing a way to view the world; this explains her effort to re-map the doctrinal landscape by which to view grace, sin, and the church. She admits that women entering Luther's "courtroom drama" of justification have been crushed by cultural constraints even before they face the wrath of God. But she goes on to say, "The story of God's judgment and mercy should, I think, be told in reverse—starting with sanctification and its rhetoric of building up instead of with justification and its initial language of undoing."[75] Justification can be revisited *after* sanctification, as the means by which to deconstruct the false selves "formed by restrictive conceptions of gender."[76]

These and other feminist theologians illuminate the paradox that exists for women in modern Christianity. With great strides forward on the one hand, and serious steps backward on the other, women have assumed leadership and, at the same time, confronted a number of challenges. The question is, then, will the paradox continue?

Conclusion

The Church of Martha and Mary

"Consider those great lives, burning with charity." Thus wrote Evelyn Underhill (1875–1941), one of the leading Christian mystics of the twentieth century. She believed that the female saints of the past should serve as the inspiration for current practices: "They represent, each in their own intensely distinctive way, the classic norm of women's ministry."[1] Underhill argued against the ordination of women, claiming that the church did not need any more officials. Rather, it needed "people in whom . . . Martha and Mary combine." Referring to the two sisters described in the Gospel of Luke, Underhill meant women whose outward actions are intimately linked to a profound interior spirituality.

A few months after her ordination in 1977 as the first African American female Episcopal priest, Pauli Murray (1910–1985) gave a sermon on Mary and Martha, using the story to contrast Martha's concern about material things with Mary's interest in spiritual matters. Murray observed that Mary was unconventional in her renunciation of the place society ascribed to her. Jesus recognized this, "and permitted her the privilege of sitting at his feet as if she were a young male divinity student, and he defended her decision."[2] Murray used the account to justify women's theological education, and, in effect, her own ordination.

Murray and some feminist theologians privilege Mary, the spiritual one, against Martha, the housewife. Even Jesus says, "Mary has chosen the better part" (Luke 10:42). Underhill and the traditionalists seem to valorize Martha, the woman engaged in the homely task of feeding her guest, "entirely free from any notions about the importance of their own status and their own work."[3] Saint Teresa of Avila, however, values both

Mary and Martha and sees the two as emblematic of the active life and the contemplative life, two sides of the same coin. "Martha and Mary walk together," she concludes.[4]

We have seen how the anonymous Marthas nurtured Christianity within their hearts and their homes until it grew into an extraordinary global faith. They continue to fill the pews, finance the church, and staff the committees at consistently higher rates than men. We have also seen the stellar Marys, those public figures whose names come down to us as guideposts. Together Martha and Mary make up the galaxy of all Christians, male and female.

Through it all—the centuries of martyrdom and suffering, of victory and accomplishment—women have shaped Christianity in countless ways. While some churches staunchly retain patriarchal structures, the exclusion of women from religious leadership is no longer taken for granted: It now must be justified through the selective use of scripture and tradition. In the nineteenth century, Catherine Mumford Booth wrote in her defense of women's right to preach,

> If commentators had dealt with the Bible on other subjects as they have dealt with it on this, taking isolated passages, separated from their explanatory connections, and insisting on a literal interpretation of the words of our version, what errors and contradictions would have been forced upon the acceptance of the Church, and what terrible results would have accrued to the world.[5]

Yet women's right to speak in church, particularly from the pulpit or the altar, remains a defining issue within Christianity today.

What the historical record tells us is that Christian women refuse to be defined by sexuality and reproduction. They are among the earliest disciples of Jesus. They are the mourners, the bone pickers, the leaders of the house churches. They are the cloistered nuns, copying religious texts in the scriptorium, and the religious sisters teaching children, feeding the poor, serving the sick and dying. They are the missionary wives who open schools in their homes, and the ministers' wives who co-pastor churches in all ways but name and title. They are the martyrs, thousands upon thousands, executed for following the gospel in which they put their trust. They are the community organizers and social activists, challenging the system, making changes. And they are the writers, thinkers, artists, and dreamers who make Christianity what it is today.

QUESTIONS FOR DISCUSSION

1. Are feminist theologians distorting or deforming the biblical record by offering different and challenging interpretations of familiar stories? Or are they simply doing what male theologians have done throughout history?

2. Do you think that the biblical character of Eve is as important to Christians today as she has been in the past?

3. Would you say that Paul and Jesus were countercultural male figures in the first century? Did they represent typical attitudes toward women? What were those attitudes?

4. Do you think Christianity spread primarily due to the activities of missionaries sent out to non-Christian lands, or primarily because of domestic proselytization? (Domestic proselytization is the phrase that describes women's evangelization of their own families and household.)

5. Male and female mystics have always had strange and astounding visions. Do you think that the revelations of medieval Christian women can be said to come from God, or are merely the product of severe physical deprivation?

6. Do you think that the idea of marriage or partnership as a vocation today would empower women or disempower them?

7. Do you think the negative effects of Christian missionization throughout the world generally outweigh the positive effects? Were the effects for women—the missionized and the missionizers— positive or negative?

8. Which view of gender relations do you think characterizes Christianity today: gender equality, gender complementarity, or gender polarity?

9. Can you identify any turning points in the history of Christianity where women had the opportunity to assume leadership positions but were denied them? Were there moments when the whole course of Christian history could have taken a different direction?

10. Do you feel that there is room in Christianity today for gender-segregated churches and for limiting ordained ministry to men? How much diversity can be allowed within Christianity for it to remain Christian?

11. Do you think the era of lifelong vows of chastity, poverty, and obedience is over? How do you explain the dramatic drop in vocations, that is, in the number of women seeking to enter religious orders?

12. Do you agree with the author that the history of Christianity is more influenced by anonymous Christians than by heroic or great women and great men?

13. Was there anything in this volume that made you think differently about the roles that women have played in the historical development of Christianity? What was it?

14. Have your views or opinions about Christianity changed as a result of reading this book? If yes, in what ways? If no, why not?

NOTES

INTRODUCTION

1. Mary-Paula Walsh, *Feminism and Christian Tradition: An Annotated Bibliography and Critical Introduction to the Literature* (Westport, CT: Greenwood, 1999), 2–3, italics in original.

2. Anne M. Clifford, *Introducing Feminist Theology* (Maryknoll, NY: Orbis, 2001), 32–34.

3. Letha Scanzoni and Nancy Hardesty, *All We're Meant to Be: A Biblical Approach to Women's Liberation with Study Guide* (Waco, TX: Word Books, 1974). See also Virginia Mollenkott, *Women, Men and the Bible* (Nashville: Abingdon, 1977); and Leonard Swidler, "Jesus Was a Feminist," *Catholic World* 212 (January 1971): 177–83.

4. Letty M. Russell, *Human Liberation in a Feminist Perspective* (Philadelphia: Westminster, 1974); and idem, *The Future of Partnership* (Philadelphia: Westminster, 1979).

5. Delores S. Williams, *Sisters in the Wilderness: The Challenge of Womanist God-Talk* (Maryknoll, NY: Orbis, 1993).

6. Mary Daly, *The Church and the Second Sex: With a New Feminist Postchristian Introduction by the Author* (1968; reprint with new introduction, New York: Harper and Row, 1975). Daly is responding to Simone de Beauvoir, *The Second Sex*, trans. H. M. Parshley (New York: Bantam, 1952).

7. Mary Daly, *Beyond God the Father: Toward a Philosophy of Women's Liberation* (Boston: Beacon, 1973), 72, italics in original.

8. Walsh, *Feminism and Christian Tradition*, 83–138.

9. Rosemary Radford Ruether, ed., *Religion and Sexism: Images of Woman in the Jewish and Christian Traditions* (New York: Simon and Schuster, 1974), 9.

10. Elisabeth Schüssler Fiorenza, *In Memory of Her: A Feminist Theological Reconstruction of Christian Origins* (New York: Crossroad, 1983), xvi.

11. Walsh, *Feminism and Christian Tradition*, 17. Walsh's book was published in 1999, and thus her magisterial bibliography ends there.

12. The word "religious" is being used as a noun rather than an adjective. A religious is a laywoman, a layman, or an ordained (male) priest in Roman Catholic Christianity who has taken vows to dedicate herself or himself to God. Historically this has meant joining a religious order or living apart from the world as a hermit.

13. Elizabeth A. Johnson, *She Who Is: The Mystery of God in Feminist Theological Discourse* (New York: Crossroad, 1992); Sallie McFague, *Models of God: Theology for an Ecological, Nuclear Age* (Philadelphia: Fortress, 1987).

14. Kathryn Greene-McCreight, *Feminist Reconstructions of Christian Doctrine* (New York: Oxford University Press, 2000), 37–39.

15. Greene-McCreight, *Feminist Reconstructions*, 59.

16. Joy Ann McDougall, "Women's Work: Feminist Theology for a New Generation," *Christian Century* 122, no. 15 (26 July 2005): 20–25.

17. McDougall takes the phrase "saving work" from the feminist theologian Rebecca Chopp.

18. Ivone Gebara, "Women Doing Theology in Latin America," in *Through Her Eyes: Women's Theology from Latin America*, ed. Elsa Tamez (Maryknoll, NY: Orbis, 1989), 37–48.

19. Theressa Hoover, "Black Women and the Churches: Triple Jeopardy," in *Black Theology: A Documentary History, 1966–1979*, ed. Gayraud S. Wilmore and James H. Cone (Maryknoll, NY: Orbis, 1979), 377.

20. Jacquelyn Grant, *White Women's Christ and Black Women's Jesus: Feminist Christology and Womanist Response* (Atlanta: Scholars Press, 1989), 205.

21. Ada María Isasi-Díaz, *Mujerista Theology: A Theology for the Twenty-First Century* (Maryknoll, NY: Orbis, 1996), 1–2, italics in original.

22. María Pilar Aquino, *Our Cry for Life: Feminist Theology from Latin America*, trans. Dinah Livingstone (Maryknoll, NY: Orbis, 1993).

23. Aquino, *Our Cry for Life*, 39.

24. Isasi-Díaz, *Mujerista Theology*, 66–73.

25. Kwok Pui-lan, "The Emergence of Asian Feminist Consciousness of Culture and Theology," in *We Dare to Dream: Doing Theology as Asian Women*, ed. Virginia Fabella and Sun Ai Lee Park (Kowloon, Hong Kong: Asian Women's Resource Centre for Culture and Theology, 1989), 94.

26. Ahn Sang Nim, "Feminist Theology in the Korean Church," in Fabella and Park, *We Dare to Dream*, 127.

27. Virginia Fabella, "Christology from an Asian Woman's Perspective," in Fabella and Park, *We Dare to Dream*, 3.

28. Mercy Amba Oduyoye, *Daughters of Anowa: African Women and Patriarchy* (Maryknoll, NY: Orbis, 1995), 173.

29. Rosemary Radford Ruether, *Sexism and God-Talk: Toward a Feminist Theology* (Boston: Beacon, 1983), 157.

30. I will be using "Hebrew Bible" and "Old Testament" interchangeably throughout the book.

31. Edith Deen, *All of the Women of the Bible* (New York: Harper, 1955), xxi.

32. Carol Meyers, ed., *Women in Scripture* (Boston: Houghton Mifflin, 2000).

33. Elsie Thomas Culver, *Women in the World of Religion* (Garden City, NY: Doubleday, 1967).

34. François Danniel and Brigitte Oliver, *Woman Is the Glory of Man*, trans. M. Angeline Bouchard (Westminster, MD: Newman, 1966), xi, 34, 35.

35. Peter Ketter, *Christ and Womankind*, trans. from 2d rev. ed. by Isabel McHugh (1937; reprint, Westminster, MD: Newman, 1952), 68, original appears in italics.

36. Ketter, *Christ and Womankind*, 83. In this passage Ketter cites Edith Stein (1891–1942), the Jewish convert to Catholicism who died at Auschwitz.

37. Edith Deen, *Great Women of the Christian Faith* (New York: Harper and Brothers, 1959).

38. Oliva M. Espín, "The Enduring Popularity of Rosa de Lima, First Saint of the Americas: Women, Bodies, Sainthood, and National Identity," *CrossCurrents* 6, no. 1 (March 2011): 7–8.

39. A more systematic approach appears in Ruether, *Sexism and God-Talk*.

CHAPTER 1. IN THE BEGINNING . . . EVE

1. Elizabeth Cady Stanton, *The Woman's Bible* (1895; reprint, Boston: Northeastern University Press, 1993), 7.

2. I have used the translation found in the New Revised Standard Version because in this instance it best indicates the meaning presented in the original Hebrew.

3. Stanton, *The Woman's Bible*, 16.

4. Phyllis Trible, "Depatriarchalizing in Biblical Interpretation," *Journal of the American Academy of Religion* 41, no. 1 (March 1973): 36.

5. Thomas Aquinas, "Selections from the *Summa Theologica*," in *Women and Religion: The Original Sourcebook of Women in Christian Thought*, rev. and exp., ed. Elizabeth A. Clark and Herbert Richardson (San Francisco: HarperSanFrancisco, 1996), 77–78; from *Summa Theologica* I.92.3.

6. Trible, "Depatriarchalizing in Biblical Interpretation," 36.

7. Susan Niditch, "Genesis," in *The Women's Bible Commentary*, ed. Carol A. Newsom and Sharon H. Ringe (London and Louisville, KY: SPCK and Westminster/John Knox Press, 1992), 14.

8. Stanton, *The Woman's Bible*, 25.

9. Trible, "Depatriarchalizing in Biblical Interpretation," 40.

10. Martin Luther, *Lectures on Genesis*, in Clark and Richardson, *Women and Religion*, 168.

11. Council on Biblical Manhood and Womanhood, "The Danvers Statement," in *Eve and Adam: Jewish, Christian, and Muslim Readings on Genesis and Gender*, ed. Kristen E. Kvam, Linda S. Schearing, and Valarie H. Ziegler (Bloomington: Indiana University Press, 1999), 389.

12. Religious studies scholars use the designations BCE and CE (Before Common Era and Common Era) for BC and AD in recognition of the fact that not all readers are Christians.

13. Pamela Norris, *Eve: A Biography* (New York: New York University Press, 1999), 4.

14. The book of Sirach (also called Ecclesiasticus) is included in the Catholic and Orthodox Old Testaments, but not in the Protestant Old Testament or Hebrew Bible. Deuterocanonical books are those that appear "alongside" the canon, although some are canonical for Catholic and Orthodox Christians. For more information about Eve in the noncanonical literature, see Alice Ogden Bellis, "Eve in the Apocryphal/Deuterocanonical Books," in *Women in Scripture*, ed. Carol Meyers (Boston: Houghton Mifflin, 2000), 82–83.

15. An apocryphal book is a religious text not considered authoritative by believers.

16. *Life of Adam and Eve*, trans. M. D. Johnson, in *The Old Testament Pseudepigrapha*, vol. 2, ed. James H. Charlesworth (New York: Doubleday, 1985), 258. Scholars date this work to sometime in the first centuries BCE and CE.

17. For a discussion of authorship of 1 Timothy, see Joanna Dewey, "1 Timothy," in Newsom and Ringe, *The Women's Bible Commentary*, 353–58.

18. The abbreviation *d.* means died; *ca.* is the abbreviation for *circa* (about) and indicates approximate dates.

19. Tertullian, *On the Apparel of Women* (*De cultu feminarum*), trans. S. Thelwall, in *Ante-Nicene Fathers*, vol. 4, American ed., ed. Alexander Roberts and James Donaldson (Grand Rapids, MI: Eerdmans, 1968), 14, italics in the translation; from *De cultu feminarum* I.1.2.

CHAPTER 2. THE WOMEN DISCIPLES IN THE KINGDOM OF GOD

1. Elisabeth Schüssler Fiorenza, *In Memory of Her: A Feminist Theological Reconstruction of Christian Origins* (New York: Crossroad, 1983), xx.

2. Paula Fredriksen, *From Jesus to Christ: The Origins of the New Testament Images of Jesus*, 2d ed. (New Haven: Yale University Press, 2000), 3.

3. Mary Rose D'Angelo, "'I Have Seen the Lord': Mary Magdalen as Visionary, Early Christian Prophecy, and the Context of John 20:14–18," in *Mariam, the Magdalen, and the Mother*, ed. Deirdre Good (Bloomington: Indiana University Press, 2005), 114.

4. Samaritans have their own holy mountain (Mount Gerizim) and their own holy city (Shechem) in opposition to Mount Zion and Jerusalem for the Jews of Judea.

5. Joanna Dewey, "The Gospel of Mark," in *Searching the Scriptures*, vol. 2, *A Feminist Commentary*, ed. Elisabeth Schüssler Fiorenza, with Ann Brock and Shelly Matthews (New York: Crossroad, 1994), 485.

6. Adele Reinhartz, "The Gospel of John," in Schüssler Fiorenza et al., *Searching the Scriptures*, vol. 2, *A Feminist Commentary*, 583.

7. Schüssler Fiorenza, *In Memory of Her*, xxiv.

8. Jane Schaberg, "Luke," in *The Women's Bible Commentary*, ed. Carol A. Newsom and Sharon H. Ringe (London and Louisville, KY: SPCK and Westminster/John Knox Press, 1992), 288.

9. Mary Rose D'Angelo, "Martha," in *Women in Scripture*, ed. Carol Meyers (Boston: Houghton Mifflin, 2000), 114–16.

10. Amy-Jill Levine, "Matthew," in Newsom and Ringe, *The Women's Bible Commentary*, 258.

11. Turid Karlsen Seim, "The Gospel of Luke," in Schüssler Fiorenza et al., *Searching the Scriptures*, vol. 2, *A Feminist Commentary*, 730. Seim and others note the significant inclusion of women throughout Luke's narrative.

12. Vasiliki Limberis, "Widow Pleading with a Judge," in Meyers, *Women in Scripture*, 449.

13. Although either "Magdalene" or "Magdalen" is correct, American Christians tend to use Magdalene.

14. Mark 6:3; Matt. 1:18–25, 2:11, 13:55; Luke 1:26–38, 1:46–55, 2:1–20, 2:22–40; Acts 1:14.

15. Katherine Ludwig Jansen, *The Making of the Magdalen: Preaching and Popular Devotion in the Later Middle Ages* (Princeton: Princeton University Press, 2000), 29. James Tabor identifies Mary the mother of James and Joses as the mother of Jesus as well in *The Jesus Dynasty: The Hidden History of Jesus, His Royal Family, and the Birth of Christianity* (New York: Simon and Schuster, 2006).

16. Deirdre Good, "The Miriamic Secret," in Good, *Mariam, the Magdalen, and the Mother*, 10.

17. Jane Schaberg argues that Mary was a victim of rape or seduction prior to her betrothal to Joseph; see *The Illegitimacy of Jesus: A Feminist Theological Interpretation of the Infancy Narratives* (San Francisco: Harper and Row, 1987).

18. Marina Warner, *Alone of All Her Sex: The Myth and the Cult of the Virgin Mary* (New York: Vintage, 1983), 47.

19. Warner, *Alone of All Her Sex*, 48.

20. Michael P. Carroll, *The Cult of the Virgin Mary: Psychological Origins* (Princeton: Princeton University Press, 1986), 58.

21. Kari Børresen, "Mary in Catholic Theology," in *Mary in the Churches*, ed. Hans Küng and Jürgen Moltmann (Edinburgh and New York: T. & T. Clark and Seabury Press, 1983), 54.

22. Schaberg, *The Illegitimacy of Jesus*, 13.

23. Rosemary Radford Ruether, *Sexism and God-Talk: Toward a Feminist Theology* (Boston: Beacon, 1983), 139–58.

24. Ruether, *Sexism and God-Talk*, 153.

25. "The Constantinopolitan Creed (381)," in *Creeds of the Churches*, 3d ed., ed. John H. Leith (Louisville: John Knox Press, 1982), 33.

26. Mark 6:3, 15:40, 15:47; Matt. 13:55, 27:56. The brothers listed are James, Joses, Juda, and Simon; the sisters are not named, but are noted in the plural.

27. Barbara Corrado Pope, "Immaculate and Powerful: The Marian Revival in the Nineteenth Century," in *Immaculate and Powerful: The Female in Sacred Image and Social Reality*, ed. Clarissa W. Atkinson, Constance H. Buchanan, and Margaret R. Miles (Boston: Beacon, 1985), 173.

28. David G. Bromley and Rachel S. Bobbitt, "Visions of the Virgin Mary: The Organizational Development of Marian Apparitional Movements," *Nova Religio* 14, no. 3 (2011): 7.

29. George H. Tavard, *The Thousand Faces of the Virgin Mary* (Collegeville, MN: Liturgical Press, 1996), 186.

30. Patricia Harrington, "Mother of Death, Mother of Rebirth: The Mexican Virgin of Guadalupe," *Journal of the American Academy of Religion* 56, no. 1 (Spring 1988): 25.

31. Virgil Elizondo, "Mary and the Poor: A Model of Evangelising Ecumenism," in Küng and Moltmann, *Mary in the Churches*, 59–65. Father Elizondo now goes by Virgilio.

32. Ivone Gebara and Maria Clara Bingemer, *Mary: Mother of God, Mother of the Poor*, trans. Phillip Berryman (Maryknoll, NY: Orbis, 1989), 122.

33. Elizondo, "Mary and the Poor," 59.

34. Warner, *Alone of All Her Sex*, xxv.

35. Dan Brown, *The Da Vinci Code* (New York: Doubleday, 2003); Michael Baigent, Richard Leigh, and Henry Lincoln, *Holy Blood, Holy Grail* (New York: Delacorte, 1982).

36. Karen L. King, with AnneMarie Luijendijk, "Jesus Said to Them 'My Wife': A New Coptic Gospel Papyrus," accessed 3 June 2014, http://www.hds.harvard.edu/sites/ hds.harvard.edu/files/attachments/faculty-research/research-projects/the-gospel- of-jesuss-wife/29865/King_JesusSaidToThem_draft_0920.pdf.

37. Jane Schaberg, *The Resurrection of Mary Magdalene: Legends, Apocrypha, and the Christian Testament* (New York: Continuum, 2002).

38. Schaberg, *The Resurrection of Mary Magdalene*, 122.

39. Stephen J. Shoemaker, "Jesus' Gnostic Mom: Mary of Nazareth and the 'Gnostic Mary' Traditions," in Good, *Mariam, the Magdalen, and the Mother*, 153–82. Also see Stephen J. Shoemaker, "Rethinking the 'Gnostic Mary': Mary of Nazareth and Mary of Magdala in Early Christian Tradition," *Journal of Early Christian Studies* 9, no. 4 (Winter 2001): 555–95.

40. Karen L. King, *What Is Gnosticism?* (Cambridge, MA: Belknap, 2003).

41. Quoted in Ann Graham Brock, *Mary Magdalene, the First Apostle: The Struggle for Authority* (Cambridge: Harvard Theological Studies, 2003), 87.

42. Quoted in Brock, *Mary Magdalene, the First Apostle*, 37.

43. Quoted in Karen L. King, *The Gospel of Mary of Magdala: Jesus and the First Woman Apostle* (Santa Rosa, CA: Polebridge, 2003), 17.

44. Quoted in King, *The Gospel of Mary of Magdala*, 17.

45. Diane Apostolos-Cappadona, "On the Visual and the Vision: The Magdalen in Early Christian and Byzantine Art and Culture," in Good, *Mariam, the Magdalen, and the Mother*, 123–45.

46. The abbreviation *p.* indicates years of papal rule.

47. Quoted in Jansen, *The Making of the Magdalen*, 33.

48. Esther de Boer, *Mary Magdalene: Beyond the Myth*, trans. John Bowden (Harrisburg, PA: Trinity Press International, 1997), 14.

CHAPTER 3. WOMEN AND THE CONVERSION OF AN EMPIRE

1. It is unlikely that Perpetua actually wrote her own memoirs, although scholars are divided on this issue. L. Stephanie Cobb, *Dying to Be Men: Gender and Language in Early Christian Martyr Texts* (New York: Columbia University Press, 2008), 94–96.
2. John Wilkinson, trans., *Egeria's Travels*, 3d ed. (Oxford, UK: Oxbow, 2006), 169–71.
3. Elizabeth A. Clark, "Faltonia Betitia Proba and Her Virgilian Poem: The Christian Matron as Artist," in *Ascetic Piety and Women's Faith: Essays on Late Ancient Christianity*, ed. Elizabeth A. Clark (Lewiston, NY: Edwin Mellen, 1986), 124–52.
4. Antoinette Clark Wire, *The Corinthian Women Prophets: A Reconstruction through Paul's Rhetoric* (Minneapolis: Fortress, 1990), 181.
5. Eldon Jay Epp, *Junia: The First Woman Apostle* (Minneapolis: Fortress, 2005), 15–20.
6. Jouette M. Bassler, "1 Corinthians," in *The Women's Bible Commentary*, ed. Carol A. Newsom and Sharon H. Ringe (London and Louisville, KY: SPCK and Westminster/John Knox Press, 1992), 328.
7. See Wire, *The Corinthian Women Prophets*.
8. Elizabeth A. Castelli, "Paul on Women and Gender," in *Women and Christian Origins*, ed. Ross Shepard Kraemer and Mary Rose D'Angelo (New York: Oxford University Press, 1999), 233.
9. Angela West, "Sex and Salvation: A Christian Feminist Bible Study on 1 Corinthians 6.12–7.39," in *Feminist Theology: A Reader*, ed. Ann Loades (London and Louisville, KY: SPCK and Westminster/John Knox Press, 1990), 72.
10. Sheila Briggs, "Galatians," in *Searching the Scriptures*, vol. 2, *A Feminist Commentary*, ed. Elisabeth Schüssler Fiorenza, with Ann Brock and Shelly Matthews (New York: Crossroad, 1994), 218.
11. Rena Pederson identifies the various individuals and groups who were called "apostles" in the New Testament; see *The Lost Apostle: Searching for the Truth about Junia* (San Francisco: Jossey-Bass, 2006).
12. Margaret Y. MacDonald, "Rereading Paul: Early Interpreters of Paul on Women and Gender," in Kraemer and D'Angelo, *Women and Christian Origins*, 238.
13. Clarice J. Martin, "The Acts of the Apostles," in Schüssler Fiorenza et al., *Searching the Scriptures*, vol. 2, *A Feminist Commentary*, 785.
14. Castelli, "Paul on Women and Gender," 224.
15. Elisabeth Schüssler Fiorenza, "Missionaries, Apostles, Co-workers: Romans 16 and the Reconstruction of Women's Early Christian History," in Loades, *Feminist Theology: A Reader*, 63, my italics.

16. Bernadette Brooten, "'Junia . . . Outstanding among the Apostles' (Romans 16:7),"
    in *Women Priests: A Catholic Commentary on the Vatican Declaration,* ed.
    Leonard Swidler and Arlene Swidler (New York: Paulist, 1977), 141; from John
    Chrysostom, *In epistolam ad romanos,* Homilia 31.2.

17. Brooten, "'Junia . . . Outstanding among the Apostles,'" 142.

18. Georgia Harkness, *Women in Church and Society: A Historical and Theological
    Inquiry* (Nashville: Abingdon, 1972), 69.

19. Castelli, "Paul on Women and Gender," 222.

20. MacDonald, "Rereading Paul," 241.

21. Margaret Y. MacDonald, *Early Christian Women and Pagan Opinion: The Power of
    the Hysterical Woman* (Cambridge: Cambridge University Press, 1996), 30.

22. Harkness, *Women in Church and Society,* 54–55.

23. Karen Jo Torjesen, *When Women Were Priests: Women's Leadership in the Early
    Church and the Scandal of Their Subordination in the Rise of Christianity* (San
    Francisco: HarperSanFrancisco, 1993), 2.

24. Karen Jo Torjesen, "Reconstruction of Women's Early Christian History," in
    Searching the Scriptures, vol. 1, *A Feminist Introduction,* ed. Elisabeth Schüssler
    Fiorenza, with Shelly Matthews (New York: Crossroad, 1993), 303.

25. Reasons for rejecting Pauline authorship of the Pastoral Letters appear in Robert
    J. Karris, "The Pastoral Letters," in *The Oxford Companion to the Bible,* ed. Bruce
    M. Metzger and Michael D. Coogan (New York: Oxford University Press, 1993),
    574.

26. Wayne A. Meeks, *The First Urban Christians: The Social World of the Apostle Paul*
    (New Haven: Yale University Press, 1983), 142–63.

27. Meeks, *The First Urban Christians,* 151.

28. Elisabeth Schüssler Fiorenza, *In Memory of Her: A Feminist Theological
    Reconstruction of Christian Origins* (New York: Crossroad, 1983), 176.

29. Bonnie Bowman Thurston, *The Widows: A Women's Ministry in the Early Church*
    (Minneapolis: Fortress, 1989), 19.

30. MacDonald, *Early Christian Women and Pagan Opinion,* 159.

31. Virginia Burrus, *Chastity as Autonomy: Women in the Stories of the Apocryphal
    Acts* (Lewiston, NY: Edwin Mellen, 1987), 4.

32. Dennis Ronald MacDonald, *The Legend and the Apostle: The Battle for Paul in
    Story and Canon* (Philadelphia: Westminster, 1983), 15.

33. Bart D. Ehrman, ed., *The Acts of Thecla,* in *Lost Scriptures: Books That Did Not
    Make It into the New Testament* (New York: Oxford University Press, 2003),
    113–21.

34. Thurston, *The Widows,* 9.

35. MacDonald, *Early Christian Women and Pagan Opinion,* 179.

36. Tertullian, *On the Veiling of Virgins* (*De virginibus velandis*), IX, in *The Tertullian
    Project,* accessed 3 June 2014, http://www.tertullian.org/anf/anf04/anf04-09.
    htm#P624_147158.

37. *Didascalia Apostolorum*, in *Ordained Women in the Early Church: A Documentary History*, ed. and trans. Kevin Madigan and Carolyn Osiek (Baltimore: Johns Hopkins University Press, 2005), 108.

38. Thurston, *The Widows*, 111.

39. *Apostolic Constitutions*, in Madigan and Osiek, *Ordained Women in the Early Church*, 111.

40. Robin Darling Young, *In Procession before the World: Martyrdom as Public Liturgy in Early Christianity* (Milwaukee: Marquette University Press, 2001), 6.

41. The abbreviation *r.* indicates years of rule or reign.

42. MacDonald, *Early Christian Women and Pagan Opinion*, 51; from Pliny's *Letters* 10.96.

43. Medieval Sourcebook, *The Passion of Saints Perpetua and Felicitas*, accessed 3 June 2014, http://www.fordham.edu/halsall/source/perpetua.asp.

44. Cobb, *Dying to Be Men*, 2.

45. Cobb, *Dying to Be Men*, 126, italics in original.

46. Young, *In Procession before the World*, 54.

47. Young, *In Procession before the World*, 6.

48. Nicola Denzey, *The Bone Gatherers: The Lost Worlds of Early Christian Women* (Boston: Beacon, 2007), xiv.

49. Burrus, *Chastity as Autonomy*, 2, 102–3.

50. Once called Montanism—after the male prophet Montanus—the movement of the Phrygian Prophets is now known as the New Prophecy, which is how the group identified itself. It flourished at the turn of the third century.

51. Burrus, *Chastity as Autonomy*, 102.

52. Cobb, *Dying to Be Men*, 25–28.

53. Rosemary Radford Ruether, "Misogynism and Virginal Feminism in the Fathers of the Church," in *Religion and Sexism: Images of Woman in the Jewish and Christian Traditions*, ed. Rosemary Radford Ruether (New York: Simon and Schuster, 1974), 176–78.

54. Karen Armstrong, *The Gospel according to Woman: Christianity's Creation of the Sex War in the West* (London: Elm Tree, 1986), 30.

55. The abbreviation *fl.* indicates the approximate time an individual "flourished," since no birth or death dates are known.

56. Lynda L. Coon, *Sacred Fictions: Holy Women and Hagiography in Late Antiquity* (Philadelphia: University of Pennsylvania Press, 1997), 79.

57. Coon, *Sacred Fictions*, 85.

58. Coon, *Sacred Fictions*, 108.

59. Burrus, *Chastity as Autonomy*, 2, 117.

60. Elizabeth A. Clark, *Women in the Early Church* (Wilmington, DE: Michael Glazier, 1983), 16.

61. Elizabeth A. Clark, "Ascetic Renunciation and Feminine Advancement: A Paradox of Late Ancient Christianity," in Clark, *Ascetic Piety and Women's Faith*, 185.

62. Torjesen, *When Women Were Priests*, 77.
63. Elaine Pagels, *The Gnostic Gospels* (New York: Vintage, 1979), 47.
64. Torjesen, *When Women Were Priests*, 157.
65. *Apostolic Constitutions*, 107.
66. *Apostolic Constitutions*, 110.
67. Denzey, *The Bone Gatherers*, 178.
68. Denzey, *The Bone Gatherers*, 176.
69. Rodney Stark, "The Role of Women in Christian Growth," chap. 5 in *The Rise of Christianity: How the Obscure, Marginal Jesus Movement Became the Dominant Religious Force in the Western World in a Few Centuries* (New York: HarperCollins, 1997), 95–128.

CHAPTER 4. SAINTS, SEERS, AND SCHOLARS IN THE MIDDLE AGES

1. Kevin Ward, "Africa," in *A World History of Christianity*, ed. Adrian Hastings (Grand Rapids, MI: Eerdmans, 1999), 197.
2. "Orthodox" is from the Greek *orthodoxos* (believing correctly), while "Catholic" is from *katholikos* (universal).
3. Alice-Mary Talbot, "The Devotional Life of Laywomen," in *Byzantine Christianity*, vol. 3 of *A People's History of Christianity*, ed. Derek Krueger (Minneapolis: Fortress, 2006), 204.
4. Lynda L. Coon, *Sacred Fictions: Holy Women and Hagiography in Late Antiquity* (Philadelphia: University of Pennsylvania Press, 1997), 100–102.
5. Liz James, *Empresses and Power in Early Byzantium* (New York: Leicester University Press, 2001), 149.
6. James, *Empresses and Power in Early Byzantium*, 151, 152.
7. "Declaration of Council of Nicaea (787)," in *Creeds of the Churches*, 3d ed., ed. John H. Leith (Louisville: John Knox Press, 1982), 56.
8. Judith Herrin, "Women and the Faith in Icons in Early Christianity," in *Culture, Ideology and Politics: Essays for Eric Hobsbawm*, ed. Raphael Samuel and Gareth Stedman Jones (London: Routledge and Kegan Paul, 1982), 75.
9. Robin Cormack, "Women and Icons, and Women in Icons," in *Women, Men and Eunuchs: Gender in Byzantium*, ed. Liz James (London: Routledge, 1997), 35.
10. Cormack, "Women and Icons, and Women in Icons," 43.
11. Talbot, "The Devotional Life of Laywomen," 204. Information in this paragraph and the following comes from Talbot, "The Devotional Life of Laywomen," except when otherwise noted.
12. Kyriaki Karidoyanes FitzGerald, *Women Deacons in the Orthodox Church: Called to Holiness and Ministry* (Brookline, MA: Holy Cross Orthodox Press, 1999), 52, 55.
13. Carolyn L. Connor, *Women of Byzantium* (New Haven: Yale University Press, 2004), 15.
14. Connor, *Women of Byzantium*, 167.
15. Connor, *Women of Byzantium*, 170.

16. Alice-Mary Talbot, "A Comparison of the Monastic Experience of Byzantine Men and Women," in *Women and Religious Life in Byzantium*, ed. Alice-Mary Talbot (Burlington, VT: Ashgate, 2001), XII.4.

17. Alice-Mary Talbot, "An Introduction to Byzantine Monasticism," in Talbot, *Women and Religious Life in Byzantium*, XI.236–237.

18. Talbot, "A Comparison of the Monastic Experience of Byzantine Men and Women," XII.10.

19. Gregory, Bishop of Nyssa, *The Life of Saint Macrina*, trans. Kevin Corrigan (Toronto: Peregrina, 1987), 26.

20. Talbot, "The Devotional Life of Laywomen," 203.

21. Thomas Cahill, *How the Irish Saved Civilization: The Untold Story of Ireland's Heroic Role from the Fall of Rome to the Rise of Medieval Europe* (New York: Doubleday, 1995).

22. Suzanne Fonay Wemple, "Women from the Fifth to the Tenth Century," in *A History of Women in the West*, vol. 2, *Silences of the Middle Ages*, ed. Christiane Klapisch-Zuber (Cambridge, MA: Belknap, 1992), 189.

23. Jane Tibbetts Schulenburg, *Forgetful of Their Sex: Female Sanctity and Society, ca. 500–1100* (Chicago: University of Chicago Press, 1998), 99.

24. Rudolf of Fulda, *Life of Leoba*, in *Medieval Sourcebook*, Fordham University, accessed 3 June 2014, http://www.fordham.edu/halsall/basis/leoba.asp.

25. Rudolf of Fulda, *Life of Leoba*.

26. Marie Anne Mayeski, *Women at the Table: Three Medieval Theologians* (Collegeville, MN: Liturgical Press, 2004), 71–72.

27. Schulenburg, *Forgetful of Their Sex*, 67.

28. Information on laywomen in the medieval church comes from Sandy Bardsley, *Women's Roles in the Middle Ages* (Westport, CT: Greenwood, 2007), 44–48.

29. Gary Macy, *The Hidden History of Women's Ordination: Female Clergy in the Medieval West* (New York: Oxford University Press, 2008), 80–81.

30. Jo Ann Kay McNamara, *Sisters in Arms: Catholic Nuns through Two Millennia* (Cambridge, MA: Harvard University Press, 1996), 210.

31. McNamara, *Sisters in Arms*, 209.

32. Jacques Dalarum, "The Clerical Gaze," trans. Arthur Goldhammer, in Klapisch-Zuber, *A History of Women in the West*, vol. 2, *Silences of the Middle Ages*, 29.

33. McNamara, *Sisters in Arms*, 211.

34. Schulenburg, *Forgetful of Their Sex*, 171.

35. Macy, *The Hidden History of Women's Ordination*, 125–27.

36. Macy, *The Hidden History of Women's Ordination*, 41.

37. Mary Martin McLaughlin, "Heloise the Abbess: The Expansion of the Paraclete," in *Listening to Heloise: The Voice of the Twelfth-Century Woman*, ed. Bonnie Wheeler (New York: St. Martin's, 2000), 4.

38. Heloise to Abelard, Letter 5, in *The Letters of Abelard and Heloise*, ed. and trans. Betty Radice (New York: Penguin, 1974), 160.

39. Elizabeth Alvilda Petroff, *Body and Soul: Essays on Medieval Women and Mysticism* (New York: Oxford University Press, 1994), 69.

40. Although several etymologies of the word "beguine" have been proposed, Walter Simons claims the likeliest is from an Indo-European word for mumbling, as in someone muttering prayers. *Cities of Ladies: Beguine Communities in the Medieval Low Countries, 1200–1565* (Philadelphia: University of Pennsylvania Press, 2001), 122.

41. Simons, *Cities of Ladies*, 61.

42. Marie A. Conn, *Noble Daughters: Unheralded Women in Western Christianity, 13th to 18th Centuries* (Westport, CT: Greenwood, 2000), 6.

43. Simons, *Cities of Ladies*, 61–90.

44. Giles Constable, *Three Studies in Medieval Religious and Social Thought: The Interpretation of Mary and Martha; The Ideal of the Imitation of Christ; The Orders of Society* (Cambridge: Cambridge University Press, 1995), 125.

45. Patricia Ranft, *Women in Western Intellectual Culture, 600–1500* (New York: Palgrave Macmillan, 2002), 91.

46. Beatrice of Nazareth, *Seven Manners of Loving*, in *Women Mystics in Medieval Europe*, ed. Emilie zum Brunn and Georgette Epiney-Burgard, trans. Sheila Hughes (New York: Paragon House, 1989), 92–93.

47. Hadewijch of Antwerp, *Poem XVII*, in zum Brunn and Epiney-Burgard, *Women Mystics in Medieval Europe*, 132.

48. Ranft, *Women in Western Intellectual Culture*, 109.

49. Mechthild of Magdeburg, *The Flowing Light of the Godhead*, in zum Brunn and Epiney-Burgard, *Women Mystics in Medieval Europe*, 59.

50. Sara S. Poor, *Mechthild of Magdeburg and Her Book: Gender and the Making of Textual Authority* (Philadelphia: University of Pennsylvania Press, 2004), 5.

51. Marguerite Porete, *The Mirror of Simple Souls*, trans. Ellen L. Babinsky (New York: Paulist, 1993), 87.

52. Caroline Walker Bynum, *Holy Feast and Holy Fast: The Religious Significance of Food to Medieval Women* (Berkeley: University of California Press, 1987), 245.

53. Bynum, *Holy Feast and Holy Fast*, 93.

54. Petroff, *Body and Soul*, 212.

55. Bynum, *Holy Feast and Holy Fast*, 142.

56. Bynum, *Holy Feast and Holy Fast*, 144.

57. Bynum, *Holy Feast and Holy Fast*, 275.

58. Caroline Walker Bynum, *Jesus as Mother: Studies in the Spirituality of the High Middle Ages* (Berkeley: University of California Press, 1982), 130.

59. Bynum, *Jesus as Mother*, 112–24.

60. Julian of Norwich, *Revelations of Divine Love*, trans. Clifton Wolters (New York: Penguin, 1966), 168.

61. Catherine M. Mooney, "The Authorial Role of Brother A. in the Composition of Angela of Foligno's Revelations," in *Creative Women in Medieval and Early*

Modern Italy: A Religious and Artistic Renaissance, ed. E. Ann Matter and John Coakley (Philadelphia: University of Pennsylvania Press, 1994), 52.

62. Wai Man Yuen, *Religious Experience and Interpretation: Memory as the Path to the Knowledge of God in Julian of Norwich's "Showings"* (New York: Peter Lang, 2003), 217.

63. The next chapter explains the plural of Reformation.

64. Rosalind Brown-Grant, *Christine de Pizan and the Moral Defence of Women: Reading beyond Gender* (Cambridge: Cambridge University Press, 1999), 2.

CHAPTER 5. WOMEN REFORMED, WOMEN RESISTANT

1. Retha M. Warnicke, *Women of the English Renaissance and Reformation* (Westport, CT: Greenwood, 1983), 17.

2. Claire Cross, "'Great Reasoners in Scripture': The Activities of Women Lollards, 1380–1530," in *Medieval Women*, ed. Derek Baker (Oxford: Basil Blackwell, 1978), 369.

3. Helga Robinson-Hammerstein, "Women's Prospects in Early Sixteenth-Century Germany: Did Martin Luther's Teaching Make a Difference?," in *Studies on Medieval and Early Modern Women*, vol. 4, *Victims or Viragos?*, ed. Christine Meek and Catherine Lawless (Dublin, Ireland: Four Courts Press, 2005), 106.

4. Charmarie Jenkins Blaisdell, "The Matrix of Reform: Women in the Lutheran and Calvinist Movements," in *Triumph over Silence: Women in Protestant History*, ed. Richard L. Greaves (Westport, CT: Greenwood, 1985), 16.

5. Robinson-Hammerstein, "Women's Prospects in Early Sixteenth-Century Germany," 109.

6. Roland H. Bainton, *Women of the Reformation in Germany and Italy* (Minneapolis: Augsburg, 1971), 61.

7. Bainton, *Women of the Reformation in Germany and Italy*, 72.

8. Lyndal Roper, *The Holy Household: Women and Morals in Reformation Augsburg* (Oxford: Clarendon, 1989), 83–84.

9. Peter Vogt, "A Voice for Themselves: Women as Participants in Congregational Discourse in the Eighteenth-Century Moravian Movement," in *Women Preachers and Prophets through Two Millennia of Christianity*, ed. Beverly Mayne Kienzle and Pamela J. Walker (Berkeley: University of California Press, 1998), 227.

10. Vogt, "A Voice for Themselves," 238.

11. Phyllis Mack, *Visionary Women: Ecstatic Prophecy in Seventeenth-Century England* (Berkeley: University of California Press, 1992), 4.

12. Mack, *Visionary Women*, 245.

13. Mack, *Visionary Women*, 344.

14. Marie A. Conn, *Noble Daughters: Unheralded Women in Western Christianity, 13th to 18th Centuries* (Westport, CT: Greenwood, 2000), 41.

15. Jo Ann Kay McNamara, *Sisters in Arms: Catholic Nuns through Two Millennia* (Cambridge, MA: Harvard University Press, 1996), 426.

16. Warnicke, *Women of the English Renaissance and Reformation*, 74.

17. Roland H. Bainton, *Women of the Reformation in France and England* (Minneapolis: Augsburg, 1973), 29.

18. McNamara, *Sisters in Arms*, 427.

19. Bainton, *Women of the Reformation in France and England*, 65.

20. Testimony of Governor John Winthrop in "The Examination of Mrs. Anne Hutchinson at the Court of Newtown," in *Womanhood in Radical Protestantism, 1525–1675*, ed. Joyce L. Irwin (New York: Edwin Mellen, 1979), 226.

21. Jon Pahl, *Empire of Sacrifice: The Religious Origins of American Violence* (New York: New York University Press, 2010), 151–55.

22. McNamara, *Sisters in Arms*, 456.

23. Stuart Clark, "Protestant Demonology: Sin, Superstition, and Society (c. 1520–c. 1630)," in *Early Modern European Witchcraft: Centres and Peripheries*, ed. Bengt Ankarloo and Gustav Henningsen (Oxford: Clarendon, 1990), 66.

24. Gustav Henningsen and Bengt Ankarloo, introduction to Ankarloo and Henningsen, *Early Modern European Witchcraft*, 10, 14.

25. McNamara, *Sisters in Arms*, 434.

26. Henningsen and Ankarloo, introduction to *Early Modern European Witchcraft*, 11–12.

27. Lyndal Roper provides the figure of fifty thousand, in *Witch Craze: Terror and Fantasy in Baroque Germany* (New Haven: Yale University Press, 2004), 6.

28. Richard Godbeer, *The Salem Witch Hunt: A Brief History with Documents* (New York: Bedford/St. Martin's, 2011), 11.

29. Bernard Rosenthal, "Dark Eve," in *Spellbound: Women and Witchcraft in America*, ed. Elizabeth Reis (Wilmington, DE: SR Books, 1998), 84–85.

30. Mary Wollstonecraft, *A Vindication of the Rights of Woman*, rev. ed. (New York: Penguin, 2004).

31. Merry Wiesner-Hanks, ed., *Convents Confront the Reformation: Catholic and Protestant Nuns in Germany*, trans. Joan Skocir and Merry Wiesner-Hanks (Milwaukee: Marquette University Press, 1996), 79n2.

32. Anna Maria van Schurman, *Whether a Christian Woman Should Be Educated, and Other Writings from Her Intellectual Circle*, ed. and trans. Joyce L. Irwin (Chicago: University of Chicago Press, 1998), 5.

33. Letter to André Rivet, in van Schurman, *Whether a Christian Woman Should Be Educated*, 42.

34. Stephanie Merrim, "Toward a Feminist Reading of Sor Juana Inés de la Cruz: Past, Present, and Future Directions in Sor Juana Criticism," in *Feminist Perspectives on Sor Juana Inés de la Cruz*, ed. Stephanie Merrim (Detroit: Wayne State University Press, 1991), 11, 31n1.

35. Sor Juana Inés de la Cruz, *The Answer/La respuesta*, ed. and trans. Electa Arenal and Amanda Powell (New York: Feminist Press, 1994), 77 (29).

36. Mack, *Visionary Women*, 303.

37. Margaret Fell, *Womens Speaking Justified (1667)* (Los Angeles: University of California, 1979).

38. McNamara, *Sisters in Arms*, 462.

39. The Catholic Church has declared only four women to be doctors of the church, that is, saints of great learning and scholarship: Teresa of Avila, Catherine of Siena, Thérèse of Lisieux, and, under Pope Benedict XVI (p. 2005–2013), Hildegard of Bingen.

40. Gillian T. W. Ahlgren, *Teresa of Avila and the Politics of Sanctity* (Ithaca: Cornell University Press, 1996), 85.

41. Teresa of Avila, *The Interior Castle*, trans. Mirabai Starr (New York: Riverhead, 2003), 292.

42. Teresa of Avila, *The Book of Her Life*, in *The Collected Works of St. Teresa of Avila*, vol. 1, trans. Kieran Kavanaugh and Otilio Rodriguez (Washington, D.C.: Institute of Carmelite Studies, 1978), 153–54.

43. Teresa of Avila, *The Book of Her Life*, 195.

44. Oliva M. Espín, "The Enduring Popularity of Rosa de Lima, First Saint of the Americas: Women, Bodies, Sainthood, and National Identity," *CrossCurrents* 61, no. 1 (March 2011): 6–26.

45. Gabriella Zarri, "Ursula and Catherine: The Marriage of Virgins in the Sixteenth Century," trans. Anne Jacobson Schutte, in *Creative Women in Medieval and Early Modern Italy: A Religious and Artistic Renaissance*, ed. E. Ann Matter and John Coakley (Philadelphia: University of Pennsylvania Press, 1994), 261.

46. McNamara, *Sisters in Arms*, 482.

47. McNamara, *Sisters in Arms*, 486.

48. Warnicke, *Women of the English Renaissance and Reformation*, 177.

CHAPTER 6. SPIRIT-FILLED WOMEN IN THE NINETEENTH CENTURY

1. Betty A. DeBerg, *Ungodly Women: Gender and the First Wave of American Fundamentalism* (Minneapolis: Fortress, 1990), 13.

2. Barbara Welter, "The Cult of True Womanhood: 1820–1860," *American Quarterly* 18, no. 2, part 1 (Summer 1966): 151–74.

3. Welter, "The Cult of True Womanhood," 174.

4. Jo Ann Kay McNamara, *Sisters in Arms: Catholic Nuns through Two Millennia* (Cambridge: Harvard University Press, 1996), 469.

5. McNamara, *Sisters in Arms*, 529.

6. McNamara, *Sisters in Arms*, 480.

7. Allan Greer, *Mohawk Saint: Catherine Tekakwitha and the Jesuits* (New York: Oxford University Press, 2005), 7.

8. Her Iroquois name was rendered Tegakouita by the French and Tekakwitha by the English, while her baptismal name, given in memory of Catherine of Siena, sounded somewhat like "Kateri" in French spoken with a Mohawk accent. See Greer, *Mohawk Saint*, xi.

9. Paula Elizabeth Holmes, "The Narrative Repatriation of Blessed Kateri Tekakwitha," *Anthropologica* 43, no. 1 (2001): 95.

10. Sergei Kan, "Clan Mothers and Godmothers: Tlingit Women and Russian Orthodox Christianity, 1840–1940," *Ethnohistory* 43, no. 4 (Autumn 1996): 619.

11. Kan, "Clan Mothers and Godmothers," 626.

12. Julie Roy Jeffrey, *Converting the West: A Biography of Narcissa Whitman* (Norman: University of Oklahoma Press, 1991), 101.

13. Mary Ewens, "The Leadership of Nuns in Immigrant Catholicism," in *Women and Religion in America*, vol. 1, *The Nineteenth Century*, ed. Rosemary Radford Ruether and Rosemary Skinner Keller (San Francisco: Harper and Row, 1981), 101.

14. Elizabeth Seton, *Selected Writings*, ed. Ellin Kelly and Annabelle Melville (New York: Paulist, 1987), 19.

15. This second date comes from Barbara Leslie Epstein, *The Politics of Domesticity: Women, Evangelism, and Temperance in Nineteenth-Century America* (Middletown, CT: Wesleyan University Press, 1981), 1.

16. Frank Baker, "Susanna Wesley: Puritan, Parent, Pastor, Protagonist, Pattern," in *Women in New Worlds: Historical Perspectives on the Wesleyan Tradition*, vol. 2, ed. Rosemary Skinner Keller, Louise L. Queen, and Hilah F. Thomas (Nashville: Abingdon, 1981), 119.

17. Baker, "Susanna Wesley," 124.

18. Earl Kent Brown, *Women of Mr. Wesley's Methodism* (New York: Edwin Mellen, 1983), 27–28.

19. Brown, *Women of Mr. Wesley's Methodism*, xii.

20. Nancy A. Hardesty, *Women Called to Witness: Evangelical Feminism in the Nineteenth Century*, 2d. ed. (Knoxville: University of Tennessee Press, 1999), 38.

21. Susie C. Stanley, *Holy Boldness: Women Preachers' Autobiographies and the Sanctified Self* (Knoxville: University of Tennessee Press, 2002), 71–72.

22. Stanley, *Holy Boldness*, 72.

23. Andrew Mark Eason, *Women in God's Army: Gender and Equality in the Early Salvation Army* (Waterloo, Ontario: Wilfrid Laurier University Press, 2003), 102–7.

24. Barbara Brown Zikmund, "The Feminist Thrust of Sectarian Christianity," in *Women of Spirit: Female Leadership in the Jewish and Christian Traditions*, ed. Rosemary Ruether and Eleanor McLaughlin (New York: Simon and Schuster, 1979), 216.

25. Eason, *Women in God's Army*, 132.

26. Lisa Joy Pruitt, *"A Looking-Glass for Ladies": American Protestant Women and the Orient in the Nineteenth Century* (Macon, GA: Mercer University Press, 2005), 145.

27. Sushil Madhava Pathak, *American Missionaries and Hinduism: A Study of Their Contacts from 1813 to 1910* (Delhi, India: Munshiram Manoharlal, 1967), 155.

28. Mary Taylor Huber and Nancy C. Lutkehaus, introduction to *Gendered Missions: Women and Men in Missionary Discourse and Practice*, ed. Mary Taylor Huber and Nancy C. Lutkehaus (Ann Arbor: University of Michigan Press, 1999), 12.

29. Pathak, *American Missionaries and Hinduism*, 147.

30. Aparna Basu, "Mary Ann Cooke to Mother Teresa: Christian Missionary Women and the Indian Response," in *Women and Missions: Past and Present; Anthropological and Historical Perceptions*, ed. Fiona Bowie, Deborah Kirkwood, and Shirley Ardener (Providence, RI: Berg, 1993), 196.

31. Basu, "Mary Ann Cooke to Mother Teresa," 196.

32. Pruitt, *"A Looking-Glass for Ladies,"* 137.

33. Sylvia M. Jacobs, "Their 'Special Mission': Afro-American Women as Missionaries to the Congo, 1894–1937," in *Black Americans and the Missionary Movement in Africa*, ed. Sylvia M. Jacobs (Westport, CT: Greenwood, 1982), 171.

34. Jacobs, "Their 'Special Mission,'" 157.

35. Bettye Collier-Thomas, *Daughters of Thunder: Black Women Preachers and Their Sermons, 1850–1979* (San Francisco: Jossey-Bass, 1998), 15.

36. Epstein, *The Politics of Domesticity*, 100.

37. Epstein, *The Politics of Domesticity*, 107.

38. Hardesty, *Women Called to Witness*, 10.

39. Hardesty, *Women Called to Witness*, 11.

40. Rumi Yasutake, *Transnational Women's Activism: The United States, Japan, and Japanese Immigrant Communities in California, 1859–1920* (New York: New York University Press, 2004), 45.

41. Yasutake, *Transnational Women's Activism*, 52.

42. Meera Kosambi, introduction to *Pandita Ramabai through Her Own Words: Selected Works*, ed. Meera Kosambi (New Delhi: Oxford University Press, 2000), 10.

43. Kosambi, introduction to *Pandita Ramabai through Her Own Words*, 12.

44. Zikmund, "The Feminist Thrust of Sectarian Christianity," 208.

45. Rosemary Radford Ruether, *Women and Redemption: A Theological History* (Minneapolis: Fortress, 1998), 150.

46. Zikmund, "The Feminist Thrust of Sectarian Christianity," 217.

47. Jean M. Humez, ed., *Mother's First-Born Daughters: Early Shaker Writings on Women and Religion* (Bloomington: Indiana University Press, 1993), 91.

48. Danny L. Jorgensen, "Gender-Inclusive Images of God: A Sociological Interpretation of Early Shakerism and Mormonism," *Nova Religio* 4, no. 1 (October 2000): 72.

49. Mary Farrell Bednarowski, "Outside the Mainstream: Women's Religion and Women's Religious Leaders in Nineteenth-Century America," *Journal of the American Academy of Religion* 48, no. 2 (June 1980): 217.

50. Stephen Gottschalk, *The Emergence of Christian Science in American Religious Life* (Berkeley: University of California Press, 1973), 166.

51. Roy E. Graham, *Ellen G. White: Co-Founder of the Seventh-day Adventist Church* (New York: Peter Lang, 1985), 101–39.

52. Zikmund, "The Feminist Thrust of Sectarian Christianity," 219.

53. Estrelda Alexander, *The Women of Azusa Street* (Cleveland: Pilgrim Press, 2005), 42.

54. Alexander, *The Women of Azusa Street*, 46.

CHAPTER 7. CHURCHWOMEN ON THE MARGINS AND
IN THE MAINSTREAM

1. Brian Kolodiejchuk, ed., *Mother Teresa: Come Be My Light; The Private Writings of the "Saint of Calcutta"* (New York: Doubleday, 2007).

2. Christopher Hitchens, *The Missionary Position: Mother Teresa in Theory and Practice* (London: Verso, 1995); and Meg Greene, *Mother Teresa: A Biography* (Westport, CT: Greenwood, 2004), 105–36.

3. Rachel Feldhay Brenner, *Writing as Resistance: Four Women Confronting the Holocaust; Edith Stein, Simone Weil, Anne Frank, Etty Hillesum* (University Park: Pennsylvania State University Press, 1997), 85, 88.

4. June O'Connor, *The Moral Vision of Dorothy Day: A Feminist Perspective* (New York: Crossroad, 1991), 11.

5. Dorothy Day, *Loaves and Fishes* (Maryknoll, NY: Orbis, 1997), xvii.

6. Day, *Loaves and Fishes*, 86.

7. Rosetta E. Ross, *Witnessing and Testifying: Black Women, Religion, and Civil Rights* (Minneapolis: Fortress, 2003), 24.

8. Ross, *Witnessing and Testifying*, 26, italics in original.

9. Quoting Nannie Helen Burroughs, in Ross, *Witnessing and Testifying*, 29.

10. Ross, *Witnessing and Testifying*, 5.

11. Ross, *Witnessing and Testifying*, 14.

12. Ross, *Witnessing and Testifying*, 15.

13. Emilie M. Townes, *Womanist Justice, Womanist Hope* (Atlanta: Scholars Press, 1993), 178.

14. Ross, *Witnessing and Testifying*, 142–65.

15. Townes, *Womanist Justice, Womanist Hope*, 185.

16. For "radical humanism," see Barbara Ransby, *Ella Baker and the Black Freedom Movement* (Chapel Hill: University of North Carolina Press, 2003), 194; for "positive theological humanism," see Rosetta E. Ross, "Lessons and Treasures in Our Mothers' Witness: Why I Write about Black Women's Activism," in *Deeper Shades of Purple: Womanism in Religion and Society*, ed. Stacey M. Floyd-Thomas (New York: New York University Press, 2006), 125.

17. Ross, *Witnessing and Testifying*, 32.

18. Ransby, *Ella Baker and the Black Freedom Movement*, 180–84.

19. Delores S. Williams, *Sisters in the Wilderness: The Challenge of Womanist God-Talk* (Maryknoll, NY: Orbis, 1993), xiii.

20. Theressa Hoover, "Black Women and the Churches: Triple Jeopardy," in *Black Theology: A Documentary History, 1966–1979*, ed. Gayraud S. Wilmore and James H. Cone (Maryknoll, NY: Orbis, 1979), 386.

21. Kyriaki Karidoyanes FitzGerald, *Women Deacons in the Orthodox Church: Called to Holiness and Ministry* (Brookline, MA: Holy Cross Orthodox Press, 1999), 143–44.

22. Lisa Joy Pruitt, *"A Looking-Glass for Ladies": American Protestant Women and the Orient in the Nineteenth Century* (Macon, GA: Mercer University Press, 2005), 120.

23. Since Vatican Council II, some men in the Roman Catholic Church have been ordained as "permanent deacons" and are not eligible for ordination as priests.

24. Bettye Collier-Thomas, *Daughters of Thunder: Black Women Preachers and Their Sermons, 1850–1979* (San Francisco: Jossey-Bass, 1998), 57–59, 91–93.

25. Carl J. Schneider and Dorothy Schneider, *In Their Own Right: The History of American Clergywomen* (New York: Crossroad, 1997), 71.

26. Schneider and Schneider, *In Their Own Right*, 72.

27. Georgia Harkness, *Women in Church and Society: A Historical and Theological Inquiry* (Nashville: Abingdon, 1972), 129.

28. Schneider and Schneider, *In Their Own Right*, 164.

29. Schneider and Schneider, *In Their Own Right*, 185.

30. FitzGerald, *Women Deacons in the Orthodox Church*, 153.

31. FitzGerald, *Women Deacons in the Orthodox Church*, 160–61.

32. See *St. Nina Quarterly*, http://www.stnina.org/.

33. Ruth A. Wallace, *They Call Her Pastor: A New Role for Catholic Women* (Albany: State University of New York Press, 1992), 5.

34. Deborah Halter, *The Papal "No": A Comprehensive Guide to the Vatican's Rejection of Women's Ordination* (New York: Crossroad, 2004), 37–39.

35. "Lay Ecclesial Ministers in the Catholic Church," *FutureChurch*, accessed 3 June 2014, http://futurechurch.org/women-in-church-leadership/women-in-church-leadership/lay-ecclesial-ministers-in-catholic-church.

36. Wallace, *They Call Her Pastor*, 19.

37. See Roman Catholic Womenpriests, http://romancatholicwomenpriests.org/.

38. Roman Catholic Womenpriests, "The Ordained Members," accessed 3 June 2014, http://romancatholicwomenpriests.org/ordained.htm.

39. Betty A. DeBerg, *Ungodly Women: Gender and the First Wave of American Fundamentalism* (Minneapolis: Fortress, 1990), vii–viii.

40. Margaret Lamberts Bendroth, *Fundamentalism and Gender, 1875 to the Present* (New Haven: Yale University Press, 1993), 156.

41. Julie Ingersoll, *Evangelical Christian Women: War Stories in the Gender Battles* (New York: New York University Press, 2003), 14.

42. Carl L. Kell and L. Raymond Camp, *In the Name of the Father: The Rhetoric of the New Southern Baptist Convention* (Carbondale: Southern Illinois University Press, 1999), 79.

43. Kell and Camp, *In the Name of the Father*, 81.

44. Southern Baptist Convention, "The Baptist Faith and Message," 2000 revision, accessed 3 June 2014, http://www.sbc.net/bfm/bfm2000.asp.

45. Pamela R. Durso, "The State of Baptist Women," *Baptist Women in Ministry*, June 2011, 6–11, http://www.bwim.info/files/State%20of%20Women%20in%20 Baptist%20Life%202010.pdf.

46. Colleen McDannell, "Beyond Dr. Dobson: Women, Girls, and Focus on the Family," in *Women and Twentieth-Century Protestantism*, ed. by Margaret Lamberts Bendroth and Virginia Lieson Brereton (Urbana: University of Illinois Press, 2002), 113–31.

47. Ronnee Schreiber, *Righting Feminism: Conservative Women and American Politics* (New York: Oxford University Press, 2008), 30.

48. Rebekah Tooley, "Walking among the Muslims," *Family Voice*, November–December 2009, 9, accessed 3 August 2013, http://www.cwfa.org/ familyvoice/2009–11/novdec09.pdf, italics in original (site discontinued).

49. Concerned Women for America, "Our Issues," accessed 3 June 2014, http://www. cwfa.org/about/issues/.

50. Schreiber, *Righting Feminism*, 30.

51. Quoting Wendi Kaiser, in Elinor Burkett, *The Right Women: A Journey through the Heart of Conservative America* (New York: Lisa Drew/Scribner, 1998), 156.

52. Burkett, *The Right Women*, 154.

53. Quoting Wendi Kaiser, in Burkett, *The Right Women*, 157.

54. Marabel Morgan, *The Total Woman* (Old Tappan, NJ: Fleming H. Revell, 1973), 117.

55. Beverly LaHaye, *The Spirit-Controlled Woman* (Eugene, OR: Harvest House, 1995), 68.

56. R. Marie Griffith, *God's Daughters: Evangelical Women and the Power of Submission* (Berkeley: University of California Press, 1997), 199.

57. Brenda E. Brasher, *Godly Women: Fundamentalism and Female Power* (New Brunswick: Rutgers University Press, 1998), 6.

58. Ingersoll, *Evangelical Christian Women*, 33–46.

59. Joni Eareckson Tada with Joe Musser, *Joni: An Unforgettable Story*, 20th anniversary ed. (Grand Rapids, MI: Zondervan, 1996).

60. Corrie ten Boom, with John and Elizabeth Sherrill, *The Hiding Place* (Uhrichsville, OH: Barbour, 1971). For best seller information, see Rhonda Renee Gamble, "Evangelical Representations of Corrie ten Boom" (M.A. thesis, San Diego State University, 1997), 52.

61. Lawrence Baron, "Supersessionism without Contempt: The Holocaust Evangelism of Corrie ten Boom," in *Christian Responses to the Holocaust*, ed. Donald J. Dietrich (Syracuse: Syracuse University Press, 2003), 125.

62. Frances S. Adeney, *Christian Women in Indonesia: A Narrative Study of Gender and Religion* (Syracuse: Syracuse University Press, 2003), 12.

63. Adeney, *Christian Women in Indonesia*, 84.

64. Heather L. Claussen, *Unconventional Sisterhood: Feminist Catholic Nuns in the Philippines* (Ann Arbor: University of Michigan Press, 2001), 184.

65. Leymah Gbowee, with Carol Mithers, *Mighty Be Our Powers: How Sisterhood, Prayer, and Sex Changed a Nation at War; A Memoir* (New York: Beast Books, 2011), 109.

66. Gbowee, *Mighty Be Our Powers*, 122.

67. Gbowee, *Mighty Be Our Powers*, 151.

68. Penny Lernoux, with Arthur Jones and Robert Ellsberg, *Hearts on Fire: The Story of the Maryknoll Sisters* (Maryknoll, NY: Orbis, 1993), 246.

69. Harkness, *Women in Church and Society*, 130.

70. Beth A. Cooper, *Under the Stained Glass Ceiling: Sexual Harassment of United Methodist Clergywomen by Laity* (San Diego: Frontrowliving, 2011), 61–62.

71. Sarah Coakley, *Powers and Submissions: Spirituality, Philosophy and Gender* (Malden, MA: Blackwell, 2002), 33.

72. Mary C. Grey, *Sacred Longings: The Ecological Spirit and Global Culture* (Minneapolis: Fortress, 2004), 74.

73. Grey, *Sacred Longings*, 142.

74. Deanna A. Thompson, *Crossing the Divide: Luther, Feminism, and the Cross* (Minneapolis: Fortress, 2004), xi.

75. Serene Jones, *Feminist Theory and Christian Theology: Cartographies of Grace* (Minneapolis: Fortress, 2000), 63.

76. Jones, *Feminist Theory and Christian Theology*, 66.

CONCLUSION

1. Evelyn Underhill, "The Ideals of the Ministry of Women," in *Mixed Pasture: Twelve Essays and Addresses*, ed. Evelyn Underhill (1913; reprint, Freeport, NY: Books for Libraries Press, 1963), 117.

2. Pauli Murray, "Mary Has Chosen the Best Part," in Bettye Collier-Thomas, *Daughters of Thunder: Black Women Preachers and Their Sermons, 1850–1979* (San Francisco: Jossey-Bass, 1998), 246.

3. Underhill, "The Ideals of the Ministry of Women," 121.

4. Teresa of Avila, *Spiritual Testimonies*, in *The Collected Works of St. Teresa of Avila*, vol. 1, trans. Kieran Kavanaugh and Otilio Rodriguez (Washington, D.C.: Institute of Carmelite Studies, 1978), 426.

5. Catherine Booth, *Female Ministry; or, Woman's Right to Preach the Gospel*, in *Holiness Tracts Defending the Ministry of Women*, ed. Donald W. Dayton (New York: Garland, 1985), 23.

WORKS CITED

Adeney, Frances S. *Christian Women in Indonesia: A Narrative Study of Gender and Religion*. Syracuse: Syracuse University Press, 2003.

Ahlgren, Gillian T. W. *Teresa of Avila and the Politics of Sanctity*. Ithaca: Cornell University Press, 1996.

Alexander, Estrelda. *The Women of Azusa Street*. Cleveland: Pilgrim Press, 2005.

Apostolos-Cappadona, Diane. "On the Visual and the Vision: The Magdalen in Early Christian and Byzantine Art and Culture." In *Mariam, the Magdalen, and the Mother*, edited by Deirdre Good, 123–45. Bloomington: Indiana University Press, 2005.

Aquino, María Pilar. *Our Cry for Life: Feminist Theology from Latin America*. Translated by Dinah Livingstone. Maryknoll, NY: Orbis, 1993.

Armstrong, Karen. *The Gospel according to Woman: Christianity's Creation of the Sex War in the West*. London: Elm Tree, 1986.

Baigent, Michael, Richard Leigh, and Henry Lincoln. *Holy Blood, Holy Grail*. New York: Delacorte, 1982.

Bainton, Roland H. *Women of the Reformation in France and England*. Minneapolis: Augsburg, 1973.

———. *Women of the Reformation in Germany and Italy*. Minneapolis: Augsburg, 1971.

Baker, Frank. "Susanna Wesley: Puritan, Parent, Pastor, Protagonist, Pattern." In *Women in New Worlds: Historical Perspectives on the Wesleyan Tradition*, vol. 2, edited by Rosemary Skinner Keller, Louise L. Queen, and Hilah F. Thomas, 112–31. Nashville: Abingdon, 1981.

Bardsley, Sandy. *Women's Roles in the Middle Ages*. Westport, CT: Greenwood, 2007.

Baron, Lawrence. "Supersessionism without Contempt: The Holocaust Evangelism of Corrie ten Boom." In *Christian Responses to the Holocaust*, edited by Donald J. Dietrich, 119–31. Syracuse: Syracuse University Press, 2003.

Bassler, Jouette M. "1 Corinthians." In *The Women's Bible Commentary*, edited by Carol A. Newsom and Sharon H. Ringe, 321–29. London and Louisville, KY: SPCK and Westminster/John Knox Press, 1992.

Basu, Aparna. "Mary Ann Cooke to Mother Teresa: Christian Missionary Women and the Indian Response." In *Women and Missions: Past and Present; Anthropological and Historical Perceptions*, edited by Fiona Bowie, Deborah Kirkwood, and Shirley Ardener, 187–208. Providence, RI: Berg, 1993.

Bednarowski, Mary Farrell. "Outside the Mainstream: Women's Religion and Women's Religious Leaders in Nineteenth-Century America." *Journal of the American Academy of Religion* 48, no. 2 (June 1980): 207–31.

Bellis, Alice Ogden. "Eve in the Apocryphal/Deuterocanonical Books." In *Women in Scripture*, edited by Carol Meyers, 82–83. Boston: Houghton Mifflin, 2000.

Bendroth, Margaret Lamberts. *Fundamentalism and Gender, 1875 to the Present*. New Haven: Yale University Press, 1993.

Blaisdell, Charmarie Jenkins. "The Matrix of Reform: Women in the Lutheran and Calvinist Movements." In *Triumph over Silence: Women in Protestant History*, edited by Richard L. Greaves, 13–44. Westport, CT: Greenwood, 1985.

Booth, Catherine. *Female Ministry; or, Woman's Right to Preach the Gospel*. In *Holiness Tracts Defending the Ministry of Women*, edited by Donald W. Dayton. New York: Garland, 1985.

Børresen, Kari. "Mary in Catholic Theology." In *Mary in the Churches*, edited by Hans Küng and Jürgen Moltmann, 48–56. Edinburgh and New York: T. & T. Clark and Seabury Press, 1983.

Brasher, Brenda E. *Godly Women: Fundamentalism and Female Power*. New Brunswick: Rutgers University Press, 1998.

Brenner, Rachel Feldhay. *Writing as Resistance: Four Women Confronting the Holocaust; Edith Stein, Simone Weil, Anne Frank, Etty Hillesum*. University Park: Pennsylvania State University Press, 1997.

Briggs, Sheila. "Galatians." In *Searching the Scriptures*, vol. 2, *A Feminist Commentary*, edited by Elisabeth Schüssler Fiorenza, with Ann Brock and Shelly Matthews, 218–36. New York: Crossroad, 1994.

Brock, Ann Graham. *Mary Magdalene, The First Apostle: The Struggle for Authority*. Cambridge, MA: Harvard Theological Studies, 2003.

Bromley, David G., and Rachel S. Bobbitt. "Visions of the Virgin Mary: The Organizational Development of Marian Apparitional Movements." *Nova Religio* 14, no. 3 (2011): 5–41.

Brooten, Bernadette. "'Junia . . . Outstanding among the Apostles' (Romans 16:7)." In *Women Priests: A Catholic Commentary on the Vatican Declaration*, edited by Leonard Swidler and Arlene Swidler, 141–44. New York: Paulist, 1977.

Brown, Dan. *The Da Vinci Code*. New York: Doubleday, 2003.

Brown, Earl Kent. *Women of Mr. Wesley's Methodism*. New York: Edwin Mellen, 1983.

Brown-Grant, Rosalind. *Christine de Pizan and the Moral Defence of Women: Reading beyond Gender*. Cambridge: Cambridge University Press, 1999.

Burkett, Elinor. *The Right Women: A Journey through the Heart of Conservative America*. New York: Lisa Drew/Scribner, 1998.

Burrus, Virginia. *Chastity as Autonomy: Women in the Stories of the Apocryphal Acts*. Lewiston, NY: Edwin Mellen, 1987.

Bynum, Caroline Walker. *Holy Feast and Holy Fast: The Religious Significance of Food to Medieval Women*. Berkeley: University of California Press, 1987.

———. *Jesus as Mother: Studies in the Spirituality of the High Middle Ages.* Berkeley: University of California Press, 1982.

Cahill, Thomas. *How the Irish Saved Civilization: The Untold Story of Ireland's Heroic Role from the Fall of Rome to the Rise of Medieval Europe.* New York: Doubleday, 1995.

Carroll, Michael P. *The Cult of the Virgin Mary: Psychological Origins.* Princeton: Princeton University Press, 1986.

Castelli, Elizabeth A. "Paul on Women and Gender." In *Women and Christian Origins*, edited by Ross Shepard Kraemer and Mary Rose D'Angelo, 221–35. New York: Oxford University Press, 1999.

Clark, Elizabeth A. "Ascetic Renunciation and Feminine Advancement: A Paradox of Late Ancient Christianity." In *Ascetic Piety and Women's Faith: Essays on Late Ancient Christianity*, edited by Elizabeth A. Clark, 175–208. Lewiston, NY: Edwin Mellen, 1986.

———. "Faltonia Betitia Proba and Her Virgilian Poem: The Christian Matron as Artist." In *Ascetic Piety and Women's Faith: Essays on Late Ancient Christianity*, edited by Elizabeth A. Clark, 124–52. Lewiston, NY: Edwin Mellen, 1986.

———. *Women in the Early Church.* Wilmington, DE: Michael Glazier, 1983.

Clark, Stuart. "Protestant Demonology: Sin, Superstition, and Society (c. 1520–c. 1630)." In *Early Modern European Witchcraft: Centres and Peripheries*, edited by Bengt Ankarloo and Gustav Henningsen, 45–81. Oxford: Clarendon, 1990.

Claussen, Heather L. *Unconventional Sisterhood: Feminist Catholic Nuns in the Philippines.* Ann Arbor: University of Michigan Press, 2001.

Clifford, Anne M. *Introducing Feminist Theology.* Maryknoll, NY: Orbis, 2001.

Coakley, Sarah. *Powers and Submissions: Spirituality, Philosophy and Gender.* Malden, MA: Blackwell, 2002.

Cobb, L. Stephanie. *Dying to Be Men: Gender and Language in Early Christian Martyr Texts.* New York: Columbia University Press, 2008.

Collier-Thomas, Bettye. *Daughters of Thunder: Black Women Preachers and Their Sermons, 1850–1979.* San Francisco: Jossey-Bass, 1998.

Concerned Women for America. "Our Issues." Accessed 3 June 2014. http://www.cwfa.org/about/issues/.

Conn, Marie A. *Noble Daughters: Unheralded Women in Western Christianity, 13th to 18th Centuries.* Westport, CT: Greenwood, 2000.

Connor, Carolyn L. *Women of Byzantium.* New Haven: Yale University Press, 2004.

Constable, Giles. *Three Studies in Medieval Religious and Social Thought: The Interpretation of Mary and Martha; The Ideal of the Imitation of Christ; The Orders of Society.* Cambridge: Cambridge University Press, 1995.

Coon, Lynda L. *Sacred Fictions: Holy Women and Hagiography in Late Antiquity.* Philadelphia: University of Pennsylvania Press, 1997.

Cooper, Beth A. *Under the Stained Glass Ceiling: Sexual Harassment of United Methodist Clergywomen by Laity.* San Diego: Frontrowliving, 2011.

Cormack, Robin. "Women and Icons, and Women in Icons." In *Women, Men and Eunuchs: Gender in Byzantium*, edited by Liz James, 24–51. London: Routledge, 1997.

Council on Biblical Manhood and Womanhood. "The Danvers Statement." In *Eve and Adam: Jewish, Christian, and Muslim Readings on Genesis and Gender*, edited by Kristen E. Kvam, Linda S. Schearing, and Valarie H. Ziegler, 387–90. Bloomington: Indiana University Press, 1999.

Cross, Claire. "'Great Reasoners in Scripture': The Activities of Women Lollards, 1380–1530." In *Medieval Women*, edited by Derek Baker, 359–80. Oxford: Basil Blackwell, 1978.

Culver, Elsie Thomas. *Women in the World of Religion*. Garden City, NY: Doubleday, 1967.

Dalarum, Jacques. "The Clerical Gaze." Translated by Arthur Goldhammer. In *A History of Women in the West*, vol. 2, *Silences of the Middle Ages*, edited by Christiane Klapisch-Zuber, 15–42. Cambridge, MA: Belknap, 1992.

Daly, Mary. *Beyond God the Father: Toward a Philosophy of Women's Liberation*. Boston: Beacon, 1973.

———. *The Church and the Second Sex: With a New Feminist Postchristian Introduction by the Author*. 1968; reprint with new introduction, New York: Harper and Row, 1975.

D'Angelo, Mary Rose. "'I Have Seen the Lord': Mary Magdalen as Visionary, Early Christian Prophecy, and the Context of John 20:14–18." In *Mariam, the Magdalen, and the Mother*, edited by Deirdre Good, 95–122. Bloomington: Indiana University Press, 2005.

———. "Martha." In *Women in Scripture*, edited by Carol Meyers, 114–16. Boston: Houghton Mifflin, 2000.

Danniel, François, and Brigitte Oliver. *Woman Is the Glory of Man*. Translated by M. Angeline Bouchard. Westminster, MD: Newman, 1966.

Day, Dorothy. *Loaves and Fishes*. Maryknoll, NY: Orbis, 1997.

De Beauvoir, Simone. *The Second Sex*. Translated by H. M. Parshley. New York: Bantam, 1952.

DeBerg, Betty A. *Ungodly Women: Gender and the First Wave of American Fundamentalism*. Minneapolis: Fortress Press, 1990.

De Boer, Esther. *Mary Magdalene: Beyond the Myth*. Translated by John Bowden. Harrisburg, PA: Trinity Press International, 1997.

Deen, Edith. *All of the Women of the Bible*. New York: Harper, 1955.

———. *Great Women of the Christian Faith*. New York: Harper and Brothers, 1959.

Denzey, Nicola. *The Bone Gatherers: The Lost Worlds of Early Christian Women*. Boston: Beacon, 2007.

Dewey, Joanna. "1 Timothy." In *The Women's Bible Commentary*, edited by Carol A. Newsom and Sharon H. Ringe, 353–58. London and Louisville, KY: SPCK and Westminster/John Knox Press, 1992.

———. "The Gospel of Mark." In *Searching the Scriptures*, vol. 2, *A Feminist Commentary*, edited by Elisabeth Schüssler Fiorenza, with Ann Brock and Shelly Matthews, 470–509. New York: Crossroad, 1994.

Durso, Pamela R. "The State of Baptist Women." *Baptist Women in Ministry*, June 2011, 6–11. http://www.bwim.info/files/State%20of%20Women%20in%20Baptist%20 Life%202010.pdf.

Eason, Andrew Mark. *Women in God's Army: Gender and Equality in the Early Salvation Army*. Waterloo, Ontario: Wilfrid Laurier University Press, 2003.

Ehrman, Bart D., ed. *The Acts of Thecla*. In *Lost Scriptures: Books That Did Not Make It into the New Testament*, 113–21. New York: Oxford University Press, 2003.

Elizondo, Virgil. "Mary and the Poor: A Model of Evangelising Ecumenism." In *Mary in the Churches*, edited by Hans Küng and Jürgen Moltmann, 59–65. Edinburgh and New York: T. & T. Clark and Seabury Press, 1983.

Epp, Eldon Jay. *Junia: The First Woman Apostle*. Minneapolis: Fortress, 2005.

Epstein, Barbara Leslie. *The Politics of Domesticity: Women, Evangelism, and Temperance in Nineteenth-Century America*. Middletown, CT: Wesleyan University Press, 1981.

Espín, Oliva M. "The Enduring Popularity of Rosa de Lima, First Saint of the Americas: Women, Bodies, Sainthood, and National Identity." *CrossCurrents* 6, no. 1 (March 2011): 6–26.

Ewens, Mary. "The Leadership of Nuns in Immigrant Catholicism." In *Women and Religion in America*, vol. 1, *The Nineteenth Century*, edited by Rosemary Radford Ruether and Rosemary Skinner Keller, 101–7. San Francisco: Harper and Row, 1981.

Fabella, Virginia. "Christology from an Asian Woman's Perspective." In *We Dare to Dream: Doing Theology as Asian Women*, edited by Virginia Fabella and Sun Ai Lee Park, 3–14. Kowloon, Hong Kong: Asian Women's Resource Centre for Culture and Theology, 1989.

Fell, Margaret. *Womens Speaking Justified (1667)*. Los Angeles: University of California, 1979.

FitzGerald, Kyriaki Karidoyanes. *Women Deacons in the Orthodox Church: Called to Holiness and Ministry*. Brookline, MA: Holy Cross Orthodox Press, 1999.

Fredriksen, Paula. *From Jesus to Christ: The Origins of the New Testament Images of Jesus*. 2d ed. New Haven: Yale University Press, 2000.

Gamble, Rhonda Renee. "Evangelical Representations of Corrie ten Boom." M.A. thesis, San Diego State University, 1997.

Gbowee, Leymah, with Carol Mithers. *Mighty Be Our Powers: How Sisterhood, Prayer, and Sex Changed a Nation at War; A Memoir*. New York: Beast Books, 2011.

Gebara, Ivone. "Women Doing Theology in Latin America." In *Through Her Eyes: Women's Theology from Latin America*, edited by Elsa Tamez, 37–48. Maryknoll, NY: Orbis, 1989.

Gebara, Ivone, and Maria Clara Bingemer. *Mary: Mother of God, Mother of the Poor*. Translated by Phillip Berryman. Maryknoll, NY: Orbis, 1989.

Godbeer, Richard. *The Salem Witch Hunt: A Brief History with Documents*. New York: Bedford/St. Martin's, 2011.

Good, Deirdre. "The Miriamic Secret." In *Mariam, the Magdalen, and the Mother*, edited by Deirdre Good, 3–24. Bloomington: Indiana University Press, 2005.

Gottschalk, Stephen. *The Emergence of Christian Science in American Religious Life*. Berkeley: University of California Press, 1973.

Graham, Roy E. *Ellen G. White: Co-Founder of the Seventh-day Adventist Church*. New York: Peter Lang, 1985.

Grant, Jacquelyn. *White Women's Christ and Black Women's Jesus: Feminist Christology and Womanist Response*. Atlanta: Scholars Press, 1989.

Greene, Meg. *Mother Teresa: A Biography*. Westport, CT: Greenwood, 2004.

Greene-McCreight, Kathryn. *Feminist Reconstructions of Christian Doctrine*. New York: Oxford University Press, 2000.

Greer, Allan. *Mohawk Saint: Catherine Tekakwitha and the Jesuits*. New York: Oxford University Press, 2005.

Gregory, Bishop of Nyssa. *The Life of Saint Macrina*. Translated by Kevin Corrigan. Toronto: Peregrina, 1987.

Grey, Mary C. *Sacred Longings: The Ecological Spirit and Global Culture*. Minneapolis: Fortress, 2004.

Griffith, R. Marie. *God's Daughters: Evangelical Women and the Power of Submission*. Berkeley: University of California Press, 1997.

Halter, Deborah. *The Papal "No": A Comprehensive Guide to the Vatican's Rejection of Women's Ordination*. New York: Crossroad, 2004.

Hardesty, Nancy A. *Women Called to Witness: Evangelical Feminism in the Nineteenth Century*. 2d. ed. Knoxville: University of Tennessee Press, 1999.

Harkness, Georgia. *Women in Church and Society: A Historical and Theological Inquiry*. Nashville: Abingdon, 1972.

Harrington, Patricia. "Mother of Death, Mother of Rebirth: The Mexican Virgin of Guadalupe." *Journal of the American Academy of Religion* 56, no. 1 (Spring 1988): 25–50.

Henningsen, Gustav, and Bengt Ankarloo. Introduction to *Early Modern European Witchcraft: Centres and Peripheries*, edited by Bengt Ankarloo and Gustav Henningsen, 1–15. Oxford: Clarendon, 1990.

Herrin, Judith. "Women and the Faith in Icons in Early Christianity." In *Culture, Ideology and Politics: Essays for Eric Hobsbawm*, edited by Raphael Samuel and Gareth Stedman Jones, 56–83. London: Routledge and Kegan Paul, 1982.

Hitchens, Christopher. *The Missionary Position: Mother Teresa in Theory and Practice*. London: Verso, 1995.

Holmes, Paula Elizabeth. "The Narrative Repatriation of Blessed Kateri Tekakwitha." *Anthropologica* 43, no. 1 (2001): 87–103.

Hoover, Theressa. "Black Women and the Churches: Triple Jeopardy." In *Black Theology: A Documentary History, 1966–1979*, edited by Gayraud S. Wilmore and James H. Cone, 377–88. Maryknoll, NY: Orbis, 1979.

Huber, Mary Taylor, and Nancy C. Lutkehaus. "Introduction: Gendered Missions at Home and Abroad." In *Gendered Missions: Women and Men in Missionary Discourse and Practice*, edited by Mary Taylor Huber and Nancy C. Lutkehaus, 1–38. Ann Arbor: University of Michigan Press, 1999.

Humez, Jean M., ed. *Mother's First-Born Daughters: Early Shaker Writings on Women and Religion*. Bloomington: Indiana University Press, 1993.

Ingersoll, Julie. *Evangelical Christian Women: War Stories in the Gender Battles*. New York: New York University Press, 2003.

Irwin, Joyce L., ed. *Womanhood in Radical Protestantism, 1525–1675*. New York: Edwin Mellen, 1979.

Isasi-Díaz, Ada María. *Mujerista Theology: A Theology for the Twenty-First Century*. Maryknoll, NY: Orbis, 1996.

Jacobs, Sylvia M. "Their 'Special Mission': Afro-American Women as Missionaries to the Congo, 1894–1937." In *Black Americans and the Missionary Movement in Africa*, edited by Sylvia M. Jacobs, 155–76. Westport, CT: Greenwood, 1982.

James, Liz. *Empresses and Power in Early Byzantium*. New York: Leicester University Press, 2001.

Jansen, Katherine Ludwig. *The Making of the Magdalen: Preaching and Popular Devotion in the Later Middle Ages*. Princeton: Princeton University Press, 2000.

Jeffrey, Julie Roy. *Converting the West: A Biography of Narcissa Whitman*. Norman: University of Oklahoma Press, 1991.

Johnson, Elizabeth A. *She Who Is: The Mystery of God in Feminist Theological Discourse*. New York: Crossroad, 1992.

Jones, Serene. *Feminist Theory and Christian Theology: Cartographies of Grace*. Minneapolis: Fortress, 2000.

Jorgensen, Danny L. "Gender-Inclusive Images of God: A Sociological Interpretation of Early Shakerism and Mormonism." *Nova Religio* 4, no. 1 (October 2000): 66–85.

Juana Inés de la Cruz, Sor. *The Answer/La respuesta*. Edited and translated by Electa Arenal and Amanda Powell. New York: Feminist Press, 1994.

Julian of Norwich. *Revelations of Divine Love*. Translated by Clifton Wolters. New York: Penguin, 1966.

Kan, Sergei. "Clan Mothers and Godmothers: Tlingit Women and Russian Orthodox Christianity, 1840–1940." *Ethnohistory* 43, no. 4 (Autumn 1996): 613–41.

Karris, Robert J. "The Pastoral Letters." In *The Oxford Companion to the Bible*, edited by Bruce M. Metzger and Michael D. Coogan, 573–76. New York: Oxford University Press, 1993.

Kell, Carl L., and L. Raymond Camp. *In the Name of the Father: The Rhetoric of the New Southern Baptist Convention*. Carbondale: Southern Illinois University Press, 1999.

Ketter, Peter. *Christ and Womankind*. Translated from 2d rev. ed. by Isabel McHugh. 1937; reprint, Westminster, MD: Newman, 1952.

King, Karen L. *The Gospel of Mary of Magdala: Jesus and the First Woman Apostle.* Santa Rosa, CA: Polebridge, 2003.

———. *What Is Gnosticism?* Cambridge, MA: Belknap, 2003.

King, Karen L., with AnneMarie Luijendijk. "Jesus Said to Them 'My Wife': A New Coptic Gospel Papyrus." Accessed 3 June 2014. http://www.hds.harvard.edu/sites/hds.harvard.edu/files/attachments/faculty-research/research-projects/the-gospel-of-jesuss-wife/29865/King_JesusSaidToThem_draft_0920.pdf.

Kolodiejchuk, Brian, ed. *Mother Teresa: Come Be My Light; The Private Writings of the "Saint of Calcutta."* New York: Doubleday, 2007.

Kosambi, Meera. Introduction to *Pandita Ramabai through Her Own Words: Selected Works,* edited by Meera Kosambi, 1–32. New Delhi: Oxford University Press, 2000.

LaHaye, Beverly. *The Spirit-Controlled Woman.* Eugene, OR: Harvest House, 1995.

"Lay Ecclesial Ministers in the Catholic Church." *FutureChurch.* Accessed 3 June 2014. http://futurechurch.org/women-in-church-leadership/women-in-church-leadership/lay-ecclesial-ministers-in-catholic-church.

Leith, John H., ed. *Creeds of the Churches.* 3d ed. Louisville: John Knox Press, 1982.

Lernoux, Penny, with Arthur Jones and Robert Ellsberg. *Hearts on Fire: The Story of the Maryknoll Sisters.* Maryknoll, NY: Orbis, 1993.

Levine, Amy-Jill. "Matthew." In *The Women's Bible Commentary,* edited by Carol A. Newsom and Sharon H. Ringe, 252–62. London and Louisville, KY: SPCK and Westminster/John Knox Press, 1992.

Life of Adam and Eve. Translated by M. D. Johnson. In *The Old Testament Pseudepigrapha,* vol. 2, edited by James H. Charlesworth, 249–95. New York: Doubleday, 1985.

Limberis, Vasiliki. "Widow Pleading with a Judge." In *Women in Scripture,* edited by Carol Meyers, 449. Boston: Houghton Mifflin, 2000.

Luther, Martin. *Lectures on Genesis.* In *Women and Religion: The Original Sourcebook of Women in Christian Thought,* rev. and exp., edited by Elizabeth A. Clark and Herbert Richardson, 163–68. San Francisco: HarperSanFrancisco, 1996.

MacDonald, Dennis Ronald. *The Legend and the Apostle: The Battle for Paul in Story and Canon.* Philadelphia: Westminster, 1983.

MacDonald, Margaret Y. *Early Christian Women and Pagan Opinion: The Power of the Hysterical Woman.* Cambridge: Cambridge University Press, 1996.

———. "Rereading Paul: Early Interpreters of Paul on Women and Gender." In *Women and Christian Origins,* edited by Ross Shepard Kraemer and Mary Rose D'Angelo, 236–53. New York: Oxford University Press, 1999.

Mack, Phyllis. *Visionary Women: Ecstatic Prophecy in Seventeenth-Century England.* Berkeley: University of California Press, 1992.

Macy, Gary. *The Hidden History of Women's Ordination: Female Clergy in the Medieval West.* New York: Oxford University Press, 2008.

Madigan, Kevin, and Carolyn Osiek, eds. and trans. *Ordained Women in the Early Church: A Documentary History.* Baltimore: Johns Hopkins University Press, 2005.

Martin, Clarice J. "The Acts of the Apostles." In *Searching the Scriptures*, vol. 2, *A Feminist Commentary*, edited by Elisabeth Schüssler Fiorenza, with Ann Brock and Shelly Matthews, 763–99. New York: Crossroad, 1994.

Mayeski, Marie Anne. *Women at the Table: Three Medieval Theologians*. Collegeville, MN: Liturgical Press, 2004.

McDannell, Colleen. "Beyond Dr. Dobson: Women, Girls, and Focus on the Family." In *Women and Twentieth-Century Protestantism*, edited by Margaret Lamberts Bendroth and Virginia Lieson Brereton, 113–31. Urbana: University of Illinois Press, 2002.

McDougall, Joy Ann. "Women's Work: Feminist Theology for a New Generation." *Christian Century* 122, no. 15 (26 July 2005): 20–25.

McFague, Sallie. *Models of God: Theology for an Ecological, Nuclear Age*. Philadelphia: Fortress, 1987.

McLaughlin, Mary Martin. "Heloise the Abbess: The Expansion of the Paraclete." In *Listening to Heloise: The Voice of the Twelfth-Century Woman*, edited by Bonnie Wheeler, 1–17. New York: St. Martin's, 2000.

McNamara, Jo Ann Kay. *Sisters in Arms: Catholic Nuns through Two Millennia*. Cambridge, MA: Harvard University Press, 1996.

Medieval Sourcebook. *The Passion of Saints Perpetua and Felicitas*. Accessed 3 June 2014. http://www.fordham.edu/halsall/source/perpetua.asp.

Meeks, Wayne A. *The First Urban Christians: The Social World of the Apostle Paul*. New Haven: Yale University Press, 1983.

Merrim, Stephanie. "Toward a Feminist Reading of Sor Juana Inés de la Cruz: Past, Present, and Future Directions in Sor Juana Criticism." In *Feminist Perspectives on Sor Juana Inés de la Cruz*, edited by Stephanie Merrim, 11–37. Detroit: Wayne State University Press, 1991.

Meyers, Carol, ed. *Women in Scripture*. Boston: Houghton Mifflin, 2000.

Mollenkott, Virginia. *Women, Men and the Bible*. Nashville: Abingdon, 1977.

Mooney, Catherine M. "The Authorial Role of Brother A. in the Composition of Angela of Foligno's Revelations." In *Creative Women in Medieval and Early Modern Italy: A Religious and Artistic Renaissance*, edited by E. Ann Matter and John Coakley, 34–63. Philadelphia: University of Pennsylvania Press, 1994.

Morgan, Marabel. *The Total Woman*. Old Tappan, NJ: Fleming H. Revell, 1973.

Murray, Pauli. "Mary Has Chosen the Best Part." In *Daughters of Thunder: Black Women Preachers and Their Sermons, 1850–1979*, by Bettye Collier-Thomas, 245–48. San Francisco: Jossey-Bass, 1998.

Niditch, Susan. "Genesis." In *The Women's Bible Commentary*, edited by Carol A. Newsom and Sharon H. Ringe, 10–25. London and Louisville, KY: SPCK and Westminster/John Knox Press, 1992.

Nim, Ahn Sang. "Feminist Theology in the Korean Church." In *We Dare to Dream: Doing Theology as Asian Women*, edited by Virginia Fabella and Sun Ai Lee Park, 127–34. Kowloon, Hong Kong: Asian Women's Resource Centre for Culture and Theology, 1989.

Norris, Pamela. *Eve: A Biography*. New York: New York University Press, 1999.

O'Connor, June. *The Moral Vision of Dorothy Day: A Feminist Perspective*. New York: Crossroad, 1991.

Oduyoye, Mercy Amba. *Daughters of Anowa: African Women and Patriarchy*. Maryknoll, NY: Orbis, 1995.

Pagels, Elaine. *The Gnostic Gospels*. New York: Vintage, 1979.

Pahl, Jon. *Empire of Sacrifice: The Religious Origins of American Violence*. New York: New York University Press, 2010.

Pathak, Sushil Madhava. *American Missionaries and Hinduism: A Study of Their Contacts from 1813 to 1910*. Delhi, India: Munshiram Manoharlal, 1967.

Pederson, Rena. *The Lost Apostle: Searching for the Truth about Junia*. San Francisco: Jossey-Bass, 2006.

Petroff, Elizabeth Alvilda. *Body and Soul: Essays on Medieval Women and Mysticism*. New York: Oxford University Press, 1994.

Poor, Sara S. *Mechthild of Magdeburg and Her Book: Gender and the Making of Textual Authority*. Philadelphia: University of Pennsylvania Press, 2004.

Pope, Barbara Corrado. "Immaculate and Powerful: The Marian Revival in the Nineteenth Century." In *Immaculate and Powerful: The Female in Sacred Image and Social Reality*, edited by Clarissa W. Atkinson, Constance H. Buchanan, and Margaret R. Miles, 173–200. Boston: Beacon, 1985.

Porete, Marguerite. *The Mirror of Simple Souls*. Translated by Ellen L. Babinsky. New York: Paulist, 1993.

Pruitt, Lisa Joy. *"A Looking-Glass for Ladies": American Protestant Women and the Orient in the Nineteenth Century*. Macon, GA: Mercer University Press, 2005.

Pui-lan, Kwok. "The Emergence of Asian Feminist Consciousness of Culture and Theology." In *We Dare to Dream: Doing Theology as Asian Women*, edited by Virginia Fabella and Sun Ai Lee Park, 92–100. Kowloon, Hong Kong: Asian Women's Resource Centre for Culture and Theology, 1989.

Radice, Betty, ed. and trans. *The Letters of Abelard and Heloise*. New York: Penguin, 1974.

Ranft, Patricia. *Women in Western Intellectual Culture, 600–1500*. New York: Palgrave Macmillan, 2002.

Ransby, Barbara. *Ella Baker and the Black Freedom Movement*. Chapel Hill: University of North Carolina Press, 2003.

Reinhartz, Adele. "The Gospel of John." In *Searching the Scriptures*, vol. 2, *A Feminist Commentary*, edited by Elisabeth Schüssler Fiorenza, with Ann Brock and Shelly Matthews, 561–600. New York: Crossroad, 1994.

Robinson-Hammerstein, Helga. "Women's Prospects in Early Sixteenth-Century Germany: Did Martin Luther's Teaching Make a Difference?" In *Studies on Medieval and Early Modern Women*, vol. 4, *Victims or Viragos?*, edited by Christine Meek and Catherine Lawless, 102–19. Dublin, Ireland: Four Courts Press, 2005.

Roman Catholic Womenpriests. "The Ordained Members." Accessed 3 June 2014. http://romancatholicwomenpriests.org/ordained.htm.

———. Website. Accessed 3 June 2014. http://romancatholicwomenpriests.org/.

Roper, Lyndal. *The Holy Household: Women and Morals in Reformation Augsburg.* Oxford: Clarendon, 1989.

———. *Witch Craze: Terror and Fantasy in Baroque Germany.* New Haven: Yale University Press, 2004.

Rosenthal, Bernard. "Dark Eve." In *Spellbound: Women and Witchcraft in America,* edited by Elizabeth Reis, 75–98. Wilmington, DE: SR Books, 1998.

Ross, Rosetta E. "Lessons and Treasures in Our Mothers' Witness: Why I Write about Black Women's Activism." In *Deeper Shades of Purple: Womanism in Religion and Society,* edited by Stacey M. Floyd-Thomas, 115–27. New York: New York University Press, 2006.

———. *Witnessing and Testifying: Black Women, Religion, and Civil Rights.* Minneapolis: Fortress, 2003.

Rudolf of Fulda. *Life of Leoba.* In *Medieval Sourcebook.* Fordham University. Accessed 3 June 2014. http://www.fordham.edu/halsall/basis/leoba.asp.

Ruether, Rosemary Radford. "Misogynism and Virginal Feminism in the Fathers of the Church." In *Religion and Sexism: Images of Woman in the Jewish and Christian Traditions,* edited by Rosemary Radford Ruether, 150–83. New York: Simon and Schuster, 1974.

———, ed. *Religion and Sexism: Images of Woman in the Jewish and Christian Traditions.* New York: Simon and Schuster, 1974.

———. *Sexism and God-Talk: Toward a Feminist Theology.* Boston: Beacon, 1983.

———. *Women and Redemption: A Theological History.* Minneapolis: Fortress, 1998.

Russell, Letty M. *The Future of Partnership.* Philadelphia: Westminster, 1979.

———. *Human Liberation in a Feminist Perspective.* Philadelphia: Westminster, 1974.

Scanzoni, Letha, and Nancy Hardesty. *All We're Meant to Be: A Biblical Approach to Women's Liberation with Study Guide.* Waco, TX: Word Books, 1974.

Schaberg, Jane. *The Illegitimacy of Jesus: A Feminist Theological Interpretation of the Infancy Narratives.* San Francisco: Harper and Row, 1987.

———. "Luke." In *The Women's Bible Commentary,* edited by Carol A. Newsom and Sharon H. Ringe, 275–92. London and Louisville, KY: SPCK and Westminster/John Knox Press, 1992.

———. *The Resurrection of Mary Magdalene: Legends, Apocrypha, and the Christian Testament.* New York: Continuum, 2002.

Schneider, Carl J., and Dorothy Schneider. *In Their Own Right: The History of American Clergywomen.* New York: Crossroad, 1997.

Schreiber, Ronnee. *Righting Feminism: Conservative Women and American Politics.* New York: Oxford University Press, 2008.

Schulenburg, Jane Tibbetts. *Forgetful of Their Sex: Female Sanctity and Society, ca. 500–1100.* Chicago: University of Chicago Press, 1998.

Schüssler Fiorenza, Elisabeth. *In Memory of Her: A Feminist Theological Reconstruction of Christian Origins.* New York: Crossroad, 1983.

————. "Missionaries, Apostles, Co-workers: Romans 16 and the Reconstruction of Women's Early Christian History." In *Feminist Theology: A Reader*, edited by Ann Loades, 57–71. London and Louisville, KY: SPCK and Westminster/John Knox Press, 1990.

Seim, Turid Karlsen. "The Gospel of Luke." In *Searching the Scriptures*, vol. 2, *A Feminist Commentary*, edited by Elisabeth Schüssler Fiorenza, with Ann Brock and Shelly Matthews, 728–62. New York: Crossroad, 1994.

Seton, Elizabeth. *Selected Writings*. Edited by Ellin Kelly and Annabelle Melville. New York: Paulist, 1987.

Shoemaker, Stephen J. "Jesus' Gnostic Mom: Mary of Nazareth and the 'Gnostic Mary' Traditions." In *Mariam, the Magdalen, and the Mother*, edited by Deirdre Good, 153–82. Bloomington: Indiana University Press, 2005.

————. "Rethinking the 'Gnostic Mary': Mary of Nazareth and Mary of Magdala in Early Christian Tradition." *Journal of Early Christian Studies* 9, no. 4 (Winter 2001): 555–95.

Simons, Walter. *Cities of Ladies: Beguine Communities in the Medieval Low Countries, 1200–1565*. Philadelphia: University of Pennsylvania Press, 2001.

Southern Baptist Convention. "The Baptist Faith and Message." 2000 revision. Accessed 3 June 2014. http://www.sbc.net/bfm/bfm2000.asp.

Stanley, Susie C. *Holy Boldness: Women Preachers' Autobiographies and the Sanctified Self*. Knoxville: University of Tennessee Press, 2002.

Stanton, Elizabeth Cady. *The Woman's Bible*. 1895; reprint, Boston: Northeastern University Press, 1993.

Stark, Rodney. *The Rise of Christianity: How the Obscure, Marginal Jesus Movement Became the Dominant Religious Force in the Western World in a Few Centuries*. New York: HarperCollins, 1997.

St. Nina Quarterly. Accessed 3 June 2014. http://www.stnina.org/.

Swidler, Leonard. "Jesus Was a Feminist." *Catholic World* 212 (January 1971): 177–83.

Tabor, James. *The Jesus Dynasty: The Hidden History of Jesus, His Royal Family, and the Birth of Christianity*. New York: Simon and Schuster, 2006.

Tada, Joni Eareckson, with Joe Musser. *Joni: An Unforgettable Story*. 20th anniversary ed. Grand Rapids, MI: Zondervan, 1996.

Talbot, Alice-Mary. "The Devotional Life of Laywomen." In *Byzantine Christianity*, vol. 3 of *A People's History of Christianity*, edited by Derek Krueger, 201–20. Minneapolis: Fortress, 2006.

————. *Women and Religious Life in Byzantium*. Burlington, VT: Ashgate, 2001.

Tavard, George H. *The Thousand Faces of the Virgin Mary*. Collegeville, MN: Liturgical Press, 1996.

Ten Boom, Corrie, with John and Elizabeth Sherrill. *The Hiding Place*. Uhrichsville, OH: Barbour, 1971.

Teresa of Avila. *The Book of Her Life*. In *The Collected Works of St. Teresa of Avila*, vol. 1. Translated by Kieran Kavanaugh and Otilio Rodriguez, 15–365. Washington, D.C.: Institute of Carmelite Studies, 1978.

———. *The Interior Castle*. Translated by Mirabai Starr. New York: Riverhead, 2003.

———. *Spiritual Testimonies*. In *The Collected Works of St. Teresa of Avila*, vol. 1. Translated by Kieran Kavanaugh and Otilio Rodriguez, 369–438. Washington, D.C.: Institute of Carmelite Studies, 1978.

Tertullian. *On the Apparel of Women*. Translated by S. Thelwall. In *Ante-Nicene Fathers*, vol. 4, American ed., edited by Alexander Roberts and James Donaldson, 14–25. Grand Rapids, MI: Eerdmans, 1968.

———. *On the Veiling of Virgins*. Translated by S. Thelwall. In *The Tertullian Project*. Accessed 3 June 2014. http://www.tertullian.org/anf/anf04/anf04–09.htm#P624_147158.

Thomas Aquinas. "Selections from the *Summa Theologica*." In *Women and Religion: The Original Sourcebook of Women in Christian Thought*, rev. and exp., edited by Elizabeth A. Clark and Herbert Richardson, 67–89. San Francisco: HarperSanFrancisco, 1996.

Thompson, Deanna A. *Crossing the Divide: Luther, Feminism, and the Cross*. Minneapolis: Fortress, 2004.

Thurston, Bonnie Bowman. *The Widows: A Women's Ministry in the Early Church*. Minneapolis: Fortress, 1989.

Tooley, Rebekah. "Walking among the Muslims." *Family Voice*, November–December 2009, 7–9. Accessed 3 August 2013. http://www.cwfa.org/familyvoice/2009–11/novdec09.pdf. Site discontinued.

Torjesen, Karen Jo. "Reconstruction of Women's Early Christian History." In *Searching the Scriptures*, vol. 1, *A Feminist Introduction*, edited by Elisabeth Schüssler Fiorenza, with Shelly Matthews, 290–310. New York: Crossroad, 1993.

———. *When Women Were Priests: Women's Leadership in the Early Church and the Scandal of Their Subordination in the Rise of Christianity*. San Francisco: HarperSanFrancisco, 1993.

Townes, Emilie M. *Womanist Justice, Womanist Hope*. Atlanta: Scholars Press, 1993.

Trible, Phyllis. "Depatriarchalizing in Biblical Interpretation." *Journal of the American Association of Religion* 41, no. 1 (March 1973): 30–48.

Underhill, Evelyn. "The Ideals of the Ministry of Women." In *Mixed Pasture: Twelve Essays and Addresses*, 113–22. 1913; reprint, Freeport, NY: Books for Libraries Press, 1963.

Van Schurman, Anna Maria. *Whether a Christian Woman Should Be Educated, and Other Writings from her Intellectual Circle*. Edited and translated by Joyce L. Irwin. Chicago: University of Chicago Press, 1998.

Vogt, Peter. "A Voice for Themselves: Women as Participants in Congregational Discourse in the Eighteenth-Century Moravian Movement." In *Women Preachers and Prophets through Two Millennia of Christianity*, edited by Beverly Mayne Kienzle and Pamela J. Walker, 227–47. Berkeley: University of California Press, 1998.

Wallace, Ruth A. *They Call Her Pastor: A New Role for Catholic Women*. Albany: State University of New York Press, 1992.

Walsh, Mary-Paula. *Feminism and Christian Tradition: An Annotated Bibliography and Critical Introduction to the Literature*. Westport, CT: Greenwood, 1999.

Ward, Kevin. "Africa." In *A World History of Christianity*, edited by Adrian Hastings, 192–237. Grand Rapids, MI: Eerdmans, 1999.

Warner, Marina. *Alone of All Her Sex: The Myth and the Cult of the Virgin Mary*. New York: Vintage, 1983.

Warnicke, Retha M. *Women of the English Renaissance and Reformation*. Westport, CT: Greenwood, 1983.

Welter, Barbara. "The Cult of True Womanhood: 1820–1860." *American Quarterly* 18, no. 2, part 1 (Summer 1966): 151–74.

Wemple, Suzanne Fonay. "Women from the Fifth to the Tenth Century." In *A History of Women in the West*, vol. 2, *Silences of the Middle Ages*, edited by Christiane Klapisch-Zuber, 169–201. Cambridge, MA: Belknap, 1992.

West, Angela. "Sex and Salvation: A Christian Feminist Bible Study on 1 Corinthians 6.12–7.39." In *Feminist Theology: A Reader*, edited by Ann Loades, 72–80. London and Louisville, KY: SPCK and Westminster/John Knox Press, 1990.

Wiesner-Hanks, Merry, ed. *Convents Confront the Reformation: Catholic and Protestant Nuns in Germany*. Translated by Joan Skocir and Merry Wiesner-Hanks. Milwaukee: Marquette University Press, 1996.

Wilkinson, John, trans. *Egeria's Travels*. 3d ed. Oxford, UK: Oxbow, 2006.

Williams, Delores S. *Sisters in the Wilderness: The Challenge of Womanist God-Talk*. Maryknoll, NY: Orbis, 1993.

Wire, Antoinette Clark. *The Corinthian Women Prophets: A Reconstruction through Paul's Rhetoric*. Minneapolis: Fortress, 1990.

Wollstonecraft, Mary. *A Vindication of the Rights of Woman*. Rev. ed. New York: Penguin, 2004.

Yasutake, Rumi. *Transnational Women's Activism: The United States, Japan, and Japanese Immigrant Communities in California, 1859–1920*. New York: New York University Press, 2004.

Young, Robin Darling. *In Procession before the World: Martyrdom as Public Liturgy in Early Christianity*. Milwaukee: Marquette University Press, 2001.

Yuen, Wai Man. *Religious Experience and Interpretation: Memory as the Path to the Knowledge of God in Julian of Norwich's "Showings."* New York: Peter Lang, 2003.

Zarri, Gabriella. "Ursula and Catherine: The Marriage of Virgins in the Sixteenth Century." Translated by Anne Jacobson Schutte. In *Creative Women in Medieval and Early Modern Italy: A Religious and Artistic Renaissance*, edited by E. Ann Matter and John Coakley, 237–78. Philadelphia: University of Pennsylvania Press, 1994.

Zikmund, Barbara Brown. "The Feminist Thrust of Sectarian Christianity." In *Women of Spirit: Female Leadership in the Jewish and Christian Traditions*, edited by Rosemary Ruether and Eleanor McLaughlin, 206–24. New York: Simon and Schuster, 1979.

Zum Brunn, Emilie, and Georgette Epiney-Burgard, eds. *Women Mystics in Medieval Europe*. Translated by Sheila Hughes. New York: Paragon House, 1989.

FOR FURTHER READING

Additional resources can be found on the companion website: http://nyupress.org/moore.

Aquino, María Pilar. *Our Cry for Life: Feminist Theology from Latin America*. Translated by Dinah Livingstone. Maryknoll, NY: Orbis, 1993.

Burkett, Elinor. *The Right Women: A Journey through the Heart of Conservative America*. New York: Lisa Drew/Scribner, 1998.

Clifford, Anne M. *Introducing Feminist Theology*. Maryknoll, NY: Orbis, 2001.

Connor, Carolyn L. *Women of Byzantium*. New Haven: Yale University Press, 2004.

Fabella, Virginia, and Sun Ai Lee Park, eds. *We Dare to Dream: Doing Theology as Asian Women*. Kowloon, Hong Kong: Asian Women's Resource Centre for Culture and Theology, 1989.

Grant, Jacquelyn. *White Women's Christ and Black Women's Jesus: Feminist Christology and Womanist Response*. Atlanta: Scholars Press, 1989.

Halter, Deborah. *The Papal "No": A Comprehensive Guide to the Vatican's Rejection of Women's Ordination*. New York: Crossroad, 2004.

Hardesty, Nancy A. *Women Called to Witness: Evangelical Feminism in the Nineteenth Century*. 2d. ed. Knoxville: University of Tennessee Press, 1999.

Harkness, Georgia. *Women in Church and Society: A Historical and Theological Inquiry*. Nashville: Abingdon, 1972.

Haskins, Susan. *Mary Magdalen: Myth and Metaphor*. New York: Harcourt Brace, 1993.

Kinzel, Beverly Mayne, and Pamela J. Walker, eds. *Women Preachers and Prophets through Two Millennia of Christianity*. Berkeley: University of California Press, 1998.

LaHaye, Beverly. *The Spirit-Controlled Woman*. Eugene, OR: Harvest House, 1995.

McNamara, Jo Ann Kay. *Sisters in Arms: Catholic Nuns through Two Millennia*. Cambridge, MA: Harvard University Press, 1996.

Meyers, Carol, ed. *Women in Scripture*. Boston: Houghton Mifflin, 2000.

Norris, Pamela. *Eve: A Biography*. New York: New York University Press, 1999.

Ross, Rosetta E. *Witnessing and Testifying: Black Women, Religion, and Civil Rights*. Minneapolis: Fortress, 2003.

Ruether, Rosemary Radford. *Sexism and God-Talk: Toward a Feminist Theology*. Boston: Beacon, 1983.

Schneider, Carl J., and Dorothy Schneider. *In Their Own Right: The History of American Clergywomen*. New York: Crossroad, 1997.

Schüssler Fiorenza, Elisabeth. *In Memory of Her: A Feminist Theological Reconstruction of Christian Origins*. New York: Crossroad, 1983.

Tada, Joni Eareckson, with Joe Musser. *Joni: An Unforgettable Story*. Grand Rapids, MI: Zondervan, 1996.

Warner, Marina. *Alone of All Her Sex: The Myth and the Cult of the Virgin Mary*. New York: Vintage, 1983.

SUBJECT INDEX

abbesses, 73–79, 136

Abelard, Peter, 78

abortion, 64, 130, 143–144, 147, 149

Act of Uniformity, 96

Adam, 21–26, 61, 122

Africa, 7, 9–10, 118, 130, 147–149; missions in, 9, 115–118

African Americans, 4, 7–8, 115, 126, 130–134, 153

African Methodist Episcopal Zion Church, 137

Alliance of Baptists, 143

Ambrose of Milan, 59

Amish, 95

Anabaptists, 92–93, 95

androcentrism, 3, 51

Angela of Foligno, 82–83

Anglican Church, 113, 138. *See also* Church of England

The Answer (La respuesta), 101

Antony (desert hermit), 60–61

Apocalypse of Moses (Apocalypsis Mosis), 24

apocryphal texts, 24, 42, 55–56, 60, 162n15. *See also* Gnosticism; *entries in non-canonical books*

Apostolic Constitutions (Constitutiones Apostolorum), 63

Aquila, 50, 51

Aquino, María Pilar, 8

asceticism, 16, 38, 48, 60–63, 72. *See also* celibacy; chastity of women; renunciation as religious discipline

Asia, 7, 9, 130, 147–148; missions in, 9, 115–116

Assemblies of God, 137

atonement, 68, 83

Augustine of Hippo, 15, 25, 59, 61

authority: of experience, 105; by gender, 3, 48, 55, 62, 141, 146; of the Holy Spirit, 107; of papacy, 64, 87; of reason, 107; of scripture, 13, 48, 107, 134

Azusa Street Revival, 125–126. *See also* revivalism

Baker, Ella Josephine, 134

baptism, 14, 49, 50, 54, 57, 92, 95, 96, 110, 125–126, 135; of Clovis, 74; by Conrad Grebel, 88

Baptist General Association of Virginia, 143

Baptist General Convention of Texas, 143

Baptist Women in Ministry, 142

Baptists, 115, 142–143. *See also* Southern Baptist Convention; Woman's Convention of the National Baptist Convention

Beatrice of Nazareth, 80–81

Beguines, 79–81, 170n40

Benedict of Nursia, 76

Benedictines, 76, 79, 148. *See also* Rule of Saint Benedict

Bible, 4, 6, 11, 13, 19–20, 36, 51–52, 78, 87–89, 93, 97, 101–102, 122, 133–134, 141–146, 154; evangelizing in, 30, 31, 44, 45, 50; as Word of God, 90, 92, 143. *See also* Hebrew Bible; New Testament

INDEX TO THE BIBLE AND
NEW TESTAMENT APOCRYPHA

Numbers in boldface indicate chapters and verses in books of the Bible or in Apocrypha.

ABOUT THE AUTHOR

Rebecca Moore is Professor of Religious Studies at San Diego State University. She is the author of *Voices of Christianity: A Global Introduction* (2005), and co-author of *A Portable God: The Origin of Judaism and Christianity*, with Risa Levitt Kohn (2007). Her most recent book is *Understanding Jonestown and Peoples Temple* (2009).